Shared Notes

Shared Notes

A Musical Journey

Martin Hayes

TRANSWORLD IRELAND

TRANSWORLD IRELAND
Penguin Random House Ireland, Morrison Chambers,
32 Nassau Street, Dublin 2, Ireland
www.transworldireland.ie

Transworld Ireland is part of the Penguin Random House group of companies
whose addresses can be found at global.penguinrandomhouse.com

First published in the UK and Ireland in 2021
by Transworld Ireland
an imprint of Transworld Publishers

A CIP catalogue record for this book
is available from the British Library.

ISBN 9781848272644

Typeset in 12.5/18pt Adobe Garamond Pro by Jouve (UK), Milton Keynes
Printed and bound in Great Britain by Clays Ltd, Elcograf S.p.A.

The authorized representative in the EEA is Penguin Random House Ireland,
Morrison Chambers, 32 Nassau Street, Dublin D02 YH68.

Penguin Random House is committed to a sustainable
future for our business, our readers and our planet. This book
is made from Forest Stewardship Council® certified paper.

To Lina

Description of a traditional folk melody

'In their small way, they are perfect as the grandest
masterpieces of musical art. They are, indeed, classical
models of the way in which a musical idea can be expressed
in all its freshness and shapeliness – in short, in the very
best possible way, in the briefest possible form and
with the simplest of means.'

Béla Bartók, *The Hungarian Folk Song*

PREFACE

WHEN, DURING THE early stage of my relationship with my wife, Lina, I started to talk about marriage, she said to me, 'But I don't know who you are!' Knowing she was a big fan of my music, I said to her, 'Do you like my music?' She said she loved it, to which I replied, 'Well, that's all I am: music.'

Traditional Irish music has been my life. I am deeply passionate about it and am always happy to talk about it. I enjoy conveying musical ideas in master classes and media interviews. Some musicians prefer not to talk about music at all, which is entirely understandable – the music itself can surely do the talking. I, however, love to think and talk about music, and though I've spent my life playing it, there is still much of it that remains a mystery to me. I never tire of trying to understand more deeply the act of making music or the very nature of the creative process itself.

When invited to write this book, I willingly embraced the idea, thinking that I might be able to convey my thoughts on music in greater and more precise detail. My initial efforts at documenting my thoughts, purely on music alone, proved difficult without context. My musical understanding and reasoning are inextricably interwoven with my personal story and journey. I had initially resisted the idea of writing a memoir, believing that maybe my life story wasn't in itself very interesting. My personal life, with all its twists and turns, however, has always been a musical story, so I eventually agreed with my publisher that a memoir was the best way to take you inside my world of music.

When I started this book, I had no real writing experience, having written little more than emails or set lists since my school days. While I was trying to figure out what shape this book might take, Lina happened to be taking an online course on autobiographical writing. She shared her insights with me, making me aware that there is an obligation towards the reader in terms of trust and honesty. I have always strived to honestly express my thoughts on music and my artistic journey. Accepting the necessity of a memoir format to convey musical ideas, however, pushed me towards telling stories of my life that are not necessarily secret but aren't widely known either. Some of these stories are a bit embarrassing to me, but without them the picture is incomplete.

There was a period of my life where I was more lost, foolish and silly than I ever thought I'd admit. My current public persona, as a professional musician in mid-career, reflects a more thoughtful and insightful person than the one I was during my years in the wilderness. Nonetheless, my career success, though modest by many standards, has still been highly improbable.

I was born into a rich music culture and a rural way of life that was about to change massively. Through the early sixties and seventies, my little part of East Clare went through massive cultural and social change. However, the musical ethos of another time still prevailed and is the foundation of my musical understanding. The environment into which I was born provided me with a cultural context rich enough in source material and inspiration to last me a lifetime. This book traces a musical thread and a life story that goes all the way from my beginnings, on a small farm with horse-drawn machinery, with a father who played the fiddle and a one-room schoolhouse, to a life of musical performance and collaboration on stages all over the world.

Traditional Irish music – which I will refer to simply as traditional music for the rest of this book – is an earthy music of deceptive simplicity that has a grounded beauty within its very DNA. Irish music is a treasury of melodic richness, and this is the story of how I've experienced this music, whether by the rustic, open-hearth fireplace of my early childhood or, later, in the sacred space of the concert stage. Through all these times, there has been an abundance of support and help from people who have shared their wisdom and thoughts with me – musicians who have lifted me to newer and higher levels, people who have believed in me, who have seen things in me I couldn't fully see myself and whose love and support has sustained me. I hope that this story can be an encouragement to those starting out in life to follow your bliss and know that even unlikely success and happiness can come to you if you are willing to follow the guidance of your heart.

INTRODUCTION

I N THE HAY shed, my father and I laid a doubled-up rope on
the ground and started evenly piling some of last summer's
hay on top of it. When there was enough hay, we took the loose
ends of the rope and pulled them over the pile of hay, running
them through the loop at the other end. We pulled the rope tight
to make a compact bunch of hay that could be swung over my
father's back. We then made a smaller one for me. Once the beart
of hay was on his back, I pulled off the loose sops of hay that were
hanging from his beart before he took off across the meadow to
feed the cattle. I then swung my smaller beart over my back and
went along with him. As we were walking towards the middle
hill, where the cattle were, my father asked me to whistle for him.
He wanted to know if I knew the tune we had worked on a few
nights before. Was the tune inside me? Was it now part of me? If
it wasn't in me, it didn't matter whether I could technically play
it on the fiddle or not.

Tunes live in my memory as remembered patterns; they live
in my body also, as if they've become part of my physical being.
When playing, they move through me, manifesting themselves

through the instrument as the final act of music-making. All the experiences of nature, the farm, the landscape, the folklore, my imagination and the memories of great moments of music have become entwined in the tunes. The deeper from within the tune comes, the more powerful it is.

I

I AM SEVEN years old and I am sitting to the side of an open-air stage in the square in Miltown Malbay, listening to my father and the Tulla Céilí Band play to a large crowd of dancers and listeners. It's the early hours of 20 July 1969, the night of the first moon-landing. Neil Armstrong and Buzz Aldrin are on the moon; we're playing at the Darlin' Girl from Clare festival. I say 'we' but really I'm just taking it all in while my father, PJ, is sitting in the middle of the band playing his fiddle. They probably didn't know where else to put me, so the side of the stage has become my perch for the night. My attention is divided between the crowd, the music and the night sky. Every now and then I strain my eyes to stare up at the moon, captivated by the fact that people are landing on this illuminated orb for the very first time. I look out at the crowd and there are hundreds of people in front of me. Most are dancing and enjoying the music, some are busy eating pig's crubeens. (These were pig's feet, the fish-and-chips of that time.) Like myself, there's a few glancing up at the moon every now and then, almost as if expecting to see a couple of tiny figures strolling across it.

Up in the sky, the world's futuristic dreams were being brought to fruition, with the Lunar Module making global history. The modern age was coming in to view, and the stable ways of life that had sustained my father's world were about to change. The music on the stage that night was in complete harmony with that old world, but how would this music stay relevant in the new times ahead? I was sitting on the cusp of a changing society, but there in Miltown Malbay revellers were simply going about their night, immersed in their own fun, making memories while the band made music.

When I cast my mind back over the first ten years of my life on our farm on Maghera mountain in Killanena, north-east County Clare, it's as if my memories place me within an older, sepia-toned era. I have attempted to hold on to as many memories as possible from my first ten years of life, but of course, with every passing year and every new step forward into the virtual world in which we now spend so much of our time, these memories and experiences seem as though they're from another world entirely.

Growing up on a farm in 1960s West of Ireland afforded me a unique type of life-education. Traditional music served as a beautiful addition to this rustic way of life. I loved the sounds of the céilí bands and the sounds of fiddles and flutes. Pop music never quite managed to infiltrate the musical realm of our house, nor did it pique my interest long enough for me to be lured in by it. I suppose as a child I was drawn to the same music my father liked. Even today, no matter what music I play or listen to, nothing resonates as deep within my soul as traditional music. When I play those tunes, there's a kind of 'coming home' experience I never have with anything else. Don't get me wrong, there are lots of musical genres that I love, but traditional music was there from the start and is entwined with me as if it has always been a deep, natural part of who I am.

I arrived into this world on Independence Day, 4 July 1962. A year and ten days after me, my brother Pat followed suit – on Bastille Day, no less! I was the eldest child, born into a household of five people: my paternal grandparents, Maggie and Martin Hayes, my parents, Peggy and PJ, and my uncle Liam, who was my father's youngest sibling. I was named Martin after my grandfather, who was also known locally as Quillan, but sadly, when I was nearly a year old, he and my grandmother passed away within six weeks of each other. I'm told I spent most of that first year either on my grandfather's knee or in my cot beside him in the kitchen. I don't remember him, but apparently he was a witty, sociable person, a bit of a character. Anyone who walked a fox on a leash through the streets of Ennis and rode a bullock to a fair must have been a character. My father always said that Quillan loved it when people visited the house, and he always kept a big roasting fire as a welcome. People who knew him would start smiling straight away when I'd ask to know more about him. I've somehow always felt a deep connection to this man.

For the seven years that followed the passing of my grandparents, the family structure remained the same. My uncle Liam continued living with us, which, growing up, meant I felt as though I had two fathers. I also felt like I had a twin, because as children my brother and I were pretty much the same size. With only a year between us, we were close friends, always playing together and even sharing a bed. Our personalities, however, were very different. Pat was easygoing and more compliant by nature, whereas I spent a lot of time battling with my parents, resisting every request, questioning everything and getting into long fights with them. These were the kind of fights that always ended up with me in tears, followed by the aggravating admonishment, *'Why can't you be more like your brother, Pat?'* He sailed right through those formative years without much trouble. When Pat did do something wrong, it was usually said to be the result of my bad example. I somehow couldn't be like him; I perceived injustice and coercion everywhere. I might be told to *'Bring a bucket of milk to the calves, now!'* Typically, I would answer, *'I will in a minute!',* to which would come the usual reply, *'What's the minute for?'* I was willing to do almost anything for anyone if asked, but when forced or commanded I would stubbornly resist. It was hard to win, and with all the trouble that I seemed to make, I began to believe that I was fundamentally bad, that I was somehow unlovable and unworthy. I was left with the impression that no child in the history of the Hayes family had ever behaved this badly and that probably no other child in the whole of County Clare ever acted like this either. Obviously, nobody tried to make me feel unlovable or wayward, but looking at the situation through a child-like lens, I simply didn't see myself as a good and lovable child. I somehow couldn't break the dynamic, couldn't just keep my mouth closed and do what I was told.

During my first seven years, my mother suffered a number of miscarriages and two stillbirths before my sister, Anna Marie, was born. My mother had a very difficult pregnancy with Anna Marie, who was very premature, weighing just 1lb 13oz at birth, and the expectation for her survival was so low that she was both baptized and confirmed on the day she was born; she was christened Anna

Marie Catherine and confirmed as Anna Marie Catherine Carmel, the names of the four nurses who took care of her and my mother, who had ended up spending six weeks bed-bound in St John's Hospital in Limerick. I have this memory of my father asking myself and Pat to get on our knees with him in the kitchen and pray for Anna Marie to survive. She was believed to have been the smallest premature baby to have survived in Ireland at that time. When she first came home, I remember my uncle Liam ominously saying that we'd all have to be much quieter, that all the running, jumping and shouting would have to stop. It didn't, but Anna Marie didn't seem to mind at all. She was a quiet baby who spent most of the time in her little cot in the kitchen. She was no trouble whatsoever. My youngest sister, Helen, would arrive into the world a couple of years later, in April 1971, with no fuss at all.

In those early years, I remember my mother being ill a lot. Along with all the agony of the miscarriages and stillbirths, she had to undergo surgery to have cysts removed from her ovaries, surgery on her gall bladder and to have growths removed from her larynx. During my mother's hospital stays, my father and uncle Liam would be responsible for cooking dinner. This was all well and good except for the fact that they were terrible cooks. It also didn't help matters that there was no refrigerator in the house. This meant that the sausages purchased earlier in the week would start to go off fast. I still associate those times with the sour sausages and potatoes my father and uncle Liam would conjure up and present on a plate before us. In my house it was considered a sin not to eat everything on your plate; you had to eat it, all of it. To overcome the sour taste of the sausages, I would cover them with the potatoes and then swallow the lot in a gulp, pretending the sausages weren't there at all. The other dreaded dinner option was boiled fatty bacon and cabbage. Bread and butter quickly became my salvation during these desperate culinary times.

Despite the lack of amenities such as a refrigerator, life felt abundant and prosperous for our family at that time, although, it goes without saying, prosperity is relative. By today's standards, and maybe even standards in other parts of Ireland at the time, we might have been considered poor, but we felt abundant. We had a garden filled with potatoes, cabbages, carrots, turnips, parsnips and lettuce, and no shortage of apple trees, plum trees and gooseberry bushes either. From the farm, we had the everyday staples such as milk, potatoes, eggs, bacon, vegetables and chicken. My mother loved flowers, so we had lots of shrubs, clipped hedges, and a kaleidoscope of flora everywhere. The sheds of the farmyard were stone-built, and always brightly whitewashed with red-painted doors and slate roofs. My father placed great pride in 'doing things right'; the aesthetics were just as important as the functionality. He liked the potato drills to be very straight, and even the dung heap near the cow house had to be shapely. It needed to look tidy even if it was just dung. The stone yard that led from the cow house had to be brushed clean every day. The flowers, the whitewashed sheds and the clean yard created a sense of harmony around the farm that gave me a reassuring feeling of well-being. You didn't need to have money to have those things.

Our house, a small cottage, sat at the confluence of two mountain streams. There was the constant sound of water gurgling over stones and the breeze blowing through the many trees that lined the avenue and yard that led up to our front door. We lived on the side of the mountain and my grandfather had been very diligent about providing shelter, which back then was seemingly much more important than a view or even access to more light. The front of our small cottage had the typical three windows and a door. Inside, to the left of the front door was the parlour, a room that was, and still is, an anomaly of the Irish house layout. There wasn't much room in any of the houses back then, but somehow there was this unused parlour where there was a cupboard with fine glassware, a few pieces of ornate furniture, a nice coffee table and a fancy fireplace. This was traditionally the room where a visiting priest or relatives from America would be taken. It was as if they might not be able to handle the more elemental life that existed, should they be taken through the door into the kitchen. The parlour stood in stark contrast to the more rudimentary nature of the farm and the rest of the house itself. It was a little haven of refinement where sherry glasses, silverware and china cups resided. It was a homage to the inner refinement of all these people.

The main room in the house was known as the kitchen. It had the open-hearth fireplace with a crane that swung in and out for hanging pots over the open fire. That was still in use when I was a young child. This kitchen/main room was a communal space where traditionally everything happened. Food was eaten and cooked there, but we played music, danced and listened to the radio there too.

There was an extension to the back of our house that was built just before my father married my mother. Prior to becoming engaged, my father had lived in the house with his parents, his sister, and brother. Until the new extension had gone up, they had all spent their entire lives in a house without indoor plumbing. My father was unsure of how to bring my mother – who was then living a much more modern life in London – into this very modest home. There was not enough money for my father to buy or build another property, and my aunt and uncle didn't have any means of moving on either, so he made the best of what he had and built an extension with two bedrooms, a bathroom and another kitchen, which we called the 'back kitchen' and which had running water and a gas cooker.

Even with these modern amenities installed, my mother was nonetheless surrendering a tremendous amount of comfort and freedom when she forfeited her life in London in favour of an abode on the side of a mountain in Clare. She was an independent-minded, free-thinking spirit, and I feel she probably struggled a lot in those early years as she tried to adapt to her new role as the 'woman of the house', where as soon as she moved in she was washing everyone's clothes by hand, baking, and preparing food for the entire household. My mother was quite a resilient woman by nature, but I still don't know how she did it.

Before going to England, and long before she met my father, my mother worked as a nurse in the psychiatric hospital in Ennis. That environment and the suffering she saw there impacted her a lot. Her next move was to join a convent in Limerick and train to become a nun. Thankfully for me, she only lasted there one year. She left after she was punished for riding a bicycle without permission. My mother concluded that the whole thing was hypocritical and not for her. She remained sceptical of all authoritarian institutions after that. I only learned of this divergence in her 'career' a few days after my father passed away, in 2001. I was sitting at the kitchen table when she passed me a photograph of herself in a nun's habit. Even the notion of her having an interest in convent life surprised me, particularly as it had always been my father who was the devout Catholic in our house, not my mother. My mother had her own mind and was very resistant towards authority and being controlled by others. The idea of her training to become a nun just seemed completely at odds with her personality. Personally, I think she joined the convent in a moment of confusion. It seems she had been very quiet, shy and withdrawn at that early stage in her life. It was only after she left the nuns, when she went to England, that she started to blossom and open up.

She liked people who spoke their minds. She had no time for people she thought might be duplicitous or phoney in some way. She was very upfront about things. If she didn't like something you said or did, she would say it. Sometimes people would be shocked, but she would just say it. She wasn't afraid to disagree with anyone and she wasn't ever going to be silenced. My mother was not your normal, everyday, run-of-the-mill farmer's wife. I remember, as a young child, picking up a book of hers with a title that mentioned something about the third eye, a book dealing with esoteric, mystical thoughts. That's a pretty common type of topic these days, but not back then. While going through her books, I recall also stumbling upon *Lady Chatterley's Lover*, a book that was banned back then.

After my mother left the convent, she travelled to London to meet up with her sisters Mary and Kate, who were already living there. She worked in a shop, initially, before securing a waitressing job at what was then a very exclusive restaurant. It was a world away from where she had come from. My mother grew up in a thatched cottage in the parish of Crusheen and had walked to school each day in her bare feet. Here she was now serving as a waitress to British aristocrats and members of the political class. The restaurant was in the centre of London, and owned and operated by BOAC (British Overseas Airways Corporation), which was the predecessor to British Airways. Back in the fifties, you could check in your luggage there, enjoy a very nice meal and then be transported directly by bus from the restaurant to your plane at Heathrow. This was during an era when flying was considered a very exclusive luxury.

My mother enjoyed the job and it really helped her integrate into British life. Her time there left her with a love for the English people; she found them to be decent and kind, and she developed many strong friendships while she was there. An advantage of working for BOAC was that she could avail herself of cheap flights to Shannon Airport, which meant she could return to Clare without the huge train and ferry journeys that most people would have to endure. During one of those visits, she went to Ennis to go to a dance. Previously, she would have gone to the modern dance hall, where the latest dance bands performed, but life in London had probably left her yearning for this deeper connection to her cultural roots, so she now felt more inclined to go to the céilí at the Queens Hotel, where my father's band was playing. She was already more than familiar with the band as her sister Biddy was in a relationship with the Tulla Céilí Band accordionist, Joe McNamara. That night was the first time she met my father. They were by all accounts enamoured with each other, but over the seven years that followed, their romance and relationship existed primarily through an exchange of letters. They would occasionally see each other when she'd return for holidays and when my father travelled with the Tulla Céilí Band to England to play the Galtymore ballroom in London and many of the other great London ballrooms where the Irish gathered.

The long, drawn-out courtship eventually began to take its toll on my mother. She wondered if they'd ever get married at all. I think my father was dragging his feet due to his home situation – how was he going to bring this modern woman into a small, crowded cottage? He was at a loss as to how he could make things work. In the end, my father broke off the relationship, reasoning that he didn't have the means to give her the kind of life to which she would have become accustomed. I have no doubt that his decision to break up was as heartbreaking for him as it was for my mother. My father's friend and Tulla Céilí Band fiddle-playing colleague Dr Bill Loughnane persisted in encouraging him to make another go of it. Meanwhile, my mother's sister Biddy wrote to my father telling him how upset my mother was about the break-up. An upcoming tour to England meant he would at least have one other opportunity to see my mother. Whatever was said must have worked because, once they'd finally met, not only were they back together by the following day, they were engaged.

The issue with the small, crowded house was resolved quite easily in the end. My aunt Philomena, who was still living there, had just become engaged to my father's musical partner and friend, Paddy Canny. After my mother and father became engaged, the idea of a joint wedding with my aunt and Paddy was proposed. Both couples were married in one big joint wedding in September 1961. Once my aunt moved out of the house, my mother moved in, and between that and the new extension, the issue of the lack of space no longer posed as much of a problem.

Paddy Canny, who was now married to my aunt Philomena, was by any definition an extraordinary musician, and one who was recognized as among the best in the country back in the fifties. In the current times of ubiquitous polished recorded perfection, our modern ears can be poorly equipped, and our patience lacking, to properly hear and fully appreciate the music of someone like Paddy Canny. His playing had an intimacy that was filled with detailed subtleties. There was an innate contentment in how he played that seemed directed inwards towards a private silence that required no listener to witness its beauty. A music of comfort and warmth that would flow effortlessly when he was in the humour for it and when the moment had been found. In County Clare, Paddy was the hero of those who knew and loved the music. *'The best of them all'* was probably the most common response to a mention of his name. Paddy had a very personal sound that was unlike that of any other fiddler. They used to say he had a 'sweep' to his music; his playing rose and fell in swells of volume, and he spoke a local musical vernacular that contained great depth for those who were familiar with that language.

Paddy's father, Pat, was the one who actually taught him. My father, at the age of eleven, then started to learn from Paddy. There was just a couple of years between Paddy and my father, and when they were young men, in the early 1940s, they would have played together as a duet around the local area for house dances. They'd strap their fiddles to their backs and cycle around our part of north-east Clare. There are stories of them getting off their bicycles on their way home in the middle of the night to play a tune that they'd heard earlier at a gathering, just to make sure they wouldn't forget it. What started out as two young men on their bicycles with fiddles strapped to their backs eventually led to them both being in the Tulla Céilí Band and travelling the world, going from the wild but humble house dance to the stage of Carnegie Hall. Paddy wasn't that interested in playing for dancers, whereas my father loved it and had developed his own rhythmic style to suit the dancers. It worked well when they played together; they had two different approaches, Paddy's long-bowed sweeping lyricism and my father's pulsing rhythm complementing each other to create a combined sweetness and drive.

Though my father had embraced the more raw, rhythmic elements of the East Clare sound, he also had a great emotional and intuitive understanding of the music. He had one particular way of describing music that covered a multitude. He would describe a piece of music played by someone as either 'having' tradition or 'not having' tradition. He might say there was no tradition in something, or that something was full of tradition. If he said something was lacking tradition, it was a euphemism for music that didn't mean anything. If it had tradition, it meant it had soul; it was music that spoke from a place of feeling. If it could bring a tear to your eye or give you goosebumps, you could be sure it was filled with tradition. This tradition is like threads of emotion and feeling handed down to us in the form of melody; a tune is nothing more than a musically encoded feeling waiting to be unlocked. In this way, the music provides a visceral-feeling connection to our past.

Many years later, as a teenager, I would take great pride when I'd hear the older fellows remark that they could hear a lot of Paddy Canny and my father in my music. I spent a lot of time trying to create a unified lyricism and pulse in my playing, trying to achieve in my own music the balance that occurred when my father and Paddy played together. I didn't want to choose one approach over the other. The music they made has woven itself into my playing in much the same way that the accent of the area is woven into the sounds and patterns of my speech. I now carry their combined styles as one. They are constantly and unconsciously with me.

My father was a farmer by profession, but he was better known as a musician and I believe he considered himself a musician first and foremost. The world of traditional music was largely filled with people who approached it from this perspective, similar to the way in which amateur sports figures or athletes might do, except as musicians they could in theory keep pursuing their passion throughout their whole life, if they wished. On one occasion, as an adult, I remember my father standing backstage after one of my concerts. He seemed to be looking at and examining my fiddle, which was sitting on a table. He turned to me and said, 'I'd love to have done what you're doing.' I'd never heard him ever say that before. I found it so moving, both in terms of his unrealized dream and his implicit endorsement of the path I had chosen. Of course, I wouldn't ever have been propelled along this path, or even taken up the fiddle in the first place, had it not been for my father's world of music and his influence on me.

When I was growing up, our house was often filled with musicians. I was by nature a night owl and never really wanted to go to bed; I still struggle with this – I have a hard time leaving the day behind. On the nights we would have musicians over, I'd make sure not to draw any attention to myself, in the hope that my mother wouldn't notice my presence. I was always afraid she'd suddenly turn and say, *'Time for bed!'* I just wanted to be in the middle of the action, be surrounded by the sounds of musical instruments. Sooner or later, of course, I would be spotted and the command to go to bed would be issued. I would agree but somehow, fifteen minutes later, I'd still be there until I was yet again told to go to bed. For many years I slept in the attic room just up the stairs from the main kitchen. My journey to bed on these occasions involved a begrudging and slow ascent to the little landing in front of my room, which overlooked the kitchen. Sometimes I'd just perch there for another while longer in my own private world, observing the scene through the bannisters until I was spotted again and told to go all the way into my bedroom. I would then leave the door cracked open while I listened to the conversation, music, and laughter down below. These were some of the most nurturing moments of my life, when I had the feeling of everything being right with the world.

Ours was very much an open house, and sometimes people we didn't even know would turn up unannounced. One of the lines you'd often hear in our kitchen was, *'I think I heard a car!'* As kids, those moments of hearing a car arrive were moments of excitement and possibility, a break in the mountainside isolation and always welcomed by us as children. We would peek out from behind the window lace to see if we could identify the car coming around the turn in the avenue leading up to our house. They'd pull up to the front wall and gate and step out of the car, by which time we'd know if we could identify them or not. No matter who it was, be they a stranger or a friend, we would go out to greet them and welcome them inside. The timing might be inconvenient but if they were coming for music, there was at least a tacit understanding that they were there because they valued traditional music, and on some level that made them friends already. It could be a musician friend from a nearby county, a folklorist from Dublin or an enthusiast from the United States or England. Either way, their arrival usually signalled the start of a big night of music in the kitchen.

Our kitchen was the place where musicians and friends from all over would congregate to play. People such as broadcaster Ciarán Mac Mathúna and lots of prominent traditional musicians, such as flute-player Peadar O'Loughlin and fiddler Tommy Potts, would all have been in our kitchen at different times throughout my childhood. My mother would be scrambling to get food ready as soon as she saw the guests strolling up the path with their instruments in tow. She wouldn't have had the easiest job, putting together a big offering of food at a moment's notice, but she always managed to make it look effortless. If there wasn't a good supply of food in the house, someone would be quietly dispatched to Kelly's Shop or to Tony McNamara's or Naughton's pubs, both of which had a grocery section as part of the bar. While musicians were being welcomed in through our front door, one of us would be darting out the back door to go pick up the ham for the sandwiches. In truth, we weren't really ever short of anything for visitors. We always had our own milk and eggs, and my mother was also a great baker, so the kitchen always had a ready-made supply of tarts, cakes and the freshest of breads.

Musicians would be playing away in our kitchen – a mixture of stories, conversation and tunes – while my mother casually put food together in the back kitchen. There always came a point in the evening where my mother would ask the visitors if they would like a cup of tea and maybe 'something small' to eat. The 'something small' was always a big spread, usually consisting of things like ham or roast beef, potato salad, fresh tomatoes and lettuce, hard-boiled eggs, beetroot and brown bread followed by one of her famous apple or rhubarb tarts. This feast was a regular occurrence in our house whenever we had guests over. In fact, all the great nights of music and family gatherings in our kitchen had some version of this delicious spread as a centrepiece.

My mother always kept the house very clean and tidy, and was comfortable with anyone walking in at any time. If my mother hadn't been as kindhearted and generous as she was, those evenings might not have occurred as frequently as they did. I always had the feeling that people liked visiting our house. She always gave a big welcome to the continuous stream of musicians that came in and out our door. Music was my father's passion, and she always encouraged this. She fully supported my father's playing and his participation in the Tulla Céilí Band. He seemed to want very little else beyond that, but she knew it was central to his happiness.

People from around the world would arrive at our house purely to get some sense of the music, to hear it played, or just to meet my father. I remember the first time the fiddler and folklorist Barry Taylor and his wife, Jacqueline, from England visited us. In the course of conversation we discovered they were camping in West Clare and that their tent had been blown down the night before, so my mother offered them a room for the night, insisting they stay. They became family friends and regular visitors to the house after that. My father and mother were very open and generous in that way and seemed to delight in these chance encounters. I remember two American musicians, fiddler Armin Barnett and whistle-player Larry McCullough, showing up for music one evening. They, too, ended up staying the night. The next morning, Armin worked on my fiddle, adjusting the bridge and doing some other bits of maintenance work on it. There would have been absolutely no way to predict that one day he would be my local fiddle-repair man when I'd live in Seattle.

Among the regular visitors in those early days was an anthropologist from Holland by the name of Jos Koning. He was secretly carrying out an anthropological study of the music culture of East Clare and in order to blend in he had learned to play Irish music on the fiddle. He convincingly passed himself off as an enthusiast who just wanted to learn this music. Other regular visitors to our house included fiddler Antóin Mac Gabhann and his wife Bernie, flute-player Jimmy Brody and his wife, Ita, concertina-player John Naughton and his wife, Rosaleen, the great set-dancer Paddy King and his wife, Rita, and accordion-player Brendan McMahon.

We also enjoyed lots of musical gatherings with just our own extended family. My mother's sister Biddy would arrive with her husband, Joe McNamara, and his accordion. My cousin, their son Christy McNamara, who also played accordion, would often be there, or maybe my aunt Julia, who was married to flute-player Willie Conroy. My musician cousins, accordion- and flute-players John and Seamus McMahon, would often come too. There were many, many nights when that small house was packed to the brim, full of people and music. We danced and played in the kitchen, and any breaks from the music were filled with storytelling. We would listen to my father telling his favourite funny stories. He might sing 'The Jolly Frog', and often a ghost story was thrown in for good measure.

There were some very special musical moments during those nights when we might just sit and listen to a visiting musician play. One thing I learned was that moments of real music were unpredictable. Much of the time a player might just be plodding along, but then there were other, special, times when the music would suddenly be transformed into a kind of powerful expression of feeling. It was these captivating experiences that became the moments by which I would define and remember these players. I could ignore hours of faltering efforts in favour of that one moment. This was when the heart of the tune was laid bare for all to enjoy, when the soul of the musician was revealed, and when the true potential had been realized. It was often a fleeting moment but for me it was the definitive one. I remember listening to John

Naughton play his concertina one night. John was an elderly local man but was affectionately always known as 'Young John'. He had moved to Dublin in his youth and had let the music slip away. He hadn't played the concertina in decades but picked it up again after his friend Jimmy Brody bought him a concertina in an attempt to encourage him back into music. He started playing as though he had never stopped all those years earlier. For me, here was someone giving a glimpse into how the local music was played in the earlier part of the century. Young John was recapturing his musical youth when he played the concertina, and his versions of the tunes were unique and fascinating to me.

One of the moments from John's playing that night is stamped on my memory. He was playing his lovely setting of the melody 'The Ships in Full Sail' when there was this transcendent moment in the second part of the melody, often referred to as the turn of the tune, where he played a series of long notes in place of a busier, more complicated section, as if distilling the phrase to its most innocent beauty. My father and I looked at each other, knowing something beautiful had just happened. Such moments didn't come as a result of technical skill – technique alone couldn't create that experience. It's difficult to explain but it required a kind of forgetting of oneself while at the same time being totally present in the act. I would end up spending a lot of my life attempting to understand the architecture of those special moments, how to get inside the tune, how to be present, how to allow the music to flow. In the end, it was mostly all about letting go.

2

THROUGHOUT MY CHILDHOOD, I listened with great interest to stories involving my ancestors being herdsmen on the slopes of Maghera mountain. My grandfather Quillan, and his father before him, were herdsmen for the Butlers of Bunnahow, the landlords of the area before Irish independence. During those times, people would send cattle to the mountain to graze the 1,100 acres that were mostly mountain bogland. Their job was to check on every herd, which meant an incredible amount of mountain walking every day. Quillan also had to feed the fish in the two mountain lakes for Lord Lingenfield, who was a regular guest of the Butlers. The house where we lived was historically the herdsman cottage. This I would later discover was evidence of our place on the lowest rung of the social ladder. It seems the family had been evicted some generations before from the more fertile lands closer to the local village of Feakle.

After Irish independence, my grandfather was given the whole mountain by the Land Commission, perhaps because he was already the person working the mountain, so he could maintain things with some continuity and because it was the easiest solution at the time. The mountain bogland couldn't be farmed in any normal way so it couldn't be given to anybody as actual farmland. So, he carried on as a herdsman, taking in cattle to graze, in addition to running the sixty-acre farm that surrounded our homestead, but it still wasn't enough to keep up with the increasing rates due on the land, and eventually he found himself in financial trouble. My father often recounted the story of walking home from school one evening and seeing all the cattle from the farm running towards him. The local sheriff was removing the animals to impound them at Flagmount on the other side of Lough Graney – a tactic to force my grandfather to pay the rates. Apparently, the evening the livestock were taken, a group of neighbours, including the local priest, banded together to go and break the cattle out of the pound. They got the cattle back, but Quillan had to appear in court in Ennis to try to resolve the situation with the rates. They were too high for land of this low quality – it was impossible to make enough money with the cattle-grazing to keep up with the payments. In the court case, Quillan got no relief. Instead, the judge gave half the mountain to the forestry department, paid Quillan ten pounds, then doubled the rates on the remaining land, which meant that the rest of the mountain would soon belong to the forestry department also. It looks like the forestry department wanted the mountain and had a plan to get it. Quillan was being forced out. The mountain was gradually sold off, bit by bit, to the forestry department. By the end, we were left just with the farm around the house.

During my childhood, my father stayed on as an overseer of the mountain for the forestry department, who now owned Maghera mountain in its entirety. This whole experience of the sheriff and the cattle left a big wound in my father's psyche. He mentioned it many times, and I think it left him a bit fearful for the rest of his life. Unfortunately the mountain is now covered in Sitka spruce trees, which always look and feel so out of place. At the top of the mountain there is now a telecommunications mast that transmits television and radio signals to most of the Mid-West region of Ireland. My father and Quillan would have helped the mast surveyors find the best path to access the top of the mountain, which my grandfather had always believed was called Maghera. It turned out that the tip of the mountain, where the mast was to be located, was actually in another townland. However, the surveyors could see that my grandfather, who loved and and identified with this mountain, was very proud of the fact that this beacon of modernity would be broadcasting to a considerable segment of the country from what he believed was his townland of Maghera, so they set about having the name of the tip of the mountain officially changed. This meant the mast would actually be located in Maghera after all. At the official opening of the transmitter, on 10 September 1963, a PR photographer for the launch shot the only photograph of me as a baby, sitting on my mother's lap. Later in life I would go on to write a tune called 'The Maghera Mountain'.

Life on the farm had a kind of rustic warmth to it in those days. We knew all the farm animals individually and each had their own name. The names usually related to their ancestry and who we bought them from originally, so we would have cows called 'Bolands' cow' or 'Brodys' cow', though others had more obvious names, like 'the spotted cow'. We would keep track of each of them, so much so that we would know their offspring for several generations. There were eight cows on the farm and my father, along with my mother and my uncle Liam, would hand-milk them all each day. Once the milking was finished, the milk was kept cool by placing the churns in the stream that ran by the house. Then, mid-morning, we'd load the milk churns onto a donkey cart, or an 'ass car' as it was better known, then transport them down to the main road along a very beautiful, winding, tree-lined avenue. On the side of the road, there was a concrete pier built especially for the milk churns, and it was here they would be left for collection. A local man was in charge of collecting the churns with his tractor and transporting them a further six miles to the creamery. There, all the cream would be extracted from the milk, after which the skimmed milk would be sent back to us later that morning. We would then fill buckets with it and use it to feed the calves.

During winter, most of these animals were housed in sheds. The cows had a combination of rushes and poor-quality hay to lie on, and a stall-full of good hay at their heads to eat. That shed was cleaned every day with a four-pronged dung fork, a barrow, a brush and a few buckets of water. New litter was spread, the stalls refilled with hay, the dung transported by barrow to the sym-metrically shaped dung hill and the cow-house yard brushed clean – all this while the cows were drinking at the stream. Work that kept the place clean and tidy was just as important as work purely related to the commercial output of the farm. It wasn't commerce, it was a way of life. It was a series of ritualistic work practices that rotated with the seasons. There was a time for sowing potatoes, a time for cutting and turning the turf, saving hay, bringing home the turf, milking cows, digging spuds, picking stones and spreading dung on the fields, and a time for blessing the land with Easter holy water on 1 May to ward off bad luck. All the work of the farm was done manually or with the help of horses or a donkey. Our two horses, Bob and Fanny, had an array of different pieces of equipment that could be attached to them: a horse car for moving things, a mowing machine for cutting hay, a swath turner for tossing and turning hay to dry, a slide rake for gathering it into heaps, a hay car for bringing the hay back to the hay shed, a plough, and a harrow for the garden.

Along with cows, our farm consisted of chickens, hens, pigs and sheep, as well as gardens of potatoes, carrots, parsnips, onions, cabbage, lettuce and turnips for our own use. We had a rhubarb garden, apple and plum trees, and gooseberry bushes that flourished every spring. Back then, children always worked the farm. It was normal and expected. You did what manual labour you were capable of. My brother, Pat, and I worked on the farm from the age of seven or eight. We worked in the fields in the summer, saving hay, helped with the picking of potatoes, cleaned out the cow house and filled the cows' stalls with hay. We also helped with the cows during calving time, and then later let those same calves out for the first time in spring. They would run and leap as if born into a completely new world. I remember having to follow one that ran for miles one day. He managed to run through briars and across fields and streams before I could eventually catch him.

Even though the Irish language had died out in my area a long time before I was born, we still used a lot of old Irish words as part of daily life on the farm. When we were saving hay or feeding cattle, the only word we knew to describe a bunch of hay that you could gather in your arms was a 'gabháil' (pronounced 'gwal'). We tied down the trams of hay with 'súgáns', and a bigger load of hay that you tied with a rope to carry on your back was called a 'beart'. You'd carry this beart across the fields to feed some of the cattle that were not housed for the winter. Pat and I did plenty of that when we were children. We often competed to see who could carry the biggest beart. We also had fields with Irish names, such as the 'gairdín', the 'reesk' and the 'páircín'.

I would have spent a lot of time with my father, helping him on the farm. There was a way to lay out a vegetable garden, a way to turn hay, a way to fix a stone wall – these were the ways it had been done for generations. A day in the bog involved more than crudely digging turf; it had to be done with precision and taste. There was an aesthetic component to it that was just as important as anything else. When my father cut turf, he went into something akin to a meditative state, a kind of deeply attentive physical mantra. He could keep tossing turf up from the turf hole for hours, not fast, just continuous. As children, it was our job to take this turf and spread it out neatly from the face of the turf bank so it could slowly harden and dry. This was hard work, and even though we liked the bog, we also dreaded this kind of day's graft. After a few weeks, we'd return to foot the turf. This footing involved taking all the recently cut sods of turf and making little pyramids of four or five of them in a way that allowed the air to move through them. In another few weeks, if the weather had been dry enough, you returned to take these little piles and transform them into a long,

triangular clamp that would then be thatched. All of these forma-
tions were architectural achievements and they said something
about who you were, how attentive and dedicated you were, and
how refined your sense of proportion and construction was. These
artistically constructed clamps of turf remained at the bog, usually
close to the bog road, until the very end of summer, when they
would all be brought home. This would be the kind of work where
you would often have the 'meitheal'. This was the old Irish term for
when the neighbours would gather to help with a big job. In this
case, they would help my father bring the turf home in one go.
Once the turf was home, it would be loaded into an open-faced
shed where, once again, it needed to be stacked in a manner that
meant the water couldn't penetrate it. This was another moment
for aesthetic judgement that required a kind of craft-knowledge
similar to that needed to build a stone wall or thatch a roof. When
this turf was stacked well it had a visually pleasing quality to it that
one could take genuine pride in.

Good constructions of turf had that same sort of elegance you
see in certain beautifully constructed stone walls. They could only
be built from a process of flow and deep engagement. There were
other rituals that came with the turf-cutting, such as making a fire
to boil water for tea in the middle of the heather-covered bog. The
scents and the primal sight of the fire, the blackened kettle, and
the taste of the tea in that setting, created a very special experience. As a child it felt like all this activity had been going on for
ever, and I thought it would continue like this indefinitely.

Eventually things began to change. The black kettle got left
behind and was replaced by a thermal flask. It made things easier,

I suppose, but something was also lost. Since then machines have started to cut turf, and with this all the ritualized work patterns have faded away. The carefully constructed clamp of turf by the bog road has been replaced by turf-filled plastic bags. The smells, the look, the textures and symmetry of many things have changed. While I can still appreciate the beauty of the bog and the value of the many old rituals to which I was able to bear witness, it doesn't take away from the fact that work in the bog could be incredibly laborious. When technology was introduced to the farm, bit by bit, to help ease the physically gruelling workload, you can be sure I was first in line to welcome it.

In my earliest childhood years, however, everything was on a smaller scale, it was more intimate. Rather than being disconnected from the farm through the use of machinery, you were constantly in physical contact with the animals, the soil, the bushes, the trees and the land you worked with your hands. If you were working the land, your hands were in the soil. If you were crossing the land, you did so by foot.

One of my earliest memories was of being in the horse cart with my father, the sound of iron-rimmed wheels and horse's hooves making a cacophony of noise along the gravel road. I remember being in the cart, wrapped in a blanket, watching my father holding the reins and guiding the horse all the way along the tree-sheltered road by the side of the valley to the Sheedys' house in Ballycroum. It was said that Ballycroum was a place full of faeries. Years later, when I would walk that same road, it seemed oddly older than other places, almost as though it had been less intruded-upon by the insensitive, hard-edged rationality of the modern world. It was soft-edged and dreamy; a place where past eras seemed to linger. It's easy to understand why people would regard this as a hospitable place for the faeries. Our part of Clare, in the rural mountainous landscapes around Feakle, Tulla and Killanena, is fertile ground for this kind of imaginative thinking – the place is filled with little mountain boreens (lanes), streams, hidden glens, groves and beautiful lakes. Growing up, there was a very rich supply of enchanted locations all around me. I felt like the place owned me, but my imagination had also laid claim to these hidden spots. I still carry them with me as mine; they are my places to visit and revisit, especially in any moment when I need to connect and to ground my music. Over the years I've often been asked if the landscape influenced or shaped the sound of my music. For me, this landscape, just like music, can simply be experienced as a feeling, and I like to imagine I can make music that is harmonious and resonates with these special places of my childhood. These enchanted locations have become musical touchstones – they are guides for me. The old people talked of faeries a lot. My early childhood years were spent in a rich, imaginative physical landscape that was entwined with invisible beings such as the faeries, the púca (or pooka) and the bean sídhe (banshee). For those unfamiliar with these entities, the banshee was a long-haired woman whose identifying signature was a wailing cry at night, usually as a warning to a local family that a death was about to occur. It was usually families with old Irish surnames that had encounters with the banshee. The púca, meanwhile, was a more nondescript dark-grey entity that lurked in the dark, an otherworldly creature that we were never given specific information about but enough to be frightened. While there were tales aplenty of people who had seen and even met the banshee, I don't recall ever hearing of anyone seeing the púca. There were even stories that my great-grandfather had once seen a leprechaun while he was out herding on the mountain. My father never liked it if I ridiculed the stories about faeries or the leprechaun; his feeling was that you didn't have to believe in them but you didn't need to disrespect them either.

For me, all of this folklore existed in the magical afterglow and memory of the local wise woman, Biddy Early. Biddy was born in 1798 and died in 1872, the same year my grandfather Quillan was born. When I was a child, her presence in the folklore and imagination of our community was so strong, it was as if she were still alive and living in Feakle. But even though we had grown up with an awareness of Biddy Early, we didn't know any great detail about her. We just knew that she was in possession of some type of magic abilities and that people couldn't agree whether it was by the power of God, or Satan, that she worked. For secularists, she is regarded as a herbalist, but for the locals I knew while growing up she was a woman with the power to cast spells, cure illnesses, and foretell future fortunes and misfortunes. The local Catholic priests were in constant battle with her for authority, trying to wield the power of the church to discredit her and shake the faith the local people had in her. Despite the best attempts of the church, people continued to have faith in Biddy and her special blue bottle in which she could see the future and conjure magical potions.

I loved the idea of having been born in the locality of Biddy Early and growing up in the living folk memory of her magical power and healing spells. Even my father, devout Catholic as he was, still had reverence and respect for the faeries and believed that Biddy probably had real powers. The area around Feakle is today a kind of mecca for herbalists, healers and free thinkers of all stripes, though I'm not sure that many of the healers and herbalists drawn to the area had even heard of Biddy or the rich faerie folklore of the place. Many of them came because they were drawn to the beauty and to feeling present in the hidden quiet spots, the echoes of older times in abandoned homesteads or the enchantment that can be sensed along the mossy banks of a tree-sheltered stream or hazelnut grove.

The Sheedys' house that we were visiting that day, which was constructed from clay, has since melted back into the earth. Bushes and briars have reclaimed the homestead, but I hold on to the memory of the times spent in that small, thatched cottage. The Sheedys, like many of the households in the area, were a different family constellation from the family unit of parents and children that is now the norm. Their household was made up of one married couple, Jim and Bobby, with no children, along with Jim's brother Paddy and sister Bridgie. They were trapped by poverty, as well as lack of opportunity and perhaps an unwillingness to emigrate. Maybe they'd left it too late to make that choice and just continued as they were. With youth populations emigrating all through the century, those left behind had also begun to run out of marrying prospects. They lived a subsistence, mostly self-sufficient life with almost no luxury and the lack of freedom to really do anything with their lives other than survive. Remarkably, they didn't seem to suffer any existential angst, but perhaps the acceptance of a situation and the refusal to fight against it brings with it a sense of contentment. For families like this, a stable routine of ritualistic work habits and a life with predictable social interaction seemed to hold it all together and give it a comforting flow.

Back then, people spent a lot of time visiting each other's homes, and Paddy Sheedy would come to our house a couple of evenings a week, bringing a bar of Fry's chocolate for us. I never had the impression that the Sheedys were unhappy, despite some obvious tensions over who was in fact the woman of the house, but then again, almost all families of every shape have tensions. The only modern amenity they had was electricity. Electricity was commonly referred to as 'the electric light'; this was the only function it had in many houses. If a house was getting electricity installed, it was said that they were *getting in the light*. The Sheedys had the light, but its only function was to replace the paraffin lamps. They'd sit by the fire in the evening, waiting until it was dark enough to justify turning on the light. The electric light brought a taste of the modern world, but in doing so slowly chased away the older, more imaginative one, the one where people would sit around the fire smoking pipes in gentle intermittent conversation and contemplation. In my grandmother Molly's house, whenever visitors would call to her thatched cottage in Crusheen they would sit around the big, open hearth, the kind with the wrought-iron crane from which a large cast-iron kettle would be hanging over the fire. Sitting around that fire in the evening, the small gathering would often begin a type of storytelling called tracing, with my grandmother often taking the lead.

Tracing involved going back through the lineage of a person, or indeed a family, local to the area and then figuring out all the relationships and connections – both marital and biological – that existed throughout the extended families in the area. This, of course, would inspire a multitude of stories about the land and about the politics involved – the disputes, the agreements and God knows what else. The upside to this storytelling was endless hours of entertainment, but the downside was that if anyone did something out of the way in the local area, the art of tracing would ensure it would not be forgotten for generations to come. Those listening to the tales in one house would then inevitably carry them forward whenever those individuals were mentioned in tracing conversations in other houses. There was no hiding your sins in those days.

Tracing was a skill, and those who had finely tuned their art over a matter of years were truly gifted at the practice. My grandmother was definitely one such individual. You could mention the name of a local family, and without any hesitation she could reel off their lineage and talk you through every connection that stemmed from their bloodline, not to mention every story that involved them. Of course, when tracing led to stories, it was almost always the case that the stories would lead to tales of folklore and supernatural encounters. Conversations about faeries, banshees, ghosts and whatnot were all told with conviction and intensity. An evening sitting around the open fire in my grandmother's cottage would produce all sorts of recollections of this nature. Some were believable, others somewhat outlandish, but back then the people telling the stories always sounded so convinced of what they were saying that you couldn't help but become drawn into this reality yourself.

As scary as these stories could be, they engaged my childlike curiosity almost as much as the music did. The idea that such otherworldly creatures could inhabit the landscape alongside us mortals just fascinated me. Even today the story of the island lights on Inchicronan lake near my grandmother's house in Crusheen is one that fascinates me. To give you an idea of the geography, there is a peninsula into Inchicronan lake that is home to a Cistercian abbey and burial ground. When it rains heavily, the water in the lake rises, sometimes resulting in the peninsula becoming cut off from the shore, at which point it becomes an island. There are five families from the parish who bury their loved ones in that cemetery, and when a member of one of those families passes away, or is about to do so, two small blue lights are often said to have been seen going from the house of the deceased across the lake to the cemetery, or vice versa.

For most of history, mankind has lived in this kind of world of mystery and magic. It's only in modern times that we have begun to close the door on this rich, imaginative landscape in favour of the rationalist, scientific view of life. But it's not really possible to escape the mysterious. All around us in our space/time continuum is a confounding physical reality where time and space are one and consciousness can influence matter in ways that seem just as mysterious to me as those stories I heard around the fireplace in my grandmother's cottage.

3

I BELIEVED I was a musician from the moment I saw the fiddle Santa had left for me on Christmas morning. I was just seven years old at the time, but I figured it must be fate. If Santa had brought me a fiddle, then he must have believed I was a fiddle-player. I had the idea that I could just pick up the instrument and play like my father. It hadn't occurred to me the level of work and practice that would be required to master even the basics, never mind play a full tune. This naivety I attribute to a fine mix of childhood optimism and the fact that my father and the musicians who played in our kitchen always made it look so effortless. I remember being at the kitchen table one morning, my father taking down his fiddle and holding it under my chin. I suppose he was first sussing me out to see if the interest was there. Though I'd never tried to play the fiddle, I was always curious about it, in the way a young boy typically wants to be like his father. I wanted to do what my father did and play the fiddle, because it meant I would be just like him. There was never one iota of pressure on me to take up the fiddle, not even after Santa had brought it to me. Receiving the fiddle on Christmas morning was certainly a gentle nudge of encouragement but I was never pressured to play it; that decision was mine alone.

On the Christmas Day I received the fiddle, I remember asking my father to show me how to play. It was then the penny dropped that this was not going to be as easy as I thought. In the coming weeks and months, my father would occasionally sit in front of me, slowly play a bar or two and ask me to follow along. It was just a matter of looking and listening. There was no actual musical instruction, just an attempt to copy what he did. I wasn't very good or fast at this, and there was no sign of any real aptitude or natural talent. I'd make a little bit of progress and then lose momentum because I wouldn't practise regularly. After a week or two I'd have to relearn the tune and start all over again. This frustrating circle of events went on for almost two years, during which I only learned a few tunes.

I must have been almost ten when my father, who was very caring and gentle, said to me one night, 'Martin, a stór. I don't think you're going to be able to do this. Maybe the fiddle isn't for you.' He just wanted to relieve me of the burden of struggling with something I didn't seem to be naturally good at. I remember being absolutely devastated. I cried myself to sleep that night at the thought of losing my dream of being a fiddle-player just like my father, but somehow this incident sparked a determination to fight for what I wanted. I began to play regularly, and gradually started to get a small selection of tunes under my belt. My father was a humble and shy man with a very modest sense of his own musical abilities. He wasn't competitive either, which was ultimately very important. Years later, in speaking with the children of some other prominent musical parents, I became aware of a more complicated dynamic that sometimes exists, where on the one hand the parent would encourage the child, but on the other, they did not want to be surpassed. This is obviously a serious impediment for anyone learning an instrument. As the years went on I always felt my father never competed with me or stood in my way. He wanted me to play better than him, which was a very generous and supportive position for him to have adopted. The result was that I never felt competitive with him either. Over time, my father and I became colleagues and friends on our musical journey. By no means am I suggesting that we didn't have the usual father-and-son difficulties – we had plenty of disputes – but they were never about music.

A big part of the initial stages in the learning process was listening and absorbing. I was pretty young when my mother's record-player from her days in London finally arrived at our home in Maghera. She obviously couldn't bring everything back with her when she came home to marry, so the items of lesser importance arrived bit by bit in the years that followed. The record-player was one of these, and with it came her collection of records. There were lots by The Shadows, Cliff Richard and the Tulla Céilí Band. I had never seen or heard any of the records my father had made. Here amongst this collection the worlds of my father and mother were mixed together, the old music of my father and the more modern musical influences from my mother's life in England.

Among these newly arrived recordings was an LP of my father and Paddy Canny with fellow Tulla Céilí Band member Peadar O'Loughlin and Dublin-based piano-player Bridie Lafferty. This was a famous record in the world of traditional music, and many musicians, like fiddlers Kevin Burke and Frankie Gavin, have spoken about its influence. I think it may have been the first LP of traditional music that was produced in Ireland. Remarkably, it very nearly didn't happen. In 1959, James O'Neill of Dublin Records asked Paddy to make an LP, but Paddy didn't feel like doing a solo recording; he wanted to make one with my father. They then invited their good friend, flute-player Peadar O'Loughlin, to join them. Bridie Lafferty from Dublin would provide the piano accompaniment. Only in the car on the way to Dublin did they begin to pick the tunes and put the selections together. I know my father played a big part in that process. When they arrived at the studio, they began to play, and after they had around two tracks recorded the engineer informed them their time was up. The studio had been booked for about two hours on the assumption that they'd simply walk in, make a forty-minute recording and then leave. With the studio booked for the remainder of the day, they had no option if they wanted to finish the recording that day other than find another studio. The next studio they found didn't have an actual engineer and could only provide them with one microphone and a young technician to turn the tape machine on and off, but they made do and positioned themselves around the microphone at distances that they felt would provide a good balance. The backbone of the recording was the two fiddles, with Peadar O'Loughlin playing the flute on about half of the tracks while Bridie played piano accompaniment on all of them. This recording has gone on to be regarded as one of the classics in traditional music, and up to that point there hadn't even been a copy of it in our house.

I would spend a lot of time in the living room with that record and a number of others, sitting with the record-player on the floor, moving the needle back and forth and learning by heart the tunes that most appealed to me. I would listen over and over, until I knew every note and flourish; I could hum, sing and whistle every single one. Even today, when I sit on a stage or find myself in a recording studio, I often go back to those same tunes that have travelled all this way with me – they feel like they have become a physical part of me. I was listening to the music of people like fiddlers Kathleen Collins and Bobby Casey, accordionist Tony McMahon, and even the Tulla and Kilfenora céilí bands. I was becoming completely lost in their music. Following the imprint of their musical ideas, I felt I began to get a glimpse into their musical consciousness. Each time I sat on the living-room floor, intently listening to their music, I picked up a little of who they were. Every now and then I would come out to the kitchen to present to my father the latest tune I'd learned. I wanted to get his opinion – or at least this is what I was telling myself. Of course, what I really wanted was his approval. He, however, would say exactly what he thought in a completely unfiltered and honest way, and the worst was that you knew it was 100 per cent what he believed. Every time I presented a tune to my father, I was encountering a musical barometer that wouldn't lie, because he was basically unable to hide his feelings. It wasn't always easy for me to hear what he had to say. If he didn't like what I played, it might hurt, but I also knew that it was a genuine opinion. This was problematic for me at the time, especially when I was just mostly looking for encouragement, a pat on the back. I'd complain and he'd say, 'But you asked!' and in the end I had to accept the cold, hard truth of what he thought. He never responded in technical terms – he'd never talk about tone, intonation, ornamentation or anything technical. His response was always about how it felt to him, or, worse still, how it didn't feel. The focus was always on what music was supposed to do for you.

Although I was regularly in the kitchen playing the latest tune I'd figured out, I spent way more time with the record-player. This model had adjustable speeds and a needle that you could flip over to play old 78rpm records, which in turn gave me access to the collection of old gramophone records that my father had been collecting since his youth. These recordings were from another time, and in some ways you had to adjust your thinking to imagine the world they came from and the world they were speaking to. Being able to envision these different eras is a useful skill in trying to make sense of this music, which was speaking to another time. The old 78s were the first widely available recorded Irish music, and mostly came from America. The most technically proficient players were the ones who got recorded, and there was a kind of bubbly, upbeat, cheerful quality to the recordings that seemed in tune with the vibrancy of the jazz age. Meanwhile, the piano-playing mimicked the vamping style of dance music popular in grand houses during the American Gilded Age of the late nineteenth century. When this stylistic influence, in combination with the best technique of the great Sligo fiddle-players, hit Ireland in these 78rpm recordings, it was a hugely attractive sound, a whole new idea of music, and a whole new level of technical proficiency. As younger musicians, my father and Paddy Canny absorbed these recordings with gusto. To our modern ears these recordings may sound a bit jolly, in a quaint and almost exaggerated way, but they nonetheless had a huge impact in every corner of Ireland and significantly shaped the direction this music would take.

There also exists a form of singing, primarily in the Irish language, that we now refer to as 'sean nós' ('the old style'). In my opinion, there is also a sean nós of the fiddle, the pipes, the flute, the whistle and concertina. Perhaps this sean nós sounded to many like a lamenting version of the music, contradicting the new upbeat music that was being predominantly recorded; this might be one reason why there was a big part of traditional music that would go unacknowledged for many decades – the subtle, plaintive music of fiddlers like Padraig O'Keeffe, John Kelly, Tommy Potts or John Doherty, who were speaking a different musical language that was mostly overrun by the influx of technically dexterous playing recorded during that era in America. There wasn't a place in this commercially recorded music for this other musical language; we didn't hear sean nós singing, we didn't hear slow airs in the sean nós style. Maybe the subtle bent notes were too granular for this recording technology or for that moment in time. The old sean nós was slowly being pushed to the margins. This doesn't take away from the excitement, energy and creativity of musicians such as the fiddle-players Michael Coleman and James Morrison, or the uilleann-piper Patsy Touhey, who were making records in America. Their influence was monumental but there was still lots of musical richness to be explored and understood in the musical styles of places like East and West Clare or Sliabh Luachra in Kerry, a region known for its very distinct style of playing; there was still music in the isolated communities of the west that spoke from a very different place. In the recordings from America we were hearing Irish music speaking to us from the New World, from a different consciousness through a new and different medium. I think it was difficult for listeners and musicians at that time in Ireland to achieve a balanced response, or at least a response where they didn't turn their backs on the sean nós expression that was giving way to a technically advanced iteration of the music. This version of the music was hugely attractive and it held sway until the sixties, when pianist-composer Seán Ó Riada, piper and broadcaster Séamus Ennis, and broadcaster Ciarán Mac Mathúna began to alert us to other, seemingly more rugged, raw and elemental expressions of traditional music. The rugged and the raw was where I went looking, but I also understood and carried with me the fiddle music of the Sligo greats. My primary default musical accent is still the East Clare music of my formative years, but I now regard traditional music's rich diversity of stylistic approaches, rhythmic ideas and emotional expression to all be part of my larger musical palette.

While I was starting to immerse myself in the music more seriously, one of my playing routines was to lock myself in the bathroom with my fiddle. The bathroom had this beautiful resonant sound which made the fiddle ring and sing in ways other rooms didn't, so that became my preferred place to play. I would sit on the side of the bathtub with my eyes closed, playing inwardly, wrapped up in a world of my own. I never overly obsessed about technical matters. It was all about immersing myself in a fantastical world of feeling and expression. Once I'd conquered the initial phase, of modest, basic competence on the instrument, practice – for the want of a better word – never again felt like just practice. Playing became a passionate pursuit, something I couldn't get enough of. I sought refuge in the music; it was a kind of medicine that I administered to myself. Initially, as a performer it was quite difficult to go out and reveal this experience publicly. It was so internal and personal. Playing in public became about my effort to turn this inward experience outward. Over time, as I grew as a musician, the greatest pleasure would eventually become the giving, the revealing and the sharing of the music. For me, the full meaning of the music is achieved in reaching out sincerely to connect with the listener. The stage has now become a place with the same musical freedom I first experienced sitting on the side of that bathtub many years ago.

4

I'M TOLD THAT in the years before I went to school, I had an inclination to escape, to run away, so I could be on my own. The immediate front yard of our house was closed off by walls, dense, impenetrable hedges and two gates. I don't know how I managed it, but I was able to wriggle my way through the bars of the gates. This great escape became a common occurrence. I wasn't running away or anything dramatic like that; sometimes I would just casually stroll to the neighbour's house in my pyjamas and wellington boots for a visit while my mother and father were milking cows, and sometimes I would take off to while away a few hours puttering around in the stream. I was sometimes missing for so long that search parties would have to be organized to find me. I seemed to have this longing for freedom, to explore a wider world. I have this memory of trying to reach for the kitchen door handle to get out; I remember only being able to touch it with the tips of my fingers, but I knew there was a world out there and that's where I wanted to be. Eventually they attached chicken wire to the gates of the yard to stop me from getting through the bars, but there was one spot they forgot to block properly. It was a gulley that went under a wall, which was there for water from the drain to flow through. Though I remember squeezing myself through this gulley, I have no recollection of anything after that, but I'm told I was later found up the hill at the back of the house with a stick in hand, following cattle. Maybe this was me acting out some epigenetic memory of the generations of Hayeses who had been herdsmen on Maghera mountain, or perhaps the faeries were calling me.

Many times in my life I'd suffer at the hand of my go-it-alone independence. I would try to solve everything on my own, single-handedly, and was unwilling to be dependent and vulnerable, when on many occasions it would have served me much better to let others help. The world seems to value self-reliance, but music, on the other hand, often asks for the opposite. There was some dynamic in our home, which I still can't fully figure out, that somehow made me want to keep my problems to myself and solve them myself, even from a very young age. I may have inherited my bold and independent nature from my mother, who was a very strong-willed person, or from my grandfather Quillan, who by all accounts was also a strong character. This streak certainly seems embedded in my DNA, and at times it can be a struggle to resist what seems like a natural inclination towards independence.

School didn't sit well with my personality or my temperament. Even before I started, I wasn't looking forward to it. I instinctively knew it was going to be a big rupture to the life I'd already got to know. I think I may have heard an ominous suggestion from my parents that the teachers would eventually put manners on me. I started school in August 1967, having just turned five the previous month. From our house, on the side of Maghera mountain, the journey to school was about two miles. To get there we would walk a small gravel road along the side of the mountain, crossing two foothills and one valley to arrive at the second valley, where the school was situated. All the children from the townlands where I grew up had walked this same road for generations. The very first day I was to go to school, my mother walked me to our neighbours the Cannys' house. Three children out of that family of six were already going to school and I was to walk with them. One of them was John Joe Canny. He was a few months younger than me and this was his first day also. Michael, James, John Joe and myself headed off from there with our bags strapped to our backs. We were all wearing short trousers and each of us had a bottle of milk and some bread wrapped in paper in our bags. I can't imagine that I had much else in my bag that morning. Tommy Woods, from the beautiful townland of Cloonagrow, would emerge a little later to the main road just at the Cannys' house. He was the oldest of us and operating at a different level; he had a bicycle and would pass us by a bit further along the road. Shortly after the Cannys' house, we'd take the small mountain road that went uphill towards McMahon's house, which was part way up our first climb. The funny thing is, even though I make reference to 'McMahon's house', it was better known as Houlihan's house; the house had been the family home of the Houlihans for generations before John Joe McMahon married into the farm when he wed Mary Houlihan. A practice that occurred quite a lot back then in rural Ireland was the nicknaming of households. Usually the purpose of this was to distinguish one family from another if they shared the same surname. Sometimes, however, it was just a nickname that had stuck. Our next-door neighbour Paddy Canny (not to be mistaken for the musician of the same name) was always known as 'The Volunteer', as a result of having joined the Volunteers during the war years. Likewise, my own family were known as 'Quillan Hayes', after my grandfather. Nicknames came about in a variety of ways, but once they stuck, you could either find yourself cursed or blessed with the one you were given, as those names lasted generations.

Four of the McMahons were going to school at the time I started: Marian, Margaret, Michael and Geraldine, which meant there was now a gang of us walking this gravel road up and down the hills, a journey we would make for many years to come in all varieties of weather. The climb after McMahon's house continued past a little avenue to the right, where John 'The Geg' Moroney's house was. We'd eventually reach our first flat stretch of road at the top. After this, we could look down towards the end of the next valley and see the entirety of the beautiful Lough Graney. Up to our left was the mountain of Maghera. We then went downhill, past Malley's Stream at the bottom, before we began another climb up towards Moroney's Flat, the second short piece of flat road on the journey. Moroney's Flat was named after another a local family of Moroneys, but nobody seems to know who the Malleys were. There is, however, something very beautiful about a family name long gone from the area, but still being remembered in the name of a picturesque mountain stream.

From Rodger's Well to Houlihan's Cross, Malley's Stream to Moroney's Flat and Bolands' Cross, it was as if various families owned these local landmarks. It's almost like an invisible rural graffiti, where the family names are engraved on the landscape. When children eventually stopped walking that road, those place names that the cartographer never knew about began to fade from everyday conversation. If we're not careful, they may soon be forgotten completely.

After Moroney's Flat we descended the steepest part of the road all the way down to Bolands' Cross, where we met the main road again and took a left for the last stretch towards the school. There was a shortcut to the school before we'd reach the main road at the back of Jimmy Collins's house and it led straight to the back of the school yard. It went through the most magnificent grove of hazelnut trees, with a beautiful stream that ran through it. I remember sunny spring mornings walking barefoot across that stream, and autumn evenings climbing those trees in search of hazelnuts. If it was too wet or mucky, we wouldn't take the shortcut. Instead, we'd continue to the main road and turn left, where just before the school all the children from the bottom of the valley would amble up a steep slope towards the main road. They were the Dillons and the O'Briens from Knockna-geeha (Cnoc na Gaoithe, the townland of the famous poet Brian Merriman), the Flahertys from Doorus, and the Moloneys and Cahills, who would come walking down from the Killanena side. I travelled this road for many years, and all the experiences and feelings it evoked are still imprinted on my soul.

Douglawn National School consisted of just one room, with a single open fireplace to heat the whole room, and two teachers who were sisters, Brid Whelan and Margaret McMahon. Brid, who was also the principal, was married and lived near Scarriff. Margaret, on the other hand, was single and lived very close to the school. Margaret taught junior infants, senior infants, first and second class; Brid taught third class right through to sixth. In Margaret's end of the room, the seats faced the back wall; Brid's classes sat facing away from us. The first thing I remember from that first day, after we'd been assigned to our seats, was that we were asked to stand up for the morning prayers. That was my very first objection to how things were being done at school: I asked the teacher (Margaret in this case) why we had to stand up to pray? I then informed her that we always knelt down at home and I had expected we might do the same in school. The first thing out of my mouth on my very first day of school was effectively a demand that the teacher explain herself to me along with the implicit suggestion that I might actually know a better way. She gave no real answer, so I just moved along with the plan and did what everyone else was doing. Following the prayers, the teacher summoned me up to her desk. I responded by asking, 'Why don't you come down to my desk?' I didn't seem to grasp the power structure at play and hadn't yet properly understood the authority of the teacher. I bent to her wishes and went up to her desk, but I don't remember what she needed to tell me or show me. During playtime, both Margaret and Brid would bring all of the younger pupils outside to play a game of Ring-a-Ring-a-Rosey. We all held hands in a circle and sang together before falling to the ground in unison. I suppose it was a way of getting us to connect in a playful way but it was lacking the kind of adventure and excitement that I liked.

I don't remember many other details about that first day at school, other than making the journey home after we'd finished. We worked our way up and down the hills until I finally got to the Cannys' house and from there was only about another third of a mile to our house. I'd made the journey to the Cannys' house with the other schoolchildren without parental support, so I was deflated to see my mother waiting for me at Cannys'. She was there to walk me home the last stretch. Before I reached her, I remember shouting out to her to go home. I had wanted to prove that, at the grand old age of five, I could do this by myself, and under no circumstances did I want my mother swooping in at the last minute to undermine my achievement. There was no way I could have understood how heartbreaking this might have been for her – it must have looked to her as if I was trying to tell her I didn't need her any more, that I didn't miss her at all during my first day of school. Of course I missed her, and frankly would have much preferred not to have had go to school in the first place, but I was eager to prove that I was grown up enough to do this journey without any help.

The school had no running water – we had one bucket of water in the play yard and one plastic cup that everybody in the school drank from. Douglawn School may not have boosted my confidence but it probably boosted my immune system. Every morning the bucket was brought by one of the older boys from a spring well close by. I had to wait many years before it was my turn to go to the well for water. Every germ and bug in the parish probably made its way through that bucket, and I'm convinced our daily use of it supercharged our resilience in the long run.

Just before lunchtime we would bring our bottles of milk close to the fire so that we'd have a warm drink with our slices of bread. The bathroom was a dry bathroom without running water at the back of the school, which I found a bit challenging. The whole scene sounds harsh, but the lack of amenities wasn't actually that bad – we simply accepted it as normal. I think my biggest problem was that I just didn't like being locked up all day and forced into a monotony of rote memorization exercises.

Our two teachers were generally kind and well-intentioned, and would administer very mild corporal punishment every now and again; you'd have to come up to the table and hold out your hand for slaps with a wooden ruler. They never hit us in any way that hurt physically, but it did hurt in other ways – the shame of being declared guilty was itself painful, and if we ever cried, it was because of that. I always felt a bit withdrawn in school and remained that way for most of my school years. I had this curious mixture of being simultaneously independent and sensitive. Sensitivity was a quality that was to be concealed. It was a weakness, a vulnerability that was best kept to oneself. This same sensitivity, on the other hand, was probably what allowed me to easily connect to the subtleties of music.

Maybe I was predisposed to a profound dislike of school. After all, I regularly heard my parents talk about how much they'd disliked it. That said, however bad I may have felt school was for me, it seems that it was much more authoritarian and violent in my parents' time. My mother often told the story of one day being falsely accused of stealing and hiding the teacher's cane, the infamous tool of coercion. Being wrongly blamed, she walked out of the classroom and went home in protest. The actual culprit did own up later, but my mother always pointed out that she never received an apology. I really wish our education had veered towards nurture and encouragement, instead of being more like an obstacle course of forced compliance and order.

Though the walk to and from school was challenging, both in terms of steep climbs and distance, it was also where I would experience the most joy. The way home was somewhat more relaxed; free from parents and teachers, we played, explored, picked fruit and climbed trees in search of hazelnuts. And even though we were usually rushing in the morning, which meant the journey tended to lack that feeling of unperturbed joy, it did sometimes have its charms. Occasionally, on our way to school, the entire valley of Lough Graney would be covered in a deep fog; a magical scene for us from our mountain road. Other mornings, we would jump over potholes coated thick with ice, walk by hedges completely covered either in dew, or, as was often the case, an astonishing shock of cobwebs that covered every hedge, sparkling under the early-morning sun. The only thing interfering with the joy of this scene was that we were, of course, on our way to school. But though getting out of school each day was a relief, we immediately faced a very steep climb. Even if I tried to drive up that hill to this day, I would only be able to do so by putting the car in first gear. Perhaps it helped that there was dinner waiting at the end of the climb!

The people we met on this mountainous journey to and from school became almost like human marker points along the way, much in the same way as we had the landscape markers like

Malley's Stream. The first house we would pass on our way home from school, a little bit up that hill, belonged to husband-and-wife Jimmy and Eileen Collins. Jimmy was a jolly, kind man who was happy to have fun, play and joke around with us, Eileen was the epitome of motherly warmth. We'd present our untied shoes to Eileen and ask her to tie them for us, after which she would often treat us to a sweet or a biscuit. We gradually got into the habit of making sure our shoelaces were loose every evening as we approached the house. I remember reaching Moroney's house another afternoon and wondering if I would be lucky enough to get a treat, if I collected the eggs from Nora May's hen house and brought them in to her. I got a biscuit that time too.

After Moroney's, we'd sometimes run into Michael Rogers, who was an old, kind, soft person with a little bit of devilment in him. He had the distinction of being the bishop's brother and having two sons who were priests. I remember him holding out his stick that he used for herding cattle – he'd ask us to jump over it. We'd individually take a run at it, but he'd just raise it as you were getting close, and of course we'd balk right at that moment. We never tired of this game of jumping the stick and he never tired of playing it with us. The next encounter were the geese at Houlihan's. When I was around five or six, these boisterous, temperamental creatures were almost as big as me. We'd try to sneak by the house as quietly as possible so as not to alert the geese to our presence, but of course they would always hear us coming. Almost as if on cue, the entire flock would charge towards us with their necks outstretched, making their threatening, hissing sound. We were terrified and ran for our lives. Sometimes they would even block the road, which in turn would force us to start climbing into fields to get around them. We felt like we just barely survived this obstacle every evening. Fortunately, the geese never caught up with us.

The final obstacle was Joe Rodgers. He was a bachelor living across the road from the bottom of our avenue, the same age as my uncle Liam, and he didn't seem to like me. He'd try to be playful and block us on the road, but his playfulness manifested in the form of neck-holds, arm-twisting and pinching. Joe was worse than the geese, which was a difficult feat to accomplish. He liked my brother Pat, though, so he'd mostly let him go free, but I wasn't quite so lucky.

The road home from school, much like life itself, brought joys and challenges along the way. The years passed and these walks to and from school became part of my relationship with the local area and with the generations of neighbours who'd walked this road before me. But as much as I enjoyed the walks and connected with the journey, I still never connected with the destination; I was never comfortable or happy in school. Any day I could avoid being there was a successful day for me, but the only way to have this kind of successful day was to be sick – or to pretend to be sick, which was nearly more work than going to school. The happenings on the farm felt more real, just as picking strawberries or climbing trees on the road home felt like a much more enriching experience than being at school itself.

When I was eight years of age, my uncle Liam, who worked in the chipboard factory in the town of Scariff, left our family home and moved to a house in Scariff with his new bride, Mary. It was a blow when Liam left. Liam was a decisive figure with strong opinions, but there was another side to him that was warm, good-humoured and sociable. I had been very close with him, and while he wasn't as soft-natured as my father, he was always very playful and affectionate with myself and Pat. We adored him.

Shortly after he got married, Liam inherited a small farm in Killanena, about four miles away. It was left to him by my grand-uncle's surviving wife, Hannie Hogan, who'd recently passed away and had no children to leave it to. Back then, houses without children seemed to be the places that changed the least. Without children introducing a new energy into the home, old ways seemed more likely to stay as they were. That was very much the case with Hannie's home. She had lived deep in a glen on the side of the mountain near Killanena Church in a house that looked like a humble version of the cottage in the film *The Quiet Man*. You had to walk across a field, then cross a stream, to reach her small, thatched cottage snuggled in between the mountains. I have early memories of that house back when my father and uncle would go there to help her with the hay and other farm work she couldn't manage on her own. I can still picture the turf fire blazing while she chopped carrots on the kitchen table, the front door open with the mountain stream running by her front yard. In those times, the inside and outside worlds of houses were not as hermetically separated as they are now. The front door would be open most of the time, and when a gabháil, or armful, of wood was brought in you could just throw it on the rugged floor in front of the fire. Indeed, the inside was often as rugged as the out-side. The only running water Hannie had was that stream itself.

There was neither electricity nor indoor plumbing; there wasn't even a gravel path that connected the house with a road. The house was sheltered by mountains on two sides. You couldn't see down into the valley from there, you couldn't see any other houses or hear any cars; instead, there was a piece of flat land in front which kept your vision pointed towards a more distant horizon. The place was completely untouched by the twentieth century.

As Liam was the only one in the family who drove a car – and sometimes drove it fast, too, much to the excitement of myself and Pat – his departure meant my father had to buy a car and learn how to drive. My father was around fifty years of age by then. He had got his driver's licence some years previously when they were handing them out freely without a theory test or even an actual driving test. You didn't even need to know how to drive, and my father had never so much as sat in a driver's seat. I remember he bought a beige-coloured second-hand Ford Anglia from Shaughnessy's Garage in Gort. I never liked the look of those cars, never liked how the back window slanted inwards instead of outwards, like all other normal cars. On the evening it was delivered, someone from the garage took my father for a drive up the road and coached him as he slowly drove back to the house. This was the first time he had driven. My uncle Christy, who drove an Anglia himself, was also there offering lots of expert advice on how to manage the car. As it turns out, Christy wasn't exactly a great driver himself.

My father decided he would attempt to drive to Mass in Feakle the following Sunday. During the week, he would practise by driving up to Paddy Canny's old house and making a turn at the crossroads, where it was possible to swing the car around fully without ever having to put it in reverse. Reversing was still a long way off, so he chose to go to Feakle Mass instead of our usual Kilclaren Mass, a route that allowed him to drive a full circle in a forward direction. All he would have to do was pull up to the side of the street somewhere close to the church, and then after Mass continue straight on towards Glendaree to complete the full circle home. Nonetheless, we were all on high alert in the car that Sunday morning when the time came to hit the road. Pat and I were on sentry duty, kneeling on the back seat looking out the back window for any cars that might be trying to pass this slow-moving vehicle. Apparently, it was too great a risk for my father to divert his attention away from the windscreen by looking in the mirror. Driving to Feakle was a collective effort and there wasn't a single moment of ease until we got home after Mass – and yet there was something in the shared vulnerability of that journey that brought us closer together as a family.

My father was not mechanically inclined. He was more connected to nature and all things natural – he was skilled with hand-held tools and the horses on the farm, and, of course, with the fiddle. He was a man from before the technological age; a gentle old soul whose more natural inclination was to inhabit the world of the generation before him. He seemed to really love and admire the old people of his childhood and spoke of them a lot. But for all my father's attributes and abilities, his command of the car was not one of them, and so his driving became a major issue for us and a source of some genuine terror at times. As time went on he became much more competent, but he was never what you'd call a comfortable driver. For a few years, our car journeys were a cramped experience, with a cot for Helen placed lengthways across the back seat, and Pat and I squashed in at either side. This was before the modern clip-in seats, or before anyone even used seat belts. Anna Marie, meanwhile, would be in the front passenger seat on my mother's knees. Once my father got the hang of driving, we went to lots of places and started visiting my grandparents in Crusheen, not to mention spending way more time with our cousins, the McNamaras.

Our house had fiddles, but the accordion ruled over at the McNamaras, as Joe had spent years playing the accordion in the Tulla Céilí Band. Mary and Christy, the two eldest of the McNamaras' eight children, also played. Whenever there were family gatherings, especially as we got older, you could be sure that between the McNamaras and myself and my father, music would form a big part of it. If we were just playing music in their kitchen during a visit, it wouldn't be out of the ordinary for them to get up and dance a set. It was a great house to visit, always a happy and vibrant energy there. As kids, we would play and chase each other late into the summer evenings, sometimes right into the dark of night. One of the eight, James, was about my age, and so naturally we developed a strong friendship. James would have spent a lot of time in our house, growing up, sometimes staying for part of his summer holidays too. The McNamaras lived about a mile and a half away, in Crusheen, about a mile and a half away from our grandparents Molly and John. My grandparents' cottage was situated a long way in from the main road, in Cappafean, a place that was supposed to be filled with faeries. It was surrounded by fields, one of which was the famous Páirc na Tarabh ('The Bull Field'), where healthy potatoes continued to grow throughout the famine without ever getting the blight. People from all over came to get seed potatoes from there.

My grandparents' home was a small, whitewashed thatched cottage. It was difficult to imagine how the eight children of my mother's family were all raised there. There was no other house in sight and by the time we'd reach the house we would be well up for the stories of faeries and ghosts that awaited us around the roasting open fire. Whenever we visited, my father, my grandfather and my unmarried uncle, Christy, who was living with them, would often decide to leave the women to their own conversation and go to Galligan's pub in Crusheen for a drink. My uncle Christy was usually the person pushing this plan – he enjoyed his few drinks more than my grandfather and certainly more than my father, who rarely drank at all. Over time, the idea of bringing the fiddles along became part of this plan. Here was a more valid excuse for going to the pub, and as a fiddler it would eventually allow me the opportunity to go along also. I think I must have been thirteen when my mother finally allowed me. Although the pub was called The Highway Inn, it was actually better known locally as Galligan's. Joe Galligan, who owned and ran the place, was a big music fan. He also played guitar, and would bring it out and join in with my father and myself. This was my first experience of guitar accompaniment with the fiddle, and I loved it. On a few occasions, brothers John and Tim Lyons would turn up and join in, as they both played accordion and sang. It started becoming a regular occurrence, and one that I would look forward to immensely.

While music and school were very much separate for me, it was actually through school that I would get my first taste of a music competition. It came about as a result of step-dancing lessons. A woman I knew only as Miss O'Loughlin used to come to the school once a week to teach us how to Irish step-dance, and while Pat and I both participated and enjoyed it, we weren't fully serious about it. I don't think anyone was. Before she'd arrive, the desks at Margaret's end of the school would be pushed back so that space could be made for the dance class. This was when we'd all start practising the steps from the previous week for the first time; no music, just us all moving around the floor in different directions, dancing to different tunes in our minds, our arms firmly pinned to our sides. With all the muddy wellingtons and shoes trampling up and down on an unpolished floor, the only result we'd achieve would be a massive dust storm. Before long, we'd lose interest and turn the practice into a different game, where we'd just start bumping into each other like bumper cars at an amusement park. Miss O'Loughlin was clearly a woman with considerable blind faith in her class: she decided we should attend a dance 'feis' in Woodford, County Galway. We were happy to go anywhere and were looking forward to this. I knew it would be a fun day; the Cannys next door were also going. My mother somehow found out that there was a music competition at the feis and suggested I bring my fiddle along and compete. I didn't mind giving it a try.

I was in for a bit of a shock when I heard Máirín Fahy play the fiddle in the competition. She was about my age but in terms of musical maturity and capacity she was light years ahead of me. I was completely taken aback, and my complacent, happy-go-lucky world of music basically collapsed that day. This was my first time hearing her perform and I was awestruck by her facility on the instrument. She was already at least as technically accomplished as most adults I'd heard up to that point. Her aunt was the very renowned fiddler Aggie Whyte, and Máirín's mother, Bridie, was also a very accomplished fiddle-player. They were from Ballinakill in Galway, which had produced many fine musicians over the years. The music competition was a foregone conclusion; I had absolutely no chance whatsoever. Years later, my mother would recall that it was after this experience that I really knuckled down. For me, the question was whether or not I could maintain the idea of myself as a musician. I was unwilling to give up on being a fiddle-player, but I didn't want to be just any kind of player, I wanted to be a really good one. My lack of achievement up to that point wasn't through any lack of enthusiasm or love for playing; I had just been lax and unfocused. I loved to play but I wasn't organized in any consistent way to make musical accomplishment a realistic possibility.

After that day in Galway, I took the fiddle from its case and never put it back. Instead it sat, out of its case, on the stairs leading up to my room. I was the only one using those stairs, so it wasn't going to be stepped on, but it meant it was now at hand for me to play at any instant I chose. I would play a little bit in the morning before breakfast, and again as soon as I came in the door from school. Playing was prioritized even before having dinner.

Needless to say, I didn't carry anywhere near the same dedication when it came to school. That was a daily obligation I viewed as more of a hindrance in my life than a help. My evenings of school homework were generously interrupted with music breaks sitting on the side of the bathtub. As soon as I hit even a mildly challenging point in my homework, or if I was faced with some homework I didn't like, I'd go straight for the fiddle instead of just knuckling down. Music was, and still is, my sustenance and my refuge.

Around that same time, innovation was starting to reach East Clare and telephone wires were making an appearance throughout the countryside. The Department of Posts and Telegraphs spent weeks putting down poles, my anticipation building as they began to edge closer to our house. On the day our phone was finally installed, I accompanied my mother to Kelly's Post Office in nearby Caher to test it out. We dialled the operator in Feakle from the post office and asked to be connected to Feakle 27 – we were calling home for the first time. My father answered. As a child, I marvelled at this. As we walked home, I looked up at the phone line stretching from pole to pole all the way along the side of the road to our house. My brain couldn't fathom how our voices managed to travel back and forth on those wires so fast. How did these wires carry sound? How could I speak to my father over two miles away and hear his immediate reply?

Though we already had a black and white television, it was the phone that seemed to kickstart a series of modernizations and changes in the house. It was followed by the refrigerator, linoleum on the kitchen floor, and a range stove that replaced the open-hearth fire, which was now closed off. On the farm, there were regular visits by inspectors from the Department of Agriculture whose job it was to 'modernize' agriculture as we entered the European Economic

Community (EEC). They advised the use of artificial fertilizers and explained how to increase production, encouraging farmers in our area to specialize in either beef or dairy. They informed farmers of the various grant schemes, not to mention the credit that was available to them in order to make this transition possible; they even showed them how to access it. It seemed you would have been foolish not to follow their advice. Small farmers were lured in by the prospect of having a real income for the first time in their lives. We followed suit and became a dairy farm. The sheep had already been gone for some time, and now also were the pigs.

Bob and Fanny were soon replaced by a small tractor, the cows were milked using a milking machine, and more hay was now growing in the fertilized fields. The farm that had eight cows when I was a child gradually increased it to forty. It really was a new farm now, with tasks being carried out in very different ways. The old, ritualistic practices were giving way to a new, commercial agriculture. The farm started to generate more income, which enabled us to afford the kinds of things that would have previously been out of reach. The tractor relieved some of the backbreaking physical labour, which we all welcomed very much. New sheds were built, we fed the animals with silage instead of hay and in the end we started buying potatoes at the shop instead of growing our own. But while the new ways of doing things were winning us over with their convenience and ease, the enchantment of the farm and its old rituals were gradually fading.

Once I'd turned eleven and was starting fifth class, another change towards modernity and convenience arrived. We learned that our small, thirty-three-pupil Douglawn School was to be closed. There were a number of schoolhouses like this around the parish and all were going to be shut and amalgamated into a new school in Flagmount, at the other side of Lough Graney. Gone were the mountain walks and geese battles – we were going to be taken to this new school by bus.

The sepia-toned memories are beginning to fade at this point; modern times were just around the corner, and my recollections from this time are now in colour. This newly built school had fancy desks, tiled floors, running water, and the height of technology in the form of indoor toilets that flushed. The simplicity of our one-roomed Douglawn school was now replaced with something bigger, unfamiliar and a bit intimidating. We felt lost among a sea of new faces as we tried to navigate our way through this new setting. Each class had its own teacher, a set-up that the students of Douglawn had certainly never experienced before. For fifth class, we had a teacher called Mrs Conway, a very warm-hearted, encouraging and kind individual whose religious fervour exceeded even that of my father. The first thing we did each morning in that class was to say the rosary. With this rosary and the one we said at home each evening, I was now up to two rosaries a day. I didn't mind the extra rosary only because of Mrs Conway's extreme kindness and encouragement, which remained constant regardless of how you were doing with the school lessons.

Around this time, feeling that I had advanced a bit since the first competition in Woodford, I had started participating in competitions again. I have a very vivid recollection of attending a 'fleadh cheoil' (music festival) in the Clare village of Toonagh when I was eleven, and once again hearing another amazing fiddle-player of my own age, this time by the name of James Cullinan. He wasn't just miles ahead of me, he was in another league entirely. I didn't get placed at all in that competition. I simply wasn't anywhere near good enough. Again, I resolved to go home and knuckle down even more.

Interestingly, even back then my playing didn't centre around the idea of technical accomplishment. The technical aspect of playing wasn't something my father really focused on. The tunes were what was passed on, and you had to gain a deeper understanding of the music by observing what was going on, just like an apprentice. Most importantly, he could tell me if what I was doing was or wasn't really working, but at that moment I just wanted to play with the same technical proficency as James Cullinan. I remember listening to the only solo recording of fiddler Brendan McGlinchey and being very taken with his technical precision. I then tried to emulate all the detailed technical parts of his playing, and arrived into the kitchen one night to show my father some tunes I'd learned from the record, tunes that I was now trying to play in McGlinchey's style. But it was my mother who spoke instead. She reminded me I had my own style and that I should follow and develop that instead. I took her advice and as I kept going deeper within myself, my own sound gradually began to emerge and I grew more confident that my efforts at going inwards were actually producing something real.

I'd keep returning to the kitchen to get some feedback, but I was mostly left to my own musical devices, learning tunes and figuring out how to play them on my own. Musically, I could try anything I liked, but in the end I'd have to see if I could get it past my father.

This always kept the focus on the essential quality of the music, on its basic functionality as a communication of feeling. We trusted each other; I even trusted him to go and buy records for me. He would often arrive home from Ennis with a new recording, though in reality it was for both of us. At this stage we were both on the hunt for new tunes to learn, and he had a very good ear for identifying melodies with real potential and depth.

Even when I was in school I was thinking of the music, the melodies dancing around in my head, never ceasing to rest. My year in fifth class passed by quite fast, and then it was on to sixth class, which was taught by Mrs Meehan, the school principal. She was very different from Mrs Conway. A robust woman with a naturally stern face, she was a frightening figure, and it was a little more difficult to daydream about music in her presence. She got our attention easily enough as she carried a metre stick, supposedly with the purpose of giving us a visual sense of the new metric system that was taking over the country. Its main purpose, however, was as a tool of compliance. This metre stick was a lot bigger than the skinny foot-long ruler that was usually used to put manners on the unruly, and at the other end of it was a big, strong woman on a mission to maintain order. If Mrs Meehan caught you doing something that she felt deserved punishment, you'd be instructed to hold out your hand while she would administer slaps with said stick. It was so heavy that she'd have to hold it with both hands, but mostly she did this to ensure she didn't actually hurt us. There'd be a twinkle in her eye and a restrained smile that told you that maybe you weren't in that much trouble after all. We all respected her – she was fair and good-humoured – yet you had the distinct feeling that you didn't ever want to see what might happen if she got really angry.

After sixth class, it was time for secondary school. The school in question, Our Lady's College in Gort, County Galway, was just over the county boundary with Clare, where I was from. I'd take the bus from my old school at Douglawn, which meant that the daily hike along the small mountain road was back again for another five years. The secondary school was one of those modern, sixties two-storey buildings with mostly glass on the front, facing the road. It was an all-boys school run by priests, with all-male teachers both lay and clergy. At the same time that I was starting secondary school, I managed to talk my way into the Tulla Céilí Band. My parents didn't think it was a great idea for me to do it, but I wore them down – begged and pleaded to be allowed to travel with the band. Once I started playing with the band at weekends, I continued to do so throughout my secondary-school years, travelling all over the country with them. While my friends were spending their weekends kicking a football, I was out all night playing with the band. I was on half pay because I was young, but I eventually worked my way up to full measure. It meant I always had pocket change when I was a teenager and I was even able to save money in the credit union.

Joining the band helped ensure I ended up feeling more connected to the world of older people than I did to my own age group. Traditional music belonged to an older demographic; teenagers my age were moving in a completely different direction. Friends or classmates at that time had no interest in this type of music that I loved. The fact was that anyone who wanted to be seen as modern made sure to get as far away as possible from this music! As you can imagine, any young person playing traditional music back then would have begun to feel quite ostracized. Being a musician in school wasn't like being good at sports. In that environment, music made me vulnerable. It was very much misunderstood and I could expect to be ridiculed if traditional music was mentioned. I kept my music to myself as much as possible, but more and more I was finding myself at the margins socially – I just didn't feel like I was fitting in. I didn't know how to; on some level maybe I didn't even want to. In some ways I was happy to feel excluded. I would rather have been connected wholeheartedly to the music than turn my back on it in order to feel more connected to my contemporaries. A big advantage to having genuine friendships and music partnerships with these older musicians – some of whom would have been sixty, maybe even seventy years of age at the time – is that I felt as though I was learning a lot. I was very moulded by the experience of being in their company and being exposed to their understanding of things, and their sense of the world – and, of course, the music. They felt quite comfortable sharing things with me because they wanted me to *get* the music. They knew I had an ear for it and a genuine interest. I think that encouraged the older musicians to share with me their thoughts and feelings about music. That was invaluable to me. Right from the beginning, the scene surrounding this music was drawing me in.

I remember one night in 1973 when we celebrated the famous accordion-player Joe Cooley's final return home from America.

He had been with the Tulla Céilí Band during its early years, emigrating to England a few years later before returning to rejoin the band for a short stint before finally emigrating to the United States. He'd started off in New York, then moved to Chicago and finally ended up in San Francisco. My father had often talked about him, how he would add some beautiful variation to almost every tune he played, often just a small alteration of a few notes but enough to lift the tune to another level.

From hearing the stories and descriptions of the moments of magic he could conjure up, I began to build my own idea of the man and his music. According to my father, before the band were going to play a dance in a local hall it would be common enough for people down the village to be looking for Cooley to bring him away to a pub and get a few tunes out of him beforehand. My father recalled, 'There were always people pulling and dragging him in some direction or other.' It would be time to start the dance and Cooley would be in full flight playing in a pub somewhere. My father would go searching for him and would then have the difficult task of breaking up the scene to get him out of the pub and back to the hall for the dance. I imagine my father arriving at the bar and finding Cooley in the corner with people gathered around him, his head thrown backwards, his chest wide open, a cigarette in his mouth, smoke and drink everywhere and people shouting, *'Good man, Joe!', 'Glory, Cooley!', 'Play "The Wise Maid"!'*

Cooley liked to start tunes slowly, with a heavy groove and just slightly behind the beat, in a way that seemed to allow him to apply maximum power – a power that would send waves of delight right through the room as he held and extended notes and put his own beautiful twists on the tune. I'm not sure I even needed to be there, because I need only to imagine this scene to feel the music going right through me. I know that the single recording of Cooley doesn't fully capture his music. Instead, I use the anecdotal stories, my father's reverential love of Joe's music, and the echo of Cooley in Tony McMahon's playing, to help construct the Joe Cooley of my imagination. He and his music are alive and well deep within me, and continue to provide me with lots of inspiration.

Dr Bill Loughnane, who was a local member of the 'Dáil' and a fiddler in the Tulla Céilí Band, had organized a homecoming concert for Cooley in the hall in Feakle. At this stage, Joe was terminally ill with throat cancer and had come home to meet his old friends one last time. I remember seeing my father hugging Joe. It had been a long time since they'd seen each other.

Dr Bill knew how to put on a big night of music. He had invited the flute-player Matt Molloy and fiddler Tommy Peoples, who would both soon go on to be a central element of the famous Bothy Band; Aggie Whyte and her sister Bridie were there, along with fiddlers Paddy Canny and Martin Rochford and flute player Peadar O'Loughlin, Dessie Mulkere on the banjo, and all the members of the Tulla Céilí Band, past and present. Dr Bill himself was the MC for the evening, and in his usual thoughtful way had also included the eleven-year-old me in this concert. This was my first time seeing Joe Cooley, and my first time playing in an actual concert. I think Dr Bill wanted to encourage me and to show people that he and his colleagues weren't the last generation playing this music, that another generation was coming on board.

I was better at playing jigs than reels and had selected a pair of my best. I was very nervous as I walked on to the stage – the hall was full and I was the centre of attention in a way I'd never experienced before. I was terrified. I sat on the chair in the centre of the stage with a microphone right in front of me and started my two jigs. My first sensation was the feeling that the ground underneath was disappearing; I couldn't feel my feet – it felt like I was floating in a kind of disembodied dream. I managed to get through the tunes without faltering and as soon as the last note was played, I made a hurried dash for the stage wing. I didn't wait for or acknowledge the applause, which somehow seemed to keep on going. I think the audience could sense my shyness and terror, and wanted to show me all the encouragement they could. Also, there weren't that many young players around at the time so I might have been a bit of a novelty. There were calls for more but there was no way I was returning. I continued to ignore all the suggestions side-stage that I should go back on. I had already run the gauntlet, I had managed to get through, and I sure as hell wasn't going to run it again.

I met Matt Molloy and Tommy Peoples in the backstage room. They asked me to play for them so I just played the same two tunes again, feeling that I still needed to make my best impression. They were in their mid-twenties but they took the time to compliment me and show an interest in this shy eleven-year-old. I never forgot that moment of kindness and encouragement. I've carried that memory with me and have tried to be careful and considerate to the eleven-year-olds I've also met along the way. The tiniest bit of encouragement can go a long way in terms of someone's confidence.

Joe Cooley finally played that night, his big heart pouring out to the audience and all the love in the hall flowing back towards him. Everyone knew why they were there; Joe was bidding them farewell, leaving them with one last experience of his soulfulness.

Later that year, Joe Cooley sadly passed away and was buried in his hometown of Peterswell, County Galway. I accompanied my father to the funeral, which was attended by a large gathering from the music world along with hundreds of people who'd simply been touched by his music. Like so many occasions when the traditional-music world would congregate, I'd find myself by my father's side listening to the conversations with his colleagues and friends, both reminiscing and discussing what was currently happening musically. These were glimpses into the shared understanding of the music. People like Peadar O'Loughlin and Tony McMahon certainly had a lot of strong opinions; others may also have had strong ideas, which they expressed in a more subtle fashion. Anything from Seán Ó Riada to The Chieftains to flamboyant fiddler Seán McGuire might come up in conversation, but on the day of Cooley's funeral there was plenty of reminiscing and talk about the special touch in Joe's own music. Dr Bill wrote a piece for the *Irish Press* about Joe Cooley and his funeral, where he listed the names of all the prominent musicians in attendance. Right there, in the middle of them all, was my name. I certainly didn't rank as being among the prominent musicians present but I imagine that when Dr Bill came to mention my father he also thought of me, and in another thoughtful gesture included my name. I was now beginning to see myself as part of this wider music community.

Whenever I listened to the older musicians discuss music, I would always hear them speak about the idea of feeling, the idea of heart, the idea of soulfulness. Listening to their thoughts helped me skip right past the idea of music as simply playing an instrument. I was seeking out the feeling of this music instead. The isolation I was experiencing from feeling disconnected from my peers, my innate feelings of unlovability and unworthiness, were all processed through the music I played. It was a release. I took the alienation of my school experience and turned it into musical fuel. Of course, it wasn't all melancholy. Music for me was also an encounter with a range of passionate experiences all the way from a gentle sadness to an exuberant joy – music can be a beautiful, poetic mixture of all the emotions. I began to play just to create an authentic musical experience for myself, an experience I seemed to really need. This in turn began to shape how I physically played the fiddle. I just kept trying, over and over, to experience that authentic feeling, my technique naturally and gradually evolving to facilitate the expression I was trying to make.

People like Junior Crehan, Tony McMahon, his brother Brendan McMahon, Martin Rochford and a multitude of other great musicians have all spoken to me about 'the feeling' in music, and once I fathomed what they meant, I recognized this 'feeling' as music's true currency. That's really what it was all about. No matter what kind of playing I heard out there in the world, if it wasn't exuding this deeper expression of music that all these musicians were talking about, then I would just pass it by. I didn't care if it was popular, if it was flashy, or if the musicians responsible for creating it were technical geniuses; if it wasn't actually speaking this deeper musical language, then it was something I didn't have to pay attention to. I took that message to heart throughout my teenage years, and viewed everything I saw or heard through that lens. I began to understand that there was a doctrine of soulfulness, feeling, depth, passion and tradition that the older, wiser souls of this music knew they were carrying. They were simply looking for more carriers, and so I felt as though they had brought me in under their wings and that such a gesture was to be cherished and respected. For me, these musical friendships with older musicians meant music became much more than playing the fiddle; I felt like I was being entrusted with something important to our culture with the expectation that I would help preserve it.

Tommy Potts is perhaps one of the most creative, soulful and fascinating musicians that the world of traditional music has ever produced. He spent a good few nights in our house, playing the fiddle for hours on end. He was a close friend of my father and Paddy Canny. All three shared a love for the music and were also very religious people. It wouldn't have been unusual for my father and Paddy Canny to go inside a church they might be passing and pray for a little while. Prayer was just as integral to their life as music, and the same was true for Potts. He was an offbeat musician who was a respected but marginal figure in Dublin's traditional music scene. He had his own way of approaching the music, with a style that was utterly unique, full of integrity, freedom and soul, his phrases, notes and flights of fancy being shaped by his intense emotional response to the melodies. He seemed to inhabit a very profound musical space while playing this music.

Potts loved to visit County Clare, and when he did, his friends Seán Reid – a piper and fiddler whose life was spent promoting the music – and Peadar O'Loughlin would each drive him around the place for a week. He treasured the opportunity to meet his friends and recharge his musical batteries. During his stay in the county, he would visit Seán's and Peadar's houses as well as Paddy Canny's house and ours, where he'd stay overnight. He knew that these musicians respected him musically and he felt comfortable coming to play for them. He had the freedom to be himself in their company. We would sit silently by the fire and along the wall of the kitchen while he played and talked for the evening. His music was very deep, and at the time much of it probably went over my head, but what was not lost on me was the level of intensity and the dedication evident in his playing. There was a distinct flavour and sound from his music that seeped into me at some level. I never forgot it. In fact, I could always hear an echo of Potts in how Paddy Canny played.

Potts's style didn't function as dance music in the normal sense; he was absorbed in the melody and the possibilities and variations he could explore inside it. He played inwardly, in almost a prayerful and devotional way, breaking the rules in pursuit of the deepest expression. It seemed that each rule broken brought him to a deeper and more profound place. His music was pure, emotional, soulful, and completely unimpeded by ego. It wasn't that he didn't have an ego; it just wasn't in his playing.

One night, my father suggested that I might play a tune or two for Potts so that he could offer me some advice. I played 'The Fermoy Lasses'. I must have been around eleven at the time so the tune would have been among the small selection that I knew how to play reasonably well. My father was looking for the best way for me to navigate my way through the tune – whether one might use, say, a finger-roll or a triplet at different points throughout. I played, and afterwards Potts took up his fiddle and played the tune himself. He played it in his own way, playing it again and again with new and different variations each time. In the end I was none the wiser about how I might approach the tune, given the seemingly infinite number of possibilities he was offering, but I had certainly internalized the idea that there was an endless array of possibilities contained within every melody. There is a saying: 'You must know the rules before you break them.' Potts knew the rules and broke them, and got to the very essence of the tune. He knew this music at the deepest possible level. There has never been anybody like him before or since.

When it came to competitions, I eventually reached a point where I wasn't prepared to adjust what I did to meet the expectations of the competition. I just wanted to get my music to a level that was satisfying and meaningful for me, and to let the chips land where they would. Two years after seeing James Cullinan at the fleadh cheoil in Toonagh, my own playing style had matured quite a lot and I finally squeaked past him to qualify for the Munster Fleadh Cheoil, which, to my great surprise, I then won. I had qualified for the first time to compete in the All-Ireland Fleadh Cheoil competition.

5

THE MAIN THING for me was that I would finally get to attend an All-Ireland Fleadh Cheoil and see this event for myself. I had heard my father on so many occasions relaying the now-mythical stories of the great céilí band competitions of the fifties at fleadhs in places like Boyle, Dungarvan, Loughrea and Athlone. I couldn't wait to get my first experience of this, which would be in Buncrana, Donegal, at the end of August.

Unfortunately, my father couldn't come to the fleadh with me because the distance meant we'd need to spend at least two nights away from home, and he needed to stay on the farm to milk the cows. My uncle James, my mother's brother, would be bringing his sons John and Seamus to the competition too – they played the accordion and tin whistle respectively. We had qualified for the trio competition together, and then John and I would be in the duet competition. (We didn't win either of those.) My mother and I travelled the long journey with them to Buncrana, which sits at the very top of Donegal. We stayed in Letterkenny on the Friday night, just when the Letterkenny Folk Festival was taking place. This was my first time seeing large gatherings of people wearing jeans, long hair, beards and headbands. There were music groups on an open-air stage singing and playing folk music that I wasn't familiar with.

We made it to Buncrana early the next morning, on time for the competition. James and the boys headed off to their events, so it was just my mother and myself in the hall where the fiddle competitions were taking place. The hall was a ballroom with a balcony, and the main floor had lines of chairs that were beginning to fill up. Directly in front of the stage, the adjudicator was sitting at a table with some assistants. I recognized him – it was the renowned fiddler Séamus Connolly, who only a year previously hadn't seen much potential in me; he hadn't placed me at all even in the less-competitive slow-airs competition at the Munster Fleadh Cheoil.

All the previous competitions that I'd ever been to had taken place in small, more intimate spaces, such as school classrooms, but here in Buncrana things were happening on a much bigger scale. There were music teachers there, along with parents and competitors. Some of the teachers and parents were checking the tuning of their children's instruments. Everybody looked like they were familiar with this situation and comfortable with it; they knew what they were doing. I wasn't even sure when to take the fiddle out of the case. Should I be tuning already? Should I be practising and warming up? My mother and I were alone in this environment. It was a bit overwhelming and we both felt like outsiders, unprepared for this moment.

Right about then, a priest made his way over to us and introduced himself as Fr Quinn. My mother knew who he was as soon as he said his name. He was a music enthusiast who had booked the Tulla Céilí Band to play in Lanesborough, County Longford, on many occasions. After looking at the programme, he had spotted the name Hayes alongside our home address and had naturally concluded that a son of PJ Hayes must be somewhere in the hall. I expect he was probably searching around to see if he could spot my father and, with some detective work on his part, somehow managed to find my mother and me. He sat with us for a while and immediately we began to feel much more at ease. In truth, most musicians and teachers in the room would have known my father and probably would have been very welcoming, but for the moment we were kind of invisible.

I think I was somewhere towards the back of the list. Lots of very fine players played their three tunes before me, almost all of them playing 'Lord Gordon's Reel'. They all did their best to play it just like the most famous fiddler of all, Michael Coleman, who had recorded this tune. The recording was regarded as his masterpiece, and playing that tune was a way of proving you could play a demanding piece where your skills could easily be observed, and where you were also declaring your veneration for the father of Irish fiddling. I had little to rely on other than my core belief that the experience and feeling of the music was a very real thing that would translate to the listeners when I played. When it was my turn to go on, I headed to the stage, my father's old fiddle in hand. I had just turned fourteen and was wearing my confirmation suit, fully decked out with shirt and tie, which probably made me look as out of place as I was feeling inside. I did my best to ignore the situation; I just wanted to play in the way I'd been doing all that time I'd been sitting on the side of the bathtub. I had very little expectation of winning, so I didn't feel I had anything to lose anyway. This was all I knew how to do, and in any case, to me this was not so much a competition as another opportunity to play out in the world. I went for it the same way I still try to do to this day, which is to let go, sink into the music, allow myself to feel it and, to the best of my ability, play from my heart. I played what were considered non-typical competition tunes at the time, including 'The Graf Spee', which Paddy Canny liked to play, and fiddler Junior Crehan's 'Golden Castle'. My playing at that point wasn't outstanding from a technical point of view but it was distinctively grounded in the music style of East Clare, and on that day I did feel as if my playing contained genuine feeling.

Once everyone had played, it was time for Séamus Connolly to deliver the results. He first talked favourably about the overall standard of performance before working his way up to giving out the placements. He named the third and second place-winners, which left me with the unsurprising feeling that my winning streak had come to a halt. I didn't really mind. I always knew that this was the more likely outcome. He then called my name. It was the most dramatic moment of my musical life so far. It was an outcome so far-fetched that I hadn't even contemplated it. Séamus Connolly talked about my playing, remarking that I had an authentic East Clare style. He mentioned Paddy Canny and my father, and said my music sounded like a continuation of theirs. My mother, who was normally very sparing with her compliments, told me how proud she was of me. Hearing her say that was on a par with hearing Séamus call out my name as the winner. I walked out of that hall, with fiddle and cup, feeling as though I was walking on clouds.

Later that year, I entered Slógadh, a competition series with Irish language and culture as the unifying theme, sponsored by the Irish-language-supporting organization Gael Linn. This had a slightly different ethos with a less competitive edge – you never felt you were there to win competitions, but they recognized your achievements and awarded you a prize that may have come in the form of a painting or some other piece of art. I still have a few Cathy Moore batiks that were given to me as prizes at Slógadh. There were sections of the event devoted to drama, choirs, rock music and sean nós singing, piping, fiddling, and so on. The band Clannad emerged from Slógadh years earlier, and in many ways they encapsulated the broad-based vision behind the event, with a reverence for the old traditions and regional styles combined with a willingness to embrace the contemporary world. This ethos resonated with me in the same way that the fleadhs probably had for my father in earlier years. I felt like I had found my tribe.

The first Slógadh event I attended was in the convent in Spanish Point, County Clare. While there, I played a few tunes for the first time with concertina player Mary MacNamara from Tulla, and we hit it off immediately. We basically had the same rhythmic approach, not to mention a common repertoire. She eschewed flash and musical pyrotechnics in the same way I did. I loved the way the fiddle and concertina blended seamlessly together, and playing with her felt effortless. Mary became my first musical partner of my own age group. We would go on to play together all through my teenage years, attending all the fleadh cheoils together and participating in Slógadh every year without fail. Mary and her siblings were in a band called the Tulla Junior Band that I was invited to join. I was now therefore also playing with Mary's brothers PJ and Andrew, and her twin sister Anita. The other members of the group were Dennis and Mary Corry, Joan Culloo and Tim Moloney. This musical connection with my own generation was a lifesaver for me. Very few young people played traditional music at that time, so we appreciated each other's support.

I would go on to spend many days and nights in the home of the MacNamaras in Tulla – it was like a second home to me in those times – and we would often rehearse in the home of Joan Culloo, who also lived in Tulla. My parents and those of the other band members gave us all tremendous freedom to practise. We certainly weren't forced to rehearse – we craved it. Musically, we were like a version of The Chieftains or Seán Ó Riada's Ceoltóirí Chualann. In fact, we played some of The Chieftains' pieces, and from this we also learned how to arrange music ourselves. I loved travelling to festivals and competitions with the Tulla Junior Band. I finally had a group of peers where I felt fully accepted, and where I could be myself.

I kept a very low profile in school and did my best to avoid the attention of the teachers. Music was an emotional refuge for me, even back then. What's more, the whole ethos of school felt like it stood in opposition to what I was experiencing and absorbing in my musical life. School felt shallow by comparison and didn't captivate my interest in the same way music did. I didn't ever get a strong sense that we were in pursuit of knowledge for its own sake; we were there to acquire the knowledge needed to pass exams and get a ticket to a better, more modern life than our parents had. The more modern life being offered didn't seem to include traditional music. My musical world was entwined with this older life that school was implicitly suggesting we needed to escape from.

I found it difficult to commit to an educational system that I now also had contempt for. I was an average-to-decent student, but I was never one who exceeded, because I really didn't embrace my academic education. When we started reading poetry in English class, however, something clicked inside. I liked this class. I preferred any class that pulled us away from the usual tedium, and poetry could do that. Our English teacher, John Conneely, was an exceptional man and I found his poetry classes to be very transporting during a time when transporting was exactly what I needed. His classes enthralled me. I remember sitting there with my hands propping up my chin while I daydreamed into the poetry he read to us. I loved Mr Conneely's dissections and discussions of the poems. Shelley, Keats, Dickinson, Wordsworth and Yeats provided windows into another world. Metaphysical poetry, meanwhile, was a welcome crack in the view of the world we were being presented with. I liked the feeling that there was an alternative way to look at the universe as a whole, and that there was a deeper level to be explored. Realizing for the first time that there was this much broader sphere of thought out there was a relief. I also remember when we read some of the prose of Edmund Burke and Francis Bacon. I enjoyed their logical questioning process. It wasn't a matter of believing their conclusions so much as admiring their capacity for clear thinking and enjoying the larger questions they pondered. I liked classes that brought us closer to the big questions in life.

Once I had deeply experienced the poetry, I had little interest in dissecting it into analysed fragments for the exam process. To this day, I have a similar problem with music. The more I have to think or apply my intellect in the act of making music, the less feeling it seems to contain. For me, poems, like music, are to be experienced. They can lift the heart, spark one's imagination and broaden one's thinking. Those classes were bright spots in an otherwise tedious and sometimes frightening school experience, which still used corporal punishment. John Conneely had the full respect and attention of the class without ever having to raise a hand or threaten anyone. He had what it took to be a good teacher and I am immensely grateful for his classes, which gave me a glimpse of my nascent spiritual and philosophical curiosity.

For a good portion of the school year, it would be dark leaving in the morning and dark when I later went the same way home. We had to wait for an hour at school each evening before the bus was available to drive us to my old school of Douglawn, from where we would then walk home. When you're walking in the dark of the unlit countryside, your night vision gradually kicks in and you don't need a flashlight. Usually there would be a few of us walking together, but sometimes I liked to walk alone with my thoughts during those late evenings. There is something about those dark winter walks that I miss: the inward, private, silent world, the wind, the rain, and the sound of my feet on the road, the lights of houses in the distance that gave a warm, reassuring impression of a huddled family warmth protected from the elements. I loved the wind and rain on those evenings too. Even in the dark of night, I found a satisfaction on that road that I couldn't get in school, except in my poetry classes.

A memorable milestone for me during those secondary-school years was making my first recordings, at the age of sixteen. I participated in two recordings, both of which were compilations produced by Gael Linn and which came about as a result of my involvement in the Slógadh competitions. I travelled to Dublin to make the recordings, and the first day was devoted to recording a collection of up-and-coming fiddle-players, of which I was the youngest. The others were Maurice Lennon, Séamus Glackin, Seán Montgomery and Séamus Thompson. The second day was solely for recording that year's Slógadh competition winners, including Mary Macnamara and me.

I was nervous, as I obviously had no experience in the studio, but I was also immensely excited as a record was a big deal in my mind; even my classmates, in spite of their opinions that traditional music wasn't very cool, would have to accept that this was a real achievement. All the players were being recorded at different times, so it was just me in the studio with the technicians, the engineer and the producer, who was the well-known fiddler Paddy Glackin, Séamus's brother. I had spent a lot of my life listening to records and now I was finally going to be on one. I remember the room where I was to play had no windows, there was foam soundproofing everywhere and it was carpeted from floor to ceiling. When I played in there, my fiddle sounded small and reedy. My practice sessions on the side of the bathtub were no preparation for this; this place was the polar opposite of the bathroom acoustics. I could feel all my desire for music and any feeling of inspiration just evaporating every minute I was in there. The final nail on the coffin was when the engineer wanted me to stop tapping my feet because the sound was travelling up through the microphone stand. For me, this was like playing with one arm tied behind my back. I know this is a confusing simile for the circumstances, but one leg tied behind my back is an even more confusing one. Without tapping my feet while I played, I began to lose connection to my rhythm. What I played that day felt like some empty version of my music; I failed to get even close to what I thought I was capable of. I was devastated by the experience. It was so painful to feel like I had blown this amazing opportunity. My lack of experience and my naivety about the recording process just caught me off guard. Sure, I was on a record now, but that wasn't going to bring me the joy I'd imagined. The whole thing just felt like a disaster.

On that first day in the recording studio, they recorded many more tunes from me than they needed for the album, allowing them the opportunity to later choose which pieces they thought worked best. I played all my best tunes for them, but this meant I was now down to the last stragglers for the second day of recording. My heart wasn't really in it any more. That first day had knocked the stuffing out of me. This second recording was being produced by the piper and broadcaster Peter Brown and recorded in a big space in the RTÉ Radio studios, which sounded much better than the dead space I had been in the day before. I recorded one solo track and a duet track with Mary MacNamara. Iarla Ó Lionáird, my future colleage in the band The Gloaming, was on that recording also. This second day's recording was a little less traumatic, but they didn't really catch me at my best, as I think the previous day's experience had left me a bit off balance.

When the *Slógadh Náisiúnta 78* record came out, it sounded better than I had expected, and the same was true for the fiddle-compilation record, *An Fhidil Scraith 1*. I had obviously played a little better than I had told myself at the time. Some of these tracks got airplay here and there. One evening, as we were walking home from school, Jimmy Collins was standing outside his house as we passed. 'I heard you on the radio today,' he said, in front of the others who were walking home with me. That was a big deal right there for my teenage sense of pride. It seemed nobody thought my playing was as appalling as I had; maybe, just maybe, I had gotten away with it.

This didn't change my understanding that the studio can be a very unfriendly place when one is heavily reliant on creating and communicating a musical atmosphere rather than just reeling out a technically perfect bag of tricks. I wasn't the first traditional musician to run into this problem in the studio. The recording process rewards flashy and technically correct playing that can be repeated and dissected without losing anything. The intangible and ephemeral parts of music are different; they can disappear fast in this environment. They're often gone before you even realize it. The magic doesn't happen on demand; it happens when the moment is right, when the atmosphere is receptive to it. I learned from an early age that one has to be prepared to accept technical imperfections in pursuit of this true essence. Unfortunately, much of our recording process and procedures tend to work in the exact opposite direction. On the album *The Liffey Banks* by fiddler Tommy Potts there is a whistling screech in the first bar of 'The Dear Irish Boy', but Potts continues and the piece is magnificently filled with emotion and soul – it has 'draíocht' (magic). If an engineer had stopped Tommy Potts at that point or asked him to repeat the tune, there is a very good chance that it would start to lose something.

Even the thought that a performance must be correct and without error is an intrusion on the process and diminishes our ability to feel things properly in the moment. When recording, the idea that we make music for another time can pull us away from making music for that very moment itself. The studio can be a hostile place, particularly when you're a musician whose only effective tool is his or her heart. If you lose that connection, you may end up reproducing and mimicking parts that were initially formed and shaped out of feeling but which are now suddenly hollow. The tune must still be delivered, but now perhaps without substance, with technique alone. I have found myself here many times, just being an empty version of myself. I have also thankfully managed on plenty of occasions to capture fully-real and present performances in the studio, though it still continues to be a struggle. So much of the magic of many humble but soulfully connected musicians has escaped into the ether when in the studio, the fleeting, ephemeral beauty being too delicate and otherworldly to hang around for the command 'Let's do that again.' The full depth of some of the older and more soul-ful musicians didn't survive such moments. This used to bother me, because I always knew there was this deeper magic that was very often getting missed or was simply failing to be expressed.

The moment of real music is a delicate and fragile moment, but the microphone and studio are built only to record quantifiable sound waves, as if that was essentially all that music really is.

I remember on one occasion, many years later in my career, being in a studio with my good friend, producer and broadcaster PJ Curtis, working on one of his projects. I view music as com-munication, and for the flow to be most effective it really helps if it can be willingly and non-judgementally received. I learned something valuable during this recording session when PJ left the control room and came into the space where I was playing. He put his headphones on and leaned forward with his eyes closed. He was 100 per cent present and actively listening to every shad-ing of every note I played. This kind of receptivity in the present moment gives you a reason to play. There was a mutual trust and respect, and I was no longer recording, I was playing directly to PJ. That's what a good producer can do for you.

6

THE BOOKINGS FOR the Tulla Céilí Band were always taken by my father, and before we got the phone the entire process was carried out by letter – three letters, to be precise. First would come the letter of request. My father would answer with his conditions, which were the provision of a piano, a supper for the band and, of course, the fee. If the person booking the band agreed to the conditions outlined, my father would then receive a final letter of confirmation that contained all the fundamentals such as the times, location and where the all-important supper would be provided.

The band would usually make their way to a céilí using two cars. One would travel there from North Clare, the other from East Clare, which would include me and my father. When I first started in the band, the accordion-player Mattie Ryan would collect us, and the drummer, Jack McDonald, would usually be with him. Jack was a kind old man who was already well into his seventies when I was starting off with the band.

With a considerable degree of precision, we would pack the car with all of our instruments, including the amplification system, with speakers and microphones, that we kept at our house.

The bass drum, meanwhile, would sit snugly in the back seat. Over the years, after Mattie had left the band, I made myself the designated expert at packing the car for my father. It was a service I happily provided as it made me a little more useful.

In those earlier years, my father would sit up front with Mattie while Jack and I were in the back seat with the bass drum. It was anything but comfortable, but still exciting, as we might be heading off to some exotic part of the country, like rural Kerry or even Mayo! Many of these journeys would take a few hours, and often we would find ourselves driving along a small country road in Galway looking for a village hall in a parish we'd never heard of or been to before. I whiled away the hours by chatting about music with Jack, who also played piano and double bass. He even gave me a couple of useful books on bowing and classical violin technique, which I read and absorbed. I mostly learned by looking and imitating, but I was very interested in getting some insight into how classical players got their tone. I didn't want to play classical music but I wanted to play traditional music with the best intonation and tone I could achieve on the instrument.

Even when I was a young, quiet fourteen-year-old in amongst those band members with their blazers, shirts and ties, I don't recall ever feeling out of place. I looked up to these men but I also felt accepted into their world. As it was, it was also mostly older people who turned up to the dances in those years, people who'd been fans since the fifties, when their musical tastes were established.

The journey home always had two predictable rituals. Firstly, my father, who was a very sincere and religious man, didn't see any reason why we shouldn't all say the rosary in the car. Traditional music tends to conjure images of wild drunken musicians, and to be fair, the basis of this preconceived notion is very often rooted in fact; however, there were also the non-drinking, morally upstanding and 'respectable' musicians who were very different. In the latter category, you could include Tommy Potts, Paddy Canny, fiddler Francie Donnellan, Peadar O'Loughlin and the renowned accordion-player Paddy O'Brien. Once you were in the car with my father, it didn't matter which camp you felt you belonged to – when my father decided to say the rosary, there was really no way out. Nobody ever objected, but then no one really knew how to object, so we'd all go ahead with it, my father leading the effort.

After the obligation of the rosary had been fulfilled, the second notable ritual of the journey home would take place: tea! Jack would bring a flask of tea, four cups, a tablecloth and a pack of wholegrain biscuits – always wholegrain biscuits. The tablecloth was for Mattie's benefit. Mattie was a mechanic by day and his car was very much his prized possession, always spotlessly clean. He didn't want any crumbly biscuits or tea to be consumed inside the car, so we'd pull in somewhere along the road and Jack would proceed to put the tablecloth over the bonnet (hood). He would then lay out the cups and biscuits. The tea would be lukewarm by this stage. This ritual could happen at two or three in the morning on the side of a road in West Limerick or Galway, and to this day, whenever I drive into the town of Adare coming from the Newcastle West side, I always look to the right side of the road, where we used to stop for tea, and reimagine that scene. An occasional car would pass, and I still wonder what they must have thought at the sight of us just casually standing there with our tea and biscuits in the middle of the night. Just as we went along with the rosary for my father, we went along with the tea ceremony for Jack. Usually, young people join bands with 'Sex, drugs, and rock 'n' roll' as their implicit motto. In my case, it was more along the lines of 'Biscuits, tea and rosaries'.

It was obvious to me even in my teenage years that the era of the céilí bands was in decline. Their heyday had come and gone, but still our band persisted when many others had fallen by the wayside. In those years of the mid-seventies, only the Shaskeen Céilí Band and the Tulla Céilí Band continued to regularly play the last of the ballroom circuit, whose peak of popularity, like that of the céilí bands, was also back in the fifties. The dance halls and ballrooms were now closing. They were beginning to be replaced by lounge bars, and smaller ballad groups, of two or three singers with guitars, were now mostly the entertainment in those venues. The ballrooms that remained open were dominated by showbands like Gina, Dale Haze and The Champions, The Indians, and Big Tom and The Mainliners. Still, every St Patrick's night and Easter Sunday, the Tulla Céilí Band would play the Classic Ballroom in Gort, just a few doors up from my school. This was a big ballroom with two separate spaces that altogether could hold about 1,000 people. The back part, where we played, only held about 200 people and was where all the older married couples were. All the young people would be in the front, dancing to a showband. Occasionally, a young couple who'd just met would escape the front part and come to the back to kiss, as if they were the only ones in the room, a sharp reminder of another reality that just wasn't happening for me.

There was a time when the Tulla Céilí Band would have played the front ballroom, but a new era was dawning and it wasn't looking too bright. Nevertheless, the band still managed to play a couple of nights a week, mostly on the weekends, in village halls, ballrooms and lounge bars mainly in the Mid-West and Midlands of the country, places from where the band could get home before three or four in the morning. (There were a few occasions when my father and I returned from a dance so late that instead of going to bed we put on our wellingtons and work clothes and started milking the cows.) Since its formation, in 1946, the band had won awards, made records, appeared on countless TV and radio shows, and toured the UK and the America. By the fifties and sixties it was one of the best-known and most respected céilí bands in the country. Some of traditional music's most esteemed musicians, such as the legendary piper Willie Clancy, the powerful and soulful accordionist Joe Cooley, the famous accordionist Paddy O'Brien and my musical hero, Tony McMahon, had passed through the band at one time or another. Though I was quite young when I first began playing with the band, I was still acutely aware of the lineage I was following.

Back in the forties and fifties, especially after the Public Dance Halls Act, which outlawed house dances, being in a céilí band was something many traditional musicians did, as house dances began to fade away. Joining a céilí band was a way of getting to play, travel a bit and be around like-minded musicians, while at the same time making a little bit of money. It could also be a tremendously powerful musical experience at times, especially in those moments when it was firing on all cylinders, with both dancers and musicians lifted together in the rhythm. Seán Ó Riada's condemnation of the céilí bands wasn't without some justification – there were many bands who simply weren't very good, and at its worst moments a céilí band can be a kind of musical abomination. Some of the bands were imitations of the Scottish country dance bands, which had almost nothing to do with the roots of our music. They were polite bands that didn't connect with the more elemental, rhythmic nature of the music we played for the good set-dancers. I loved good set-dancers. The best ones had their own style, they had personality in their dancing and they connected to the music – not just the basic rhythm but the flow of the melodic line itself. They weren't restricted to specific moves in the manner that we see in step-dancing or céilí-dancing. It wasn't a performance as such; each dancer found his or her way to respond to the music, they could be themselves and they could lose themselves. A lot of things have to go right for all of this to come together properly. Rhythm is one of those things that needs to be tight but not too much so; it needs to breathe and it needs everyone to find the centre, simultaneously feeling the nuance of the syncopated groove in such a way that everyone gets swept along. Making moments of euphoric energy and connection is what the céilí band is all about.

The Tulla Céilí Band had seen a continuous turnover of people since its foundation. As each person left and another replaced them, the new member would be slowly absorbed into the swing and groove. Over time, many musicians would pass through the band, yet the unique rhythm remains to this day. The bands I preferred had a raucous, thunderous power with driving rhythm. Some things are not supposed to be refined to the finer detail and I think a céilí band is perhaps one of those things. It functions best with a kind of looseness that can respond and react to the uniqueness of each moment. The band sometimes needs to slowly work itself into sync. Often this can be ignited by the powerful rhythm of great set-dancers. When it's going well there is a dialogue, a back-and-forth between musician and dancer, each informing the other.

I remember many years ago, in Miltown Malbay in County Clare, looking down from the stage at the set-dancer Willie Keane from Mullagh. He looked as if he was suspended in the air, only coming down to the ground in moments of his choosing. He would land with a crack of his shoe, with perfect timing. He was lifted by music and a joy to watch. A percussionist on the dance floor, he was music in motion, and if you were wise enough to take a musical cue from him he'd show you where the heart of the groove really was. There was a period in the Tulla Céilí Band where myself and Mary MacNamara's younger brother, Andrew, were really enjoying the wildness of making a powerful rhythm as we tried to sweep up the dancers into a frenzy. One night, in the Spancilhill Inn in Clare, the band had crowded on to a very small stage, only maybe a foot off the ground. This never bothered anyone in the band as we actually liked being bunched up in a small space; it meant we could play much tighter. Jimmy and Kathleen Moloney were there with all the family – Geraldine, Breda, Kitty and Michael Anthony. They were all mighty dancers. In fact the place was filled with great dancers that night. As the night wore on, the place became steamy, the dancers and musicians were sweating and were collectively moving past some threshold where there was no longer any separation between us. The music, the band and the dancers were all just parts of one larger experience.

Tony McMahon, who in his role as a TV producer had done more for the promotion of traditional music on television than anybody else, was there that night. He was completely animated and excited by the whole thing. He could see that something elemental and primal was taking place, that there was a euphoric energy and connection between musicians and dancers, a connection that was now largely absent in the wider world of this music, as the set-dancing tradition was dying out in most parts and whole generations of musicians were losing the connection to the natural rhythms of the dancer. I remember Tony saying the whole experience needed to be filmed or documented in some way; something needed to be done to portray the energy and excitement of this interaction. Some years later, Tony would make a landmark recording with concertina-player Noel Hill in a pub in Knocknagree. Tony and Noel brought some of the best set-dancers they could and recorded this incredible album simply titled *In Knocknagree*, which in many ways captures the same atmosphere between dancer and musician that was happening that earlier night in the Spancilhill Inn.

Throughout my teenage years, even when public interest in céilís was declining, I still did my best to make sure I was there playing with the Tulla Céilí Band. We mainly toured up and down the west of Ireland, playing parish halls and old ballrooms, and sometimes we went to England to play the old haunts from the late fifties, places like London's Galtymore ballroom in Cricklewood, National Ballroom in Kilburn, and Gresham Ballroom on Holloway Road. We also went to Irish centres in places like Liverpool, Manchester and Birmingham. All of this exposed me to the touring life of a musician and everything that came with it.

The céilí band had a role to play but it couldn't satisfy all of my musical needs. Even though I really enjoyed the sound and power of a good céilí band, I was well aware of the deeper, more sensitive level of the music that couldn't be delivered in this situation. There was the music of the heart, which my father and I regularly talked about at home. While the céilí-band era was in decline, a new iteration of the music was emerging. Seán Ó Riada and his band, Ceoltóirí Chualann, had re-examined and dug deeper into more elemental aspects of Irish music. He managed to create a new performance model, one that would become the basis for many ensembles, including The Chieftains and Ceoltóirí Laighean. The countercultural folk revival in the US and UK was also influencing and fuelling a new hybrid blend of folk and Irish traditional music. People like Christy Moore, Liam O Flynn, Dónal Lunny, Mary Black, Matt Molloy, Paul Brady, Andy Irvine, Mick Moloney, Kevin Burke and Johnny Moynihan were making new sounds – a new generation putting their stamp on the music. The blend of the fiddle, flute and accordion, with harmonic and rhythmic support coming from piano and drums, was becoming a thing of the past. There was a new sound, with guitars, bouzoukis and mandolins interwoven with pipes, fiddles and flutes. This music was no longer connected to the communal dance tradition; it was beginning to speak to a new urban and educated audience. The Bothy Band, Planxty and De Dannan were the new sound. Sometimes I really wished I were part of this new wave of Irish traditional music instead of the céilí-band world that was beginning to fade, but at least I was actually out playing music and I was grateful for that. However, I was beginning to get a taste of what it meant to become obsolete. It was a strange experience to be having, especially at that stage of my life, when really I was only just getting started.

Years later, there would be a revival of set-dancing and the céilí band would enjoy a comeback, but it would no longer occupy the prime position it had once held in the fifties and sixties. The Tulla Céilí Band are still going strong and continue to attract the very best of the dancers. For many of the new wave of dancers, the band is a direct connection to the older era of set-dancing. There is a solid melodic core to traditional music, from which new forms emerge that speak for each new generation. This is how traditional music has survived. We return to the melodic bedrock over and over again; we push the reset button and a new sound gradually emerges. Whether it's the Tulla Céilí Band, The Chieftains, the Bothy Band, Lúnasa or The Gloaming, we work with much of the same core material. We all drink from the same well but our different generational worlds of experience and influences give us the opportunity to create new resonant, and more relevant, sonic worlds for the times we live in.

With something as beautiful and deep as this music there is a natural inclination and instinct towards preserving the music in some stable and unchanging form, but for a tradition to be truly alive it also needs to evolve and be continuously relevant. On a personal level, it's often difficult to achieve this balance, but when we look at the music overall, its competing strands tend to operate as a kind of self-regulating and balancing influence. Irish music has never been able to achieve a consensus of definition, but ironically this lack of consensus is in my opinion one of its most powerful assets. It allows and necessitates all these different proponents of the music to exist simultaneously: traditionalists, neo-traditionalists, innovators, commercial opportunists, academic folklorists, ethnomusicologists, and mostly people who just want to enjoy a few tunes without any debate or headache. This lack of consensus creates a space of musical freedom.

There were two venues in County Clare in the mid-seventies where the bands and musicians of this new folk revival would play: The Merriman Tavern in Scariff and The Highway Inn in Crusheen. One night not long after I turned fifteen, Joe Galligan invited me to play a few tunes in his pub, The Highway Inn – the same pub I had occasionally visited whenever my uncle Christy managed to persuade my father and grandfather to go. Joe's regular music night had progressed into a folk club of sorts, one that hosted acts such as De Dannan, Séamus Ennis, Andy Irvine, Noel Hill and so on. Among those in attendance that night was my musical hero, Tony McMahon. I used to watch Tony on a television programme called *Bring Down the Lamp*, and even at age seven I completely got the passion and feeling of his music. I was ten when I first met Tony, and my reaction was probably on a par with a child meeting their sports idol. I was in Dublin with my father, who was recording an album with the Tulla Céilí Band at the time, and as we were walking down O'Connell Street we met Tony McMahon walking towards us. I was absolutely thrilled to meet the man. Five years later and here he was, listening to me play.

After I'd finished, he made a beeline for me. I remember him smiling broadly as he approached me, something that put me at ease, as it was clear he'd enjoyed what he'd heard. His exact words to me were: 'Don't ever change what you're doing.' I don't think he meant that I shouldn't change my playing; I understood it as meaning that I shouldn't change direction or abandon the feeling of the music. Over the next few years he invited me on to just about every television series he was producing. To have Tony championing my music as a young fiddle-player was the best possible endorsement I could have wished for. What made his support so important to me was that I had revered his music right from the beginning. I always understood his music and he now understood mine.

Tony's sister and Mary's mother, Ita MacNamara, was also a big influence on me. She encouraged me enormously. I spent a lot of time in Ita's house, so she became like a second mother to me. She was a very discerning listener, someone who'd spent time in her youth listening to Joe Cooley play music in her kitchen, a time she often talked about. I loved to play for her; it was easy to pick up on her receptivity to heartfelt expression. Reaching her musically was a reassurance that my own internal experience of the music was real, not just some part of my own imagination. It was a confirmation that was very valuable to me.

Tony was also very good at spotting real musical value in some of the older, more humble musicians who weren't flashy players and who were often overlooked. He would pay a lot of attention to the great talents of Micho Russell, Joe Bane and Bill Malley, seeing beauty and soul in very rugged and humble vessels. These musicians may have been regarded as unsophisticated, but they were nonetheless speaking a language of the soul that was quite deep. Tony helped me to recognize the quality and depth of things that were naturally all around me. I was already inclined to search for musical value among overlooked musicians, and many times what they may have lacked in technical sophistication they made up for with insight and imagination. Tony eliminated any doubt or uncertainty I might have felt in seeking out musical understanding from those kind of sources. I would learn all the old music of my locality, understand all the old ways of playing. I would engage with all of the old local musicians I knew, including my father, Joe Bane, Bill Malley, Martin Rochford, Paddy Canny, John Naughton, Jimmy Brody, Martin Wood and fiddler Vincent Griffin.

As I followed those musicians, particularly those from the older generations, I think their playing, their knowledge and their understanding just filtered into me. There was so much to absorb, because even in my own locality there wasn't uniformity. There were lots of different styles. There was music for listening to and music for dancing to. I concentrated a lot of my musical efforts in pulling together listening and dance music into a single style. I wanted to draw together the dance of the music and its expressive lyricism into one way of playing. Paradoxically, after completely immersing myself in the music of my locality I ended up playing an East Clare style of music that nobody else was playing. I had also ended up assimilating influences from the various other instrumental styles that were all around me, such as concertina-, accordion- and whistle-playing. I also enjoyed what was happening musically during the seventies in the folk world of traditional music – I loved Planxty, De Dannan, the Bothy Band and so on – but I quite consciously blocked them from being a musical influence or affecting my direction. I was quite dedicated to delving deeply into how the old musicians played and I wanted to absorb those old forms into my playing.

Joe Bane was a local musician whose humility and uncomplicated, sweet expression on the tin whistle really brought home to me the idea that music doesn't always have to be complex or clever to be good. He only lived about a mile away from Paddy Canny's house and I got to know him quite well. He was a reclusive, quiet man who never married and didn't travel much, but he was highly regarded locally for his tin whistle- and flute-playing. He played for years with Bill Malley from the next townland over, and together they became a very popular duet for local house dances. To my ears, their music was always earthy, rugged and real. Unlike my father and Paddy Canny, Bill and Joe didn't appear to be influenced by the recorded music from America. They had older and simpler melodies that fitted perfectly with the uncomplicated simplicity of their playing. Joe's style had an uncluttered directness, a bit like the better-known West Clare whistle-player Micho Russell. My abiding memory of Joe is of watching him in his kitchen, contentedly playing the tunes of his youth. There was a warmth and soothing self-satisfaction in his music, a natural beauty and creativity in some of the partially remembered and reconstructed melodies. He found clever and simple ways to navigate certain passages, sometimes unconsciously reinventing sections of a melody that might have gradually evolved over his lifetime to become his own personal take on the tune. I loved listening to his reconstructed versions of the tunes, as well as the obscure melodies of his youth. Many of the older players weren't virtuosos but they nonetheless often had deep and valuable insight into the music. For me, understanding and deciphering their musical intention became just as important as the notes they were actually playing. Despite the simple, direct beauty expressed by musicians like Joe, many of these humbler musicians had musical aspirations for a tune that was beyond their technical capacity to deliver. I could sometimes patch together in my mind a musical image of the tune as they imagined it, just from talking with them and hearing descriptions of what they liked or how a particular note really made the tune worthwhile. When they'd sing tunes to me I would get another view into their musical intention. Martin Rochford was a local musician who always gave beautiful, deeply felt expressions of any tune he lilted to me. The combination of their playing and their musical visions would become a guide for me, a kind of road map to the deeper levels of the music.

In the hands of any musician in an aural tradition, tunes will naturally evolve. In times before recordings, and before notated versions of the tunes became commonly available, melodies couldn't be fixed and stable; they were bound to evolve and change. I imagine they were in a permanent state of mutation, if for no other reason than the fallibility of human memory. Sometimes the mutation might be very slight, but would still be enough to have an impact. I know this from my own experience of playing variations of a melody; over time, it becomes easy to forget the original lines. Just imagine somebody learning a new tune from a musician from another area at a house dance where they both happen to meet. There is a very good chance that when the person who has just learned the tune plays it the next day, some notes will have already changed. There now exists a slightly altered version which, when passed along to some other area, may undergo further alteration. If the name of the tune happens to be forgotten or confused, we could end up with a tune somewhat similar to the original but now possibly with a new name. In the end, we technically have a new tune. Every melody is in permanent motion, in continuous development, imitating life and nature itself in a continuous evolutionary flow. This in turn means that each tune has at some level a history of collective composition. It seems reasonable to expect tunes to stabilize in one area, among one group of musicians, for a time, while some variant may be taking hold in another location. This is entirely my theory of how the transmission of tunes took place before recorded music, based on living examples of individual musicians who sometimes unintentionally develop their own versions of tunes, as well as my own experience where tunes naturally, and often unintentionally, evolve in my own hands. While the tunes are now well documented and stable as a result of recordings and widely available transcriptions, the possibility to vary and reimagine these tunes still exists today.

Another big anomaly in traditional music was that a lot of players weren't skilled performers. This might sound surprising to anybody who imagines that being a good musician and a good performer are the same thing. Many of these musicians knew the music well and could play their instruments, but they didn't have much experience in performance situations. I would come to know players who had the capacity to deliver soulful moments of beauty when in an intimate and safe setting, but the second the spotlight was shone on them and they found themselves in the unfamiliar environment of a recording studio or on a stage, their effort often became little more than an attempt to avoid making mistakes. In circumstances where they were unable to access their full depth, these musicians would then have very little to offer. This can be very confusing for uninitiated listeners who may have heard of the importance of some carrier of the tradition but get nothing from the musician's playing when they encounter it on a stage or in a recording. Sometimes we have to listen past the surface sound, the faltering technique, and seek the emotional feeling and intent. That's what it's all about. It is the opposite of ready-made, accessible pop music that can catch your attention when you're not even listening. Traditional music sometimes requires a more active kind of listening.

The music of people like Joe Bane, Junior Crehan or Martin Rochford didn't come rushing out to meet you when they played; it was more of an invitation. You were being asked to take a step towards them, to answer that invitation. This intimate music has always been difficult to access – you had to be in the kitchen with Junior Crehan or the corner of the bar with Martin Rochford to catch those moments in a visceral way. This kind of playing was less of a musical performance and more of a direct human communication where something of their spirit and soul was being revealed to you. There are some recordings of the old players that manage to capture that elusive essence – recordings like Tommy Potts's *The Liffey Banks*, Willie Clancy's *The Minstrel from Clare*, Micho Russell's *Ireland's Whistling Ambassador*, Darach Ó Catháin's eponymous sean nós album or *The Star Above the Garter*. But sadly, I know first-hand that there are many more musicians whose musical spirits were never adequately captured in a way that did them justice.

Even though, in my teens, I enjoyed a very different type of music to other kids my age, my connection to music was really no different from theirs. People enjoy different types of music, regardless of genre, because of the power and meaning it holds for them. Many people around me just didn't get that taste for traditional music – I think to their ears it was a series of barely discernible and repetitive patterns that all sounded the same. Lots of people didn't have enough exposure and simply didn't come close enough to the music to get swept up in its more powerful moments that make sense of the whole thing. Not many people actually knew this music. It was a very marginal pursuit.

7

DURING MY TEENAGE years there were plenty of moments outside school that were hugely rewarding and which compensated for the alienation I always felt while I was there. Going to music competitions was a great way for me to connect musically with my own generation. But on some level, of course, the idea of a music competition is a flawed one. First of all, it goes against the supposed communal, non-competitive ethos of the music. There is also the other problem, which is that music and the value in music are difficult to measure, and that the adjudicator's evaluation and conclusion is based on their subjective response. The danger is that competition by nature pushes us in the direction of quantifiable technical perfection, which can easily encourage a music that's lacking in deeper meaning. We don't want to start evaluating music like judges do in the sports world; this is not synchronized swimming or ice skating. That said, whether I now believe competitions are good or bad, I competed in a lot of them throughout my teenage years. I needed to be part of the music scene with people my own age, and I certainly harboured no philosophical objection to competing or winning back then.

Around that time, Fr Burke was replaced by a new school principal, Fr Carney. The Tulla Céilí Band had been offered a tour of the UK that was taking place during a school term. Once again I begged my parents to let me go. For the quiet life, they eventually relented and said I could play on the tour on the condition that I got permission from the principal. I think the tour was going to take around ten days but there was a long bank-holiday weekend in the middle, so I fudged the request and asked for just four days off during the first week. I knew there were going to be a few additional days I would miss, but I figured I would deal with that later. I can't even remember what excuse I came up with, but I do know I didn't breathe a word about England or going on tour. Whatever reason I offered, it worked, and Fr Carney gave me the green light.

A few days later, we flew from Shannon Airport to London. When we landed, we hopped on to a shuttle bus that brought us into the airport terminal. I sat down, taking it all in. Seated directly across from me on the bus, looking right at me, was Fr Carney, who I was sure I had fooled only a few days earlier. I couldn't believe what I was seeing. To my astonishment, he never said a word. In fact, he even smiled at me. I suppose he guessed what I was up to and may have thought I was getting the education I actually needed. My father didn't see him and I said nothing.

Heading off on a trip with my fiddle in tow was what I lived for. While I appreciated my other realities, such as the farm, I didn't love them, and I certainly didn't live for them. I knew from a young age that, as the eldest son, I was expected to take over the farm from my father, but I began to feel that my life would not be going in that direction. The stories of my father's travels to London and New York had from an early age seeped into my consciousness. My own travels only reinforced my desire to explore the world further. The visits to our house by broadcasters and musicians from Dublin and from other countries were an opening to another world and somehow I wanted to go there.

I wanted to pursue this musical passion on some level, even if it wasn't going to be my career. I knew I wanted to be free to move around in the world and it felt like the farm would restrict that freedom. So, when I was around fourteen or so, I approached my brother, Pat, with a proposal of sorts. We agreed that I would forfeit the farm in favour of making my own way in the world, and he would take it on instead. It was absolutely the right decision. Even though I liked the farm in many ways, I didn't show an aptitude or even a willingness when it came to the work involved. Pat, on the other hand, loved feeding the calves and was very engaged with what was happening on the farm. I was a bit of a daydreamer and I remember that when we were giving the skimmed milk to the calves each day, there was always the risk that I would feed the same calf twice. It's not that I was incapable of the task, it's just that it never held my interest or sparked any kind of curiosity in me. Pat would never make such a mistake because he was far more interested and engrossed in the farm work. He seemed to prefer the solid and predictable, whereas I needed adventure.

It was obvious from early on which one of us was really the farmer. Even as a kid, Pat would play with toy farm animals whereas I never would. Similarly, the fiddle was of little interest to him, though both he and my sister Helen played a little bit. Helen progressed a good bit further than Pat and could play reasonably well. She also became a really fine singer and a music connoisseur – she is still someone whose musical opinion I value a lot. I suspect Pat and Helen's reluctance to push further with the fiddle may have been somewhat rooted in their memories of my apparent struggle during the learning process. They may have thought that all those hours I spent in the living room and sitting on the side of the bathtub looked like too much hard work. It never felt like work to me, but it might have looked like it. Anna Marie cleverly avoided the whole thing. When Pat and I finally informed our parents of the decision we had reached, they didn't argue. They, too, could see which of us was the farmer.

East Clare at this time was still remote and isolated. Families had occupied the same land and houses for generations, which meant everyone knew everyone else. I can distinctly recall the very first time I could see the make-up of the area beginning to change. I was up the hill with my father, helping him to open a drain, when we saw this stranger walking across our main meadow. We couldn't make out the face, but we could easily tell just from the stride alone that it was not one of our neighbours. As he got closer, we could see that he had long hair and a beard. He was also wearing leather trousers. He started waving at us and saying something we couldn't quite make out. My father and I walked towards him, a bit confused but curious. He introduced himself as Bill Sampson. I have no idea if it's even politically correct any more to call someone a hippie, but back then Bill was a hippie. The counterculture movement that had swept through the UK and the US had finally reached Maghera.

Bill and his wife, Anne, were from England but wanted desperately to move to Clare. They were interested in buying an old house up the road and had found out it belonged to my father. The old house in question was where Paddy Canny had grown up. Paddy had left there maybe twenty years previously and the house was in poor condition. It came into my father's possession during the Land Commission divide. The Land Commission was originally set up to distribute the land of the big estates among the tenant farmers and was still operating into the 1990s, purchasing land and distributing it among farmers, helping them consolidate and expand their holdings into more viable farms. Back then, no one renovated old houses, so my father didn't even see the property as an asset, but Bill had a kind smile and appeared to be a gentle soul, so my father agreed to sell it to him for some nominal price. Bill and Anne wanted to move in as soon as possible, so we all got involved in cleaning out the house, lighting fires in the fireplaces to try to rid the place of the damp that had set in since it was last inhabited. There were plenty of fireplaces in the house but no running water or electricity, so there was a long way to go in terms of making it fit for living. My parents, however, felt a responsibility for looking after them, so we did everything we could to try to make the place habitable. My father then offered to give them a lift to Mass the following Sunday. This was almost certainly the kind of help they didn't need, but they were very good-humoured about it and came along to Mass in Kilclaran. In the door of the church they marched alongside my father and mother. You can be sure their presence was well noticed and quietly discussed among the locals afterwards. My father hadn't thought to ask Bill and Anne if they wanted to go to Mass, or even if they were Catholic, but there they were, sitting in the pew taking it all in. I think it only dawned on my father that they were of a different denomination when he realized they were unsure of when to sit and when to stand. After Mass, he asked them what they thought of the experience, and only then asked them what religion they were. Bill explained he himself was a Quaker. My father, wanting to respond quickly in some knowing way, immediately replied, 'Oh! Just like President Nixon!' Bill laughed, saying something about Nixon not being a very good Quaker. My father, even if he tried, couldn't have come up with a comparison more diametrically opposed to everything that he and the entire counterculture movement stood for.

Bill and Anne became good friends of the family and would visit our house quite a lot, even becoming part of our Christmas gatherings. Bill would sometimes even help us with the silage and hay, and whenever their parents visited from England, they would stay with us as Bill and Anne's place was just a little bit too rustic at that time. My father and mother could see that Bill and Anne, despite their rustic way of living, hailed from an educated and professional middle-class background. During my teenage years, I would always call in to visit them whenever I was dispatched to count the cattle in 'Canny's place', as we called it, which was the land around the house where Bill and Anne were now living. It was around then that I managed to get my first bicycle, and I loved to cycle up to the top end of the valley to count the cattle and maybe visit Bill and Anne. (I'd then free-wheel the entire way home afterwards.) I loved calling in to see Bill and Anne, as it would allow me to experience this other reality that seemed completely free and unbound by all tradition and cultural expectations. I tried to imagine that kind of freedom, that liberated way of thinking that was no longer bound by the cultural and religiously conservative norms that governed my life. It was there that I first began to hear about environmentalism and alternative energy sources. Bill and Anne fitted into our world just fine. They seemed to enjoy the company of local elderly people, who were living in older ways, people like their nearest neighbours, Paddy, Tom and Mary Jones. The Joneses were siblings who cut hay by hand with a scythe and didn't have a car, electricity or running water. Both houses lived with the same amenities, and they liked and respected each other, even if they lived in two alternative consciousnesses.

Bill and Anne were the first of many people who moved to the area. Eventually there was a significant number of people from the UK and all over Europe who were seeking an alternative life in the quiet, secluded valleys of East Clare. They cared for this environment and even became a vital support to the music culture of the area. Many of the great nights of music in Pepper's Bar in Feakle, where my father and his fiddle-playing colleague and friend of many years, Francie Donnellan, played regularly, were kept alive and vibrant thanks to the number of musicians who moved here. These 'blow-ins' were as vital to the music sessions in Pepper's as the locals were, both as players and listeners.

The listener is the other part of the musical equation. A good listener in a conversation can get others to really open up, and a good listener to music can, in a similar way, draw the music out of you. With traditional music, a good listener sometimes knows just as much about the music as the players do. Danny Connors was a locally revered connoisseur who never played a note, and yet he knew more than most musicians. He certainly knew when music was real or not. Geraldine Moloney was another person with this innate ability. Geraldine was Mary MacNamara's closest friend and a great set-dancer. The three of us spent a lot of time together in our youth. Geraldine was one of those discerning listeners who spent many an hour listening to Mary and me play. This was not any kind of passive listening; this was listening with your heart and soul. It's a different kind of interaction. She could somehow draw the music out of you as if asking you to give your very best and most deeply felt expression of the music. There were times when the music reached a place where I could even spot the tears starting to well in her eyes. Her mother Kathleen was the same. If Kathleen was listening to music that was starting to hit her deep, you would see her come close to tears – but not tears related to tragedy or sadness. The experience I'm talking about comes from having your soul touched, with tears produced by that truly human moment when the melancholic and joyful cannot be separated and the player and listener are united. Melancholic music has a feeling of profundity for me. It doesn't make me feel sad; it touches my soul and makes me feel completely alive and joyful, as if the very deepest part of me is awakened by it. Mary MacNamara and I were once playing in a duet competition at another fleadh in Buncrana. It was as if things just suddenly started to click, and we landed in this perfectly comfortable groove that had both momentum and ease. From the way we were effortlessly phrasing the tunes together, it was obvious that at a deeper level both of us were feeling them in the same way. It wasn't long before I could tell that the entire room had joined in with our experience. It was no longer a competition; for me it was a shared moment of musical connection to be savoured. That one experience has stayed with me my whole life. It became for me what a performance can, and should, be about. We won the competition that evening but that fact was just incidental, almost irrelevant.

My teenage experience was first and foremost about my musical life, the thing I willingly pursued with dedication and all of my passion, the one thing I loved to do. Everything else was simply what I was obliged to do. During secondary school I had a stable rich musical life that ran parallel to my predictable and manageable school life. The real world of adulthood was around the corner, however, and my contained bubble of music would soon be in a vulnerable position.

8

MANY PEOPLE WHO have seen me perform over the years
might naturally assume that I'd always planned to become
a professional musician, that I have studied music in some formal
manner. Back in my teenage years, however, there was absolutely
no support for the idea of being a professional traditional musician. There was no real model for such a way of life and no
obvious way to start if I wanted to. Even if I'd just wished to continue with music on some academic level, there were no third-level
courses relating to traditional music, so really there were no
opportunities for someone like me to study music. To enrol in
any of the existing third-level music courses, you'd need to be
capable of playing at least some Mozart in order to get past the
audition process. I was very far removed from that world. I
remember my father commenting as we were watching some
orchestral performance on television, some years earlier, 'Wouldn't
that be a nice life for you?' His question was met with an emphatic
'No!' I didn't have that passion for classical music, though this
would change massively in years to come.

The summer following the end of secondary school, my mother
began to sense a lingering uncertainty in me. She picked up on

that ever-present doubt that would persistently creep in whenever I thought about the direction I should be taking. I had gone from having my day planned out to now suddenly having the freedom to go about my day or my life however I wished. It was a relief to have secondary school behind me, but with that relief came an overwhelming insecurity and the constant questioning of where I should go from there. My mother suggested I apply to some third-level colleges, such as those in Limerick, which was the closest city with a few third-level options. Further education had always been part of the plan; I just didn't know what I wanted to study. Still, going to college was the pragmatic choice.

I decided to apply to the National Institute of Higher Education, now known as the University of Limerick, to study business. Looking back, it seems obvious that I should have considered studying a course relating to the arts, but that didn't make sense to me at the time. If I couldn't pursue my musical passion in college, why would I pursue an education in some other area of the arts, where I had neither direct experience, passion nor skills? In the end I chose Business Studies, because it was in theory about money – money that could potentially buy me the freedom to do what I wanted, which was to play music. Music was my deepest passion but the idea that I could have a music career, that I could follow my actual passion and make a living from it, seemed so ludicrous that I never gave it any thought. If anything, I was going to try very hard not to have a career as a musician. I had accepted the more practical prevailing opinion – that one should get an education and pursue music as a hobby. A career in traditional music looked to me more like failure in life.

Unfortunately, nothing about the business course I had chosen sparked my curiosity or ignited any passion within me. My interest in business studies lay only in making money. The premise was all wrong from the beginning. I was looking at education as an escape route out of the farm, and a means to continue my fiddle-playing dreams, which I was certain could never support me financially. My view at the time was so linear that I couldn't see college as serving any other purpose. The concept of studying something I might have interest in for its own sake just never occurred to me. In some sense I was already doing that with my music; college was just about finding a way to make money. I was viewing education purely and singularly through the utilitarian lens of career and job opportunities.

Unlike my musical life, when it came to the academic work I never had one of those moments where I suddenly found the motivation to invest the work necessary. I had never had good study habits in secondary school, with my evening studies often yielding far too easily to the welcome distraction of music, and frankly those habits didn't change much in college either. While in Limerick, I lived with Paddy and Nora McMahon, who were distant relatives of the family. In the evenings I studied in their front room. I would spend hours in there studying, sitting at a table with my small boombox right in front of me, as if I could read a textbook and listen to music at the same time. It was as if I couldn't do anything that didn't somehow involve music. There were far more music notes entering my mind than any notes I'd taken during lectures, but I just carried on nursing the illusion that I was earnestly studying. My passion was music, and I didn't have another passion to replace it with, other than perhaps politics, which was connected to my upbringing through my father's involvement in politics at a local level. But I didn't examine that pursuit very closely and it came nowhere near to being the deep or soulful passion that music was for me. Today, that same college has a music programme as part of its Irish World Academy, which is designed for people exactly like me. If that choice had been available back then, it would have been ideal. I'd have had an opportunity to study this music on my terms and would likely have done that. It would have allowed me to start my creative journey much earlier instead of taking the long, circuitous path that I did. That said, our life experiences are what mould us into the people we become, so perhaps the journey, with all its turbulences, served its purpose after all. Sometimes we're just not ready to handle our own gifts, and having to fight for something also has real value.

As my Business Studies course progressed, I still had no real passion for the subject, though certain parts stoked my curiosity, particularly the modules in psychology, sociology and economics. And even though I opted not to pursue politics academically, the college offered me the opportunity to delve further into this interest. Just like my Catholicism, my political view was an inherited belief system, a loyalty to identity more than anything else. I wouldn't get to know my real political inclinations or my own spiritual truths until many years later. If you came from a small farm in East Clare, there was a strong likelihood your family identified with Éamon De Valera's Fianna Fáil. My father was a big De Valera supporter all his life and was an active member of the local Fianna Fáil party. My mother's and father's families had both provided safe houses for revolutionaries on the run during the War of Independence, with both sides of the family remaining loyal to De Valera's anti-treaty side during the Civil War. I met De Valera as a child and my father received Christmas cards from him; I also went along with my father to De Valera's funeral. Pat has carried on that part of the family tradition, having been a local Fianna Fáil councillor for most of his life. Though I seemed to be rebellious by nature, I never rebelled against my bubble of music, Catholicism and Fianna Fáil. I think they came in that exact order of priority, but they all seemed to be harmonious parts of my identity and that of my family also.

My father and I would talk politics throughout my teenage years, although it was more of a discussion where we evaluated how articulate, effective or decent we saw particular politicians – decency was very important to my father and would form the basis of his opinion of a politician. From a young age, I read the political pages of the paper. I also watched and listened to political programmes on the television and radio. At the time, I suppose I was simply responding to my father's world, and instead of rebelling against it I embraced it, which perhaps was rebellion in itself, but a rebellion against the norm of my own generation. Every Sunday, on the way home from Mass in Feakle, we'd buy a few newspapers – two for ourselves and one for our neighbour Paddy Canny, 'The Volunteer'. I could never hold off reading the newspaper until we got home; I would have to start there and then in the back seat of the car and continue on to the inevitable point of feeling carsick. The routine was that we'd stop at Paddy's house and I'd take the paper inside, where he and I would then have a chat about politics, maybe even a bit of a debate. It wasn't so much that we disagreed on any fundamental issue; it was more that often I considered his viewpoints to be quirky, and even entertaining at times. We'd chat for about fifteen or twenty minutes, but the weird thing about this weekly Sunday ritual was that his children, who were my school mates, would have to observe this seemingly serious and respectful adult-type conversation taking place between their father and me. I can't imagine what they would have been thinking, but it couldn't possibly have been positive. Who could blame them? I was already standing there in the kitchen, talking about the politics of the moment and the carry-on of the government, looking like some kind of politician-in-waiting with my jacket, shirt and tie. I never wore the same style as my school peers though I knew this was setting me apart. It wasn't that I didn't get it. It was my rebellion against the contemporary world. The truth was that I was every bit as such a social misfit as any city skinhead or punk was, only just in the completely opposite direction. I couldn't help myself. I was the kind of teenager that girls looked at and immediately crossed off their lists as a potential boyfriend. I had no clue about modern music, about pop culture of any kind, but I didn't care, because I knew I didn't belong to that world or identify with it in any way.

I'd leave The Volunteer's house and walk the rest of the road home, where my mother was preparing Sunday lunch. Deep down, I knew there was something wrong with this picture – my mother preparing lunch while 'the men' talked politics, as if it were somehow unquestionably clear and obvious that preparing lunch was solely a woman's responsibility and talking politics was the men's realm. As children and teenagers, we did almost as many chores inside the house as we did on the farm, but my brother and I never considered it our realm, as such, whereas the women seemed tied to this role, no matter what. On Sundays, I often had the task of shining the doorknobs and candle sticks with Brasso, and of course setting the table for lunch and doing the wash-up afterwards, but I would also try to carve out time to continue reading the Sunday newspapers. When I'd finish the political section of one paper, I'd swap it with my father to read the political page of the other. We'd comment back and forth to each other about what we had just read, and once we had finished, it would almost be time for the main Sunday political programme on the radio at 1 p.m., which we would listen to with devoted attention. Even just thinking back on that radio programme, I can almost smell the little saucepans of Bisto gravy and peas, the roast beef sizzling away in the oven, as my father and I listened to host Gerald Barry interviewing politicians who were either defending some position from the preceding week or laying out some new agenda or line of attack for the next one. This part of the Sunday ritual concluded with us listening to the end of the programme as we sat down to a table of floury potatoes, peas and carrots lined up alongside the slices of tender roast beef, the steam still rising from the gravy. Sunday lunch was always followed by a cup of tea and a slice of apple or rhubarb tart, which my mother would bake using our own fruit from the garden. It's not the standard picture that comes to mind when one thinks of Irish politics, but for me the origins of my interest are firmly attached to that wonderful Sunday ritual.

Throughout my teenage years, I always accompanied my father to the local Fianna Fáil meetings. It wasn't an obligation forced upon me; I genuinely enjoyed sitting and listening to the old men discuss and strategize who would make a good candidate for particular positions, whose seat was under threat, whose support they needed, who could provide a network of contacts or who was secretly in which camp. I found it all incredibly intriguing. It was all about tactics and political smarts and capabilities. It was more akin to finding yourself supporting a sports team. Listening to these older people talk politics was also similar to how I absorbed musical viewpoints from being around older musicians.

Our local Fianna Fáil TD (member of parliament) was Dr Bill Loughnane – the same man who had organized the welcome-home concert for Joe Cooley when he returned from America. Dr Bill was also our local GP and a fine fiddle-player who spent years performing in the Tulla Céilí Band. He was an important figure in my life, always encouraging me as a budding musician and, later on, in my political activities. He was also a remarkably charismatic man. I remember, on one particular occasion, playing at a dance in Feakle with the Tulla Céilí Band when I observed Dr Bill walking into the hall. As soon as he arrived, you could sense it. A different type of energy came over the room. He had a presence, and everyone felt it. I watched closely from the stage as he moved through the crowd, shaking hands and chatting excitedly with people, no doubt referring to each one by name and asking them about something specific that he knew was going on in their lives. He had the most incredible memory when it came to people's names and their personal stories. Anyone he spoke with always felt as though he took a great interest in them and, knowing Dr Bill, this interest would have been genuine. By that stage, I had occupied the political realm long enough to know that anyone could fake the niceties; anyone could turn on the charm and work the room as if everyone there would be heading to a ballot box straight after. I had a pretty good instinct for identifying those who were sincere from those who were outright charlatans. Dr Bill was one of the good ones. That night onstage, I watched as people started to sidle up beside him, anticipating that moment of connection with him. Eventually, he made it on to the stage. I ended up giving him my fiddle so he could play a few tunes. After a while, he gave it back to me and then sang a few songs with the band. Larger than life, he added something very special to the evening.

Dr Bill didn't function like any regular member of parliament; he was almost like a social worker, who loved people and would try to solve their problems with advice, reassuring stories, his doctor's bag or his political connections. His political speeches were always entertaining, with a minimum of political rhetoric and flavoured with lots of jokes and stories. I think I wanted to be Dr Bill. I found myself basically mirroring his political positions and leaning towards the more republican views of his colleagues, such as Neil Blaney and Kevin Boland. I even liked Charles Haughey, who took over the leadership of Fianna Fáil, and the country, in 1979. Dr Bill was a supporter of Haughey's and had played an important part in the lead-up to him taking power. Everyone had a different opinion of Haughey. At the time, most people knew he was slightly shady. For some, he was simply a likeable rogue, a clever businessman, maybe a perjurer for a noble cause; or, depending on your political background, an unscrupulous bully or an outright crook. Opinions of such a character will always vary but I think a great deal of Fianna Fáil supporters at the time preferred to imagine him as the inheritor of some older and more genuine republicanism, a decisive man of ability and charisma whose other shortcomings could be overlooked, his unaccountable wealth evidence only of his cleverness. He was in many ways an effective and able politician who did many good things, but who also failed to act at times when he knew better. In the end, his achievements were overshadowed by significant personal moral failings that also prevented him from fully realizing his political potential. His political leadership ultimately had a lasting and very corrosive impact on the party he led.

The political curiosity that was rooted in my formative years gradually began to overtake my interest in my studies. By nature and force of habit, I was not a dedicated or disciplined student and had skated through most of my school life by doing the bare minimum. Perhaps in the same way that I had used music as a distraction from my school homework, I turned to political involvement as a distraction from the tedium that accompanied such necessary modules as accounting and statistics. One of my economics lecturers in college was Pat Cox, who at that point was a member of Fianna Fáil and would eventually become president of the European Parliament. He was a brilliant lecturer, and his classes were very engaging. Another lecturer there was future politician Willie O'Dea. Willie taught law and would often deliver lectures on the law side of business studies. I had joined the Fianna Fáil cumann (branch) on campus, and Pat Cox and Willie O'Dea were also members at the time. There were so few of us that we were nearly all officers, the others being Micheál Ó Móráin from Connemara, Sean Nolan from Sligo and Jim Ó Dwyer from Tipperary.

In 1981, during my first year in college, I asserted myself at one of the party meetings of East Clare Fianna Fáil in Scariff and spoke out about some issues relating to the interests and concerns of young people. I think the people gathered there were a bit surprised at my audacity but were also impressed that someone so young had managed to speak coherently and effectively. One of the many benefits of having spent most of my teenage years onstage was being unfazed by the prospect of public speaking.

I don't think the people there that night cared too much about the point I was making but were more impressed by the fact that I was a capable speaker and that I was young and therefore a good image for the party, so they signed me up to do some church-gate speeches. In the lead-up to the upcoming general election, I was to make a political speech outside church gates around East Clare as people were leaving Sunday Mass. I suppose I had a vague idea that there might be a possible future for me in politics, even if I couldn't yet properly see how that might materialize. As I canvassed during that election race, part of me wondered if the day would come when I might be on the ballot sheet myself. I certainly didn't dislike the idea. But while I felt it would do no harm to keep my options open, it wasn't something I discussed openly. If anything, I kept these aspirations a safely guarded secret. I just didn't feel as though I wanted that ambition of mine to be 'out there', so to speak. I preferred to see how things would naturally progress and let the cards fall where they may.

I was eighteen when I gave my first political speech, in front of the church in Ogonnelloe, East Clare. I was nervous because I was aware that many people there would be opposed to the ideas I was about to express. I received word from Dr Bill that I was to announce his securing of some kind of funding or support for the local chipboard factory in Scariff, which was struggling at the time. I made that announcement and I also parroted plenty of Fianna Fáil rhetoric along with a list of the current political talking points that nobody had to prompt me on. Part of the Fianna Fáil ethos and identity was a muted republican nationalism that was difficult to articulate during this time of strife in Northern Ireland. This republicanism traced its lineage right back to the foundation of the party, the Civil War, the War of Independence and the Easter Rising. This all lined up harmoniously with my identity as a traditional musician, our music often being presented as evidence of our unique cultural identity, a justification of our right to independence. I hadn't yet fully scrutinized many of the inherited political positions and views I was offering that day – maybe that's why it was possible for me to deliver my speech with passion.

It's interesting for me now to muse over the make-up of my political beliefs back then and what they really were. My political position, like my music, was simply part of my upbringing and identity, and I formed whatever intellectual arguments I could muster, selectively choosing facts to back up my 'political position'. This approach doesn't fundamentally differ from basic debating skills, where you learn how to represent any position you are asked to defend. Deep down I had a sense that there was something a bit dishonest in this point-scoring approach – making policy arguments on some issue as if that was the sole reason for my political involvement, when I was actually fighting to defend my deep-rooted identity and perhaps my own political ambition. My friend and totally sincere fellow musician Dennis Cahill quotes a funny, albeit somewhat cynical, saying about sincere musical performance, which I think can also apply to being a politician: 'Once you've learned how to fake sincerity, you have it made!' In college, I found myself parroting party political positions, defending them with every conceivable argument and with as much sincerity as I could muster. I was accepting party orthodoxy and views that I had not yet properly examined for myself. I was already in the party, and once you were in the club you never really had to answer any question regarding the source of your political ideology. You just had to show and prove loyalty.

As well as immersing myself in politics during my first year in college, I was also a member of the Students' Union Executive Committee. All this activity allowed me to test out the waters politically, but more importantly it subconsciously provided a way for me to avoid studying accounting and statistics. Politics did indeed take me away from studying accounting and statistics, but so much so that I was barely passing my exams. In the summer of 1981, another welcome distraction came my way in the form of an invitation to go to the Lorient Music Festival in Brittany, France. I travelled there with the Lewis family – John and Breda, and their children, Patsy and Liam, all of whom I knew well through various music sessions and fleadh cheoils. A flute-player from Galway named Seán Moloney travelled with us also. The Lewises lived in Galway too, having moved over from England. They were all wonderful musicians who played in the East Galway style, which is stylistically very close to how we played in East Clare. This was my first trip to France and only my second time on the Continent. The trip marked my first encounter with pungent cheese, not to mention my first time eating 'mountain oysters', neither of which you would find in Maghera too easily!

Our performance was a musical joy to me. It was this lovely combination of two fiddles, two flutes, concertina and mandolin, playing lots of lovely tunes composed by Paddy Fahey along with many other beautiful melodies from East Galway, with just the perfect pace. Unfortunately, this performance proved to be far from the most memorable event of this trip for me. I was what was known then as a 'pioneer'. For readers unfamiliar with this term, a pioneer was someone who had taken a pledge not to drink alcohol. All Catholic children took this pledge at their Confirmation ceremony when they were in their final year of primary school. The priests in school made sure that we had the opportunity to join this temperance movement, and though it was supposedly voluntary, it was the kind of opportunity you couldn't actually turn down. To show your commitment, you wore a badge pinned on to your lapel or somewhere on your sweater. Many people in my family had kept this pledge their whole lives. My uncle, Liam, always wore his pioneer badge, as did my father for most of his life, but in later years he removed it and would enjoy an occasional drink, though he didn't actually care much for alcohol. A history of drink problems in previous generations of the family meant a residual family fear of alcohol remained.

I regularly wore my pioneer badge and didn't have any problem in abstaining. I didn't feel any real pressure to drink. However, something changed during that festival. All of the performers and their families from all over the Celtic world would have their lunch in the Palais des Congrès. Everybody seemed to be drinking wine with lunch, and it looked very civilized, so I thought, *Why not? I'll try a glass! What harm could it do?* Soon after the first few sips, I began to experience an unfamiliar, slightly intoxicated feeling. I liked it a lot, so much so that I decided to have another few glasses, after which things started to get a bit out of focus, shall we say?

That is where I should have stopped, but no. I decided that then was the best time to also try a few beers. That whole day is still a distorted mix of haziness and total memory lapses. I know I disappeared into the town on my own, embarking on a one-man drinking spree. By the time I somehow miraculously made it back to my tribe, I was completely drunk and just had to go to bed. This was an incredibly telling first experience with alcohol. I woke up the next day with an incredible hangover and a clear decision in my head that I would never do this again.

Something happened to me that day that caught me off-guard. It was as if my buttoned-down reality as the compliant, socially conservative misfit began to crack once I had a drink; I was no longer in control. Word of my escapade spread fast, with even my friends back in Ireland hearing of my breakout. At the time, those who knew me were genuinely fascinated by what had happened, and most were disappointed to have missed it. After I arrived back in Ireland, I noticed a few chancing their arms at buying me drinks, in the hope of getting a repeat performance. They never got it, but I didn't exactly return to my pioneer ways either. Merely a week or so after being home from France, the barman was handing me a drink, and the promise I had made myself to never drink again was quickly forgotten.

The France episode might have been the catalyst for a period of self-reflection, a pointed moment of realization that I was unhappy and needed to start instigating change in my life, and I should for sure have avoided alcohol. Instead, around this time my identity as a competent, though undedicated, college student slowly started to fracture as I began to drink. I suppose there was an incredible amount of pent-up frustration, even anger and pain, at being such an oddball, such a social misfit. I started to feel resentful, as though I had allowed myself to be moulded into some socially compliant cultural manikin at the cost of a normal teenage life. It was also becoming obvious that my studies had no real meaning for me. My life very gradually became a cycle of Students' Union politics, Fianna Fáil politics, partying and attending class, where I was doing the minimum amount of work necessary to get by.

Drinking seemed to distract me from my problems, but it also weakened my resolve to keep up with my studies and it didn't take very long for me to start losing control of my academic life. Soon, things began slipping away from me on that front, and when they did I would continue to turn to alcohol to soothe the inner disquiet rather than facing my problems. I still played with the Tulla Céilí Band at the weekends, but anything I earned from a night of playing was used to sustain my partying in the nights that followed. I was now also playing banjo in the band, a useful instrument rhythmically but without any soulful attraction for me. I had slowly begun to lose my connection to the real music that I had once lived and breathed.

9

GOING ALL THE way back to my early teenage years, I had presented myself, at least outwardly, as a competent, articulate and intellectually capable individual who also happened to be a very good musician. I never dedicated myself to the academic side of things, though; instead I was always telling myself that I was just about to really knuckle down on the academic front, but I never did. At this point, however, my academic life was skirting close to the edge of failure. It was all rapidly coming apart at the seams, and the illusion of my academic competence was now facing the possibility of being shattered. I was disheartened and stressed enough to know I needed help, so I sought out a student counsellor. During our appointment, I described to him how I was feeling, and explained what was going on in my life. I have no doubt he imparted some words of advice during the session, but the only thing I can remember from this encounter is what he said to me as I was leaving the room: 'Don't do anything foolish, now, OK?' I was alarmed by his response. I got the distinct impression that he sensed I was suicidal or, at the very least, verging on it. The shocking part of all this was that I'd actually understated to him just how low I was really feeling. I wasn't suicidal, but it did rattle me to know that my situation was potentially bad enough for somebody to think it was plausible for me to have that response.

I still had plenty of capacity for self-delusion to sustain me while my life and studies continued spiralling out of control. I knew my life was becoming a bigger mess than I'd originally thought. It was now common for me to wander into bars in Limerick city for a few drinks on my own. This kind of drinking had nothing to do with socializing. One evening in a pub, an interesting bar owner struck up a conversation with me. Over the course of our conversation, he asked what I was studying and was curious about my future plans. As always, my plans were vague. I mumbled something about starting a business or getting some kind of corporate job in marketing or something like that. It didn't sound very convincing to him, so he pushed me a little further and started quizzing me about what I wanted out of life. Then the conversation turned a little bit more philosophical. He told me that I was getting it all wrong, that I hadn't identified what would make me happy. He started espousing the value of a contented simple life, posing the question why, instead of joining the corporate world or starting a complicated business, I didn't open a small sweetshop, or something simple where life didn't have to be too difficult. He asked me if I'd heard of Wayne Dyer, the American New Age spiritual writer. I wasn't familiar with Dyer. The bar owner recommended one of Dyer's books to me, which I didn't follow up, but I didn't forget the conversation I'd had that evening. For the first time, it caused me to truly contemplate the fundamental question of where my own happiness lay and to take stock of the fact that I was clearly on a path or trajectory that wasn't heading in that direction. Granted, the conversation didn't result in me immediately making any fundamental, life-changing decisions – it would take a bit more work to make that happen – but it did plant a seed.

During this turbulent time, I lost an important influence in my life. On 18 October 1982, Dr Bill died suddenly. I'd been chatting with him that same night after a party meeting in the West County Hotel in Ennis, just before I caught the bus back to Limerick. That was the last time I saw him. He was in good form as we spoke, so to wake up to hear that he had passed was a huge shock, and news that I couldn't quite grasp. Dr Bill was an incredible character who had deeply touched many people's lives, including mine, and for him to suddenly disappear from all our lives felt like a great loss.

I stayed involved with politics for a couple of months after that, but I was beginning to find it difficult to muster much enthusiasm. Maybe my loyalty to Dr Bill had kept me there longer than I would have stayed otherwise. I was in my third year of college by this point. The sense of allegiance and identity that was previously sufficient to sustain my involvement was no longer enough – defending Charlie Haughey was becoming too much of a stretch. In November 1982, the final election of a trilogy, I campaigned for the Fianna Fáil candidate Michael Herbert in the Limerick East constituency. I knew he didn't have a great chance of being elected, but at least I felt I was supporting a good, honourable man. In the end, he lost out. Some time after that election, I stood up at a Fianna Fáil meeting in Ennis and announced that I was quitting, that I didn't think the party actually spoke to the needs of my generation, that it wasn't open enough or transparent enough, that the republicanism of liberty, equality and fraternity was now just rhetoric. That was my last Fianna Fáil meeting. I had essentially closed the door on a political future. It was somehow liberating to finally challenge some of the orthodoxy of my upbringing and to speak a political truth that wasn't also self-serving.

I had also lost heart with college. I knew that if I graduated, I was only going to scrape by, and given the economic climate of that time, scraping by wasn't going to cut it. Even if I succeeded, I already knew I didn't want to work in a job that involved accounting, sales or marketing – not that it would have been likely, one way or another, as there were virtually no jobs available. The only jobs I stood to be hired for were some menial, low-paying ones that would have been available to me even without a university education. I felt stuck. It seemed pointless continuing on with college, but quitting seemed like an admission of defeat and I don't think I could bring myself to actually admit to the world that I had failed. As tough as I found things, it still seemed easier to trudge on in the hope that things would miraculously improve. With everything that was going on in my life at that time, I became quite depressed, though I managed to keep it under wraps. I didn't share my feelings with anyone, thinking it was wiser to keep things to myself after the student counsellor imagined I might be suicidal. I kept a bounce in my step, looked and acted normal, but in reality I was starting to unravel. I wasn't coping very well; sometimes I couldn't cope at all. I was having a difficult time mustering the willpower to continue studying topics that didn't interest me, and it seemed too late to transform my studying habits for it to make any meaningful impact on my academic life.

My nights of drinking inevitably led to me skipping some classes. I only had to do this a couple of times before I somehow started to find it acceptable. The battle between getting up and attending an accountancy lecture or staying in bed and sleeping off a hangover was lost before it had even begun. I failed two of the modules, which meant I would have to spend the summer studying so I could resit them at a later date.

That summer, in 1983, was spent back home with my parents, feeling a bit down and unable to summon the enthusiasm or willpower to study for the exams I had failed. Instead, I basically ignored the situation. I didn't tell anyone what was really happening and not much was said around the house about what was going on. I was an adult, after all, even if I wasn't exactly handling things in a very adult way. In the end, I didn't study and I didn't retake the exams. I was done with college. I felt a deep sense of shame. I had been the first one in my family to attend college, yet here I was unceremoniously walking away and leaving it all behind. I was letting a lifetime of potential opportunity and prospects just slip away, and I knew I couldn't turn it around. I had failed, and that was a very painful realization for me.

Once the summer had passed, notices started going up about a six-month 'Start Your Own Business' course taking place in the local hall in Feakle. The programme was a series of lectures and workshops being run by a firm of high-powered management consultants and led by local man Jim Nugent. Jim had become very successful in the world of business consultancy and was now returning to help give others a start. My mother came to the rescue. She knew I felt dejected, and probably sensed I was depressed too, so in a bid to motivate me she told me about the course and suggested I attend. The attendees were paid a small stipend and the consultants would guide, teach and empower them in the direction of entrepreneurship. It seemed like a good fit for me, so I signed up. The course turned out to be a very necessary fresh start for me, an opportunity to rebuild my self-esteem and move on from my educational misadventure. I started to think about self-education as the way forward. My solution was like a mantra of sorts: learn to do what you need to do, find the knowledge necessary to solve the task at hand, be brave, take a risk, learn by doing.

The concepts presented by these consultants were easy for me to grasp as they were more like a synopsis of what I'd already learned in Limerick. Unlike the college work, however, I actually enjoyed this course. I liked the community feeling that arose from having a group of young people collectively engaged in an activity that encouraged self-reliance. Also involved was an organization called Tuath Éachta Cooperative, which was founded and led by a very dynamic young local solicitor, Mahon Slattery. The organization pulled both young and old people together with ambitious and progressive plans on how to develop the local area economically, socially and culturally. I became good friends with Mahon and was very taken by his energy and vision of local self-reliance. There were many meetings in the hall in Feakle, where we talked about creating local food and crafts cooperatives, new agriculture, and so on. The ultimate goal would be for us to create either individual small businesses or some larger cooperative enterprise, all of which might be located in a local building where these businesses could work together, sharing overheads. The classes were actually a bit of a boost for me. It was all very exciting and I dived in head first.

For a small locality, the level of innovation, creativity and resourcefulness was remarkable. Among the locals who had particular enthusiasm for this effort was a fascinating man, Fr Harry Bohan. Fr Harry had previously been the driving force behind the creation of a housing project in the village, and he had developed his own rural resource organization and centre. He had even started a bank with the goal of supporting, sustaining and developing rural communities. Fr Harry was very interested in what was happening in Feakle at this time. The consultancy company running the course had managed to secure a lot of money to pay the management consultancy fees, but when the time came for people to launch their business ideas, there was almost no funding available other than the smaller loans that Fr Harry was able to help provide. One of my fellow students, Con McGuinness, started doing some ironwork, while another, Susan Minogue, who had taken Business Studies at the University of Limerick at the same time as me, started a craft business making moulded wall-plaques geared to the tourist market. My business venture started up after one of the consultants read about a company in Tipperary called Quality Kitchens that were producing frozen shepherd's pies and various other one-dish meals in nice earthenware dishes. The consultant suggested to me that I should take a look. The company that produced these dishes was new and had only supplied samples so far, but they were already looking for partners and for people to come on board as distributors. The fact that they had already won some new-business awards made them seem like a good bet. I had a meeting with them and by the end of the meeting I had persuaded them to give me the distribution rights for the Mid-West region of the country. There wasn't anything else happening for me, so I figured, why not sell frozen food? My only goal was to make a profit. I believed that my lack of money meant I had nothing to lose, so I might as well jump in and be an entrepreneur. I wasn't really wondering how good this might be for society, or even how truly nourishing the meals were.

I now needed to buy a van with an ice box, which meant I had to get a loan. I put the jacket, shirt and tie back on and managed to talk the bank manager in Tulla into giving me a partial loan. Fr Harry loaned me the remainder. I bought a Ford Transit flatbed van and then went to Francie Ó Halloran in Ennis, who had a big frozen-food business, and got an ice box from him to put in the back. I drove away that day all set up to start transporting frozen food.

The kitchen in Tipperary was still only in the phase of providing samples and hadn't yet swung into full production, so for now I was just going to take samples with me and see what business I might be able to drum up. My idea was to supply businesses, factories and workplaces with an opportunity to provide tasty warm lunches for their employees without having to invest in a full-on catering operation. All that was needed was a freezer and a couple of microwaves. The meals actually tasted good – at least, they did to my unsophisticated palate – and they also looked good in those earthenware bowls. It all looked fairly straightforward.

I made a connection with a factory in Ennis called Studio Eyewear that had a good number of employees. Their managing director seemed interested in my idea so we made a plan that I would turn up one day at lunchtime to provide Quality Kitchens' samples to the workers and see if they might like these meals and want them on a regular basis. If all went well, I'd just have to swing by every now and again to keep the freezer stocked up. I had calculated that it might not take very many of these outlets for me to make a reasonably comfortable living.

For the initial sampling in Studio Eyewear, I had managed to lease a few microwaves and install myself in a room in the premises where I could get all the meals heated up just in time for lunch. To help speed the process along, I even had a friend make some wooden racks that would allow me to put four or five meals in one microwave at a time. I wanted to have my timing just right, so in the previous few days I had experimented with a microwave to find out how long it would take to heat up one of the meals, which I think was around eight minutes. With lunchtime looming, I started heating up the meals, four at a time. After the eight-minute timer went off, I took out the first batch, but something wasn't right. They were barely warm. I put them back in and rolled the dial to heat them for another few minutes but still they came out lukewarm. By now, hungry workers were starting to gather in the room, all with the expectation of a hot meal waiting for them.

It turns out there was one detail I'd overlooked. You can't put four meals in a microwave and expect them to be reheated at the same speed as just one meal. It takes almost four times as long. I hadn't realized my mistake, however, and was mystified as to why my microwaves were letting me down at this crucial moment. I kept putting them back in for just a little while longer but, with the clock ticking, lunchtime was starting to get a little tight for those who were waiting. I yielded to the pressure of the hungry employees, who were asking how much longer it was going to take, and started handing out the lukewarm samples. It was the best I could do in the circumstances. I had hoped that maybe the dishes were piping hot on the inside, but the shriek of alarm that came from the back of the room quickly shattered that particular sliver of hope: 'There's ice in my dish!' Five words no one in the food industry ever wants to hear after serving up a hot, or in my case lukewarm, meal. This revelation of course sparked off a frenzy of food-poisoning panic. People started to slowly return their dishes. Hungry and annoyed, they naturally had no interest in hearing about my microwave woes. It was bad enough that they hadn't brought their own lunches that day, but now there was the added fear that they might have been poisoned by my efforts. There wouldn't be any need for a follow-up survey to see how the meals had been received.

It was a rough start, but I reassured myself that there would be other opportunities. It was just going to take a bit of time to set them up. In the meantime, I could work on figuring out the microwave equation. I continued organizing try-outs, bringing samples to various places. Things were starting to look positive. It wasn't exactly taking off like wildfire, but there was enough initial interest for me to think the idea had some real potential. I was making progress with building up possible future sales and I was constantly thinking about the places I could pitch to next. Everything was on the up – until I arrived home one evening to find a letter telling me that Quality Kitchens had gone out of business. They never even managed to make it to regular, full production. There I was with a van full of samples and a business plan that was suddenly going nowhere. I started to look around for another supplier. The only company I could find that came close to being able to replace Quality Kitchens was a company called Lydon House. I set up a meeting with them and took a look at their products. I now found myself in the TV dinner business, replete with aluminium food trays. I was descending down to the lower levels of the frozen foods universe.

Lydon House was a well-established company, and I wasn't in a position to say their product wasn't suitable. This was the only supplier I might be able to use to replace Quality Kitchens if I intended to avoid going out of business myself. I had to start all over again, with new samples, and so another tour of product demonstrations began. After just a couple of months of trying to reboot my business plan, I received a letter. I opened it up, the Lydon House letterhead greeting me as I unfolded the page. The division of their company that made the TV dinners was closing down. It wasn't that surprising – the economic environment all round was very challenging at that time. It was starting to turn comical at this point. It seemed as if the universe was trying to block my adventures in frozen food. The possibilities for Martin Hayes, future Frozen Food Baron, were looking dim. I had, at that point, been in talks with some bars about providing them with frozen dinners that they could sell on to their customers. Instead, I had to abandon taking that idea any further and just start to sell the samples to anyone I could so I could make some pocket change. I remember pulling into Slattery's Pub in the Clare village of Bodyke and asking the owner, Mike Slattery, to pop a few dinners into the microwave. I didn't have the heart to charge the locals, so I forced a smile and said they were on the house. I sat there with my roast-beef TV dinner, feeling disheartened and discouraged by the direction things were taking, but at least someone was getting a free lunch. Maybe all of this was life forcing me back on to the right path, but at this point I wasn't yet ready to heed the real clues that were being offered to me.

My next venture was the video business. My friend Matt Purcell, from Feakle, had called me up one evening and told me of his idea to set up a video production company. He said he'd like me to be part of it, along with our mutual friend Mahon Slattery. He explained his idea was to make news/current affairs/sports videos to distribute to the Irish expat communities in America and possibly the UK. The videos were to be tailored to the perceived needs of the Irish diaspora scattered around the world. We imagined them being watched in Irish bars and community centres. I was set to travel to the States that autumn with the Tulla Céilí Band. We'd be touring Irish centres and ballrooms in big Irish-American cities like New York, Chicago and Boston, and I knew it would be a good opportunity to see if this video idea had traction with the Irish immigrant communities there. In the meantime, we got the equipment and started doing more utilitarian tasks, like filming weddings and creating industrial training videos, just to get the practice and also generate some income.

We actually had a lot of fun and some good times creating videos. But even though I now had this involvement in a video business, I was still kicking around the idea that I could set up some kind of operation to produce the frozen dinners, since all the suppliers had gone out of business. Maybe a kitchen could be established in Feakle? I had no fundamental attraction to frozen food; I just happened to be driving around in a van with an ice box and no particular use for it. I was somehow still unwilling to let go of the frozen food idea. The bigger question should really have been, how the hell did I end up obsessing about a frozen foods business? My mother nonetheless indulged my attempt to keep the business plan alive by seeing if we could actually make a decent lunch that could be frozen and reheated. We made some samples that tasted at least as good as the Lydon House ones, but we didn't have the facilities to do this at the scale we'd need.

Life after secondary school was not going well. I seemed to be failing at every turn. I was still having nightmares about my time at Limerick University. In one nightmare, I was trying to find my locker at the university, a mundane inconvenience that in real life would merit little reaction other than annoyance, but in the dream I'm panicked to a point where the anxiety is palpable even through the filter of my dreamlike state. Searching for my locker was a reminder of some unfinished business, of the fact that I'd failed to complete the task. I could bury this in my waking hours but not in my dreams.

The funny thing is, my former college wasn't quite finished with me either. Many years later, towards the end of 2015, I was doing some concerts in Tokyo when I received an email asking me if I'd like to accept a position on the governing body of the university. I was shocked but flattered. I reread it a few times, savouring the offer as though it would somehow help remedy the regret I felt over my squandered educational opportunity. It transpired that Michael McNamara, a Labour TD and music enthusiast, had suggested to the minister of education, Ruairí Quinn, that he nominate me to this post. I didn't think that my schedule would allow me to accept the honour, but, wanting to relish the idea a little longer, I wasn't ready to decline it just yet. When I subsequently returned from Japan, another letter was waiting for me. This one was from Quinn himself, thanking me for having accepted the position. I hadn't figured out if I'd be able to give the time to the role, but it seems my failure to promptly say 'No' had been construed as a 'Yes', and so to the board I was appointed. On my way to the first meeting, I curiously wondered if the people on the governing body had any clue that I'd attended college there. Did they know I'd flunked out? We never had that conversation. I enjoyed my time on the board, connecting with the university in this new way during a much more mature and confident phase of my life that left me with a contented feeling of having come full circle.

One Sunday in the summer of 1984, I attended a sports day in Scariff organized by Macra na Feirme, an organization for young

Irish farmers. I was only going along because my friends Matt Purcell and Mahon Slattery had asked me to accompany them; I had no connection to the organization. There were lots of unusual events taking place there, such as competitions to judge the weight of cattle and for tossing hay sheaves. There was also a competition where participants had to try to build the tallest tower of hay bales. Each team would criss-cross the bales two by two on top of each other and continue with this construction in the hopes of being the highest or, at the very least, the last tower standing. More often than not, the hay towers would collapse, plunging the architect perched on top into the mound of hay bales that had given way beneath them. It actually looked like good fun, so a few of us decided to give it a go. As we got ready to begin, it was decided that I would be the person on top, constructing the tower. I was the lightest of us, so it made sense. I was certainly up for anything, but as my friends passed me bales of hay, and as my slightly shaky tower began to get higher, I could feel myself questioning just how safe this game really was. Everyone may have treated the activity as perfectly normal, but maybe that familiarity had bred a false sense of security. Still, I put my concerns aside and kept on constructing my tower with great precision. It was looking like we might actually win the competition, when suddenly I could feel the tower beginning to lean. I think I had packed the thing too tight, and instead of crumbling downwards it buckled in such a way that I was thrown from the top. I didn't land in the hay, but on the hard ground beside it. Afterwards, a few people remarked that they'd heard my shinbone crack. Lying on the ground in pain, but even more so in shock, I lifted my leg with the help of my hands. My left foot had contorted into an entirely new position, pointing in a direction it shouldn't have been, like a cartoon character after a fall. I was in a lot of pain, but I tried to be humorous and even light-hearted about the situation. I asked a local horse trainer who was standing beside me what he might do in a similar situation with a horse. 'I wouldn't have a horse that fucking stupid,' came the reply. I suppose he had a point. You'd rarely see a horse falling from a tower of hay bales.

Rather than wait for an ambulance, Matt Purcell and a few friends loaded me into the back of his car to take me to the hospital. Another local man, Éamonn Fennessy, came along to hold my leg in place on the bumpy road to A&E. As I was being wheeled down the corridor, I asked the people pushing the trolley to stop at a public phone I had spotted along the way. I called home to tell my parents what was happening and to let my father know that I wouldn't be able to play with the Tulla Céilí Band that night. I played down the situation, but I have no doubt they could hear the agony breaking through my voice.

Being in the hospital should have brought some relief for my injury – a broken shinbone and dislocated ankle – either physical, from plenty of pain-numbing medication, or psychological, from knowing that I was in the one place that would help fix the mess I had made of my leg. It brought neither. Hospital staff were thin on the ground on a Sunday evening, when they made what in hindsight seems to have been the mistake of prematurely straightening my foot and putting it in a full cast. The pain became excruciating that night as my leg began to swell inside the plaster. I was crying out for relief, but there was a general staff shortage at the time, so no one was really there to pay attention. The following morning, when someone finally called into my room and opened the cast, my leg was completely covered in blisters from the pressure of the swelling. They knew from the X-ray that I needed surgery on that leg, so I was moved to Croom Orthopaedic Hospital. However, the surgery had to be put on hold until the blistering cleared up. Unfortunately, while they were waiting for signs of improvement on the blister front, they failed to continue observing my leg as closely as they should have been, and unbeknown to me or anybody else, some kind of bacterial or fungal growth was taking over from the blisters. A nurse came in to check my leg one day, no doubt expecting to see a great improvement, and instead she saw the makings of a science experiment. I didn't realize it, but I was perilously close to losing my foot. A look of panic came over her face and within minutes my antibiotics were being quadrupled to try to quell the infection before the scheduled surgery, which had to be delayed yet again. Back then, you could drink beer and smoke cigarettes when in hospital, so there I was in my bed, my leg raised, my six-pack of beer, an ashtray and a carton of cigarettes to keep me company. I was there for over two weeks. It wasn't so much 'a stay' but 'a saga', and one that involved me leaving with metal pins in my leg and an infection that would last many years.

10

DURING THOSE FEW weeks lying on my back, I had plenty of time to mull over my deteriorating business and my financial situation. I had borrowed money to buy the van and to cover insurance and all the other expenses that one might incur when starting a small business, but interest rates on my borrowings were now heading towards 18 per cent. The damage to my leg meant I couldn't drive, as I couldn't physically push the clutch pedal, so I had no chance of continuing with what I had been doing before the accident. Things were not looking too good.

That November, the Tulla Céilí Band was to travel to the States for a tour. This wasn't my first time touring America with the band but it was every bit as exciting as the first, and proved a welcome distraction from my professional and medical predicaments. Those tours didn't really make any money, but they were fun to do and gave me a taste of adventure that I enjoyed.

After a difficult year, I headed off with the band in November 1984 for another return to the States, this time hobbling on crutches but nonetheless still able to enjoy the tour and appreciate the experience. We got from place to place by minibus, sometimes by train, and for longer legs of the journey we would fly. At a few of the gigs we met old emigrants that my father knew from his childhood. Conversations were dominated by talk of memories, with random questions as to what had become of various people and where they had ended up. In some of these people, the Irish accent had faded to nothing more than a soft lilt, diluted by the American twang that had taken hold over the years. In others, the accent was as strong as if they had never left at all.

We had a good time on that tour, travelling from city to city, often staying in people's homes, and playing the various Irish venues filled primarily with Irish emigrants from the forties, fifties and sixties. However, this kind of touring just seemed to reinforce the idea that there wasn't really much of a career opportunity for me as a musician. The world that I found myself in wasn't connected to the folk movement in America. I knew that there was some other folk circuit out there but I had no connection to it and people in that folk world had no idea who I was. We were almost entirely inside an Irish bubble. I was still working on making a go of the video business, and while in America I made some contacts, albeit tentative ones. It seems people were not hungering to hear the latest news from Ireland as much as I'd expected. They were, however, interested in seeing the Tulla Céilí Band, which for many brought back memories of their youth back home. Emigrants remember their home country as it was when they left, and the music of the Tulla Céilí Band was a medium through which many could access that period of their lives again. I remember from my friend and author Tim O'Grady's beautiful book and emigrant story, *I Could Read the Sky*, that on the day somebody emigrates there's often a line drawn between the past and future, and that, for a lot of people, much of their life from then onwards is spent looking back. It's a poignant statement as there's so much sadness contained within it when you think of the volume of people who emigrated out of necessity, rather than choice, never having the means to return. Some people can easily make the transition, but for others emigration was a very painful experience. For many, music would have been a nostalgic link to their past.

While we were on tour, the band accordionist, Gerry Carey, met an Irish girl living in New York. As big as the Irish community was in New York, it turned out Gerry had managed to meet a girl from Kilmihil, which is in Clare. Her name was Maggie and Gerry was besotted, so much so that about a month after we returned from the tour, he gave me a call to say he was hoping to return to America the following February for a few months to earn some money playing, with his brother Christy on drums and a singer-guitarist called George Benn, and they wondered if I might join them. The plan was to earn money as a group by playing many of the same venues we'd played with the Tulla Céilí Band. Gerry then told me that Christy and George would only go if I was willing to. This little bit of subtle pressure was no harm but unnecessary all the same. My business plans had already collapsed and the video idea wasn't showing signs of making money anytime soon either. I had no reason not to go. I also figured that I could continue my efforts to make contacts for the video business while in America. Maybe I could make some money there and pay off some of my debts.

If you had asked me at that moment, I would have said I was heading to the States for just a few months, but some other part of me had a nagging sense that it might be for longer, and my actions seemed to bear this out. As soon as I had made the decision to go, I knew the frozen food idea was over for good. I set about selling my van to local man Con McGuinness, who had been on the entrepreneur course with me, and I returned the ice box to Francie Ó Halloran. I had agreed to sell my very old and beat-up Citroën CX2000 to my friend Andrew MacNamara but the car slid on a sheet of ice and crashed before I could seal the deal. I had to let it go for scrap value. I didn't make much money on these transactions, but just enough to get me to America with some spare change in my pocket for essentials. I discovered some time later that Gerry had actually told Christy and George that I was the one willing to travel to America but only on the condition that they would agree to go also. Gerry had cleverly leveraged all of us into agreeing to this tour, as he knew none of us would want to disappoint the others. Maggie was a lovely woman – we all loved her and completely understood why Gerry was willing to go to such lengths to see her again – so in truth none of us were really reluctant to go on this trip. Gerry knew that but he was just making sure.

Gerry, Christy and George mainly performed in lounge bars, playing a blend of traditional music and covers of popular country music, for which Gerry, normally an accordionist, would then play bass guitar. The group was well suited to playing weddings and other social events. I had developed strong contacts throughout the Irish music communities in various US cities, so before we went to America we checked in with all of these and started lining up gigs.

After our arrival in the country, we based ourselves in a motel in Dearborn, a suburb of Detroit. This was where Fr TJ Moloney, who was helping us put the tour together, lived. These were times of adventure, fun and excitement. Breakfast at the diner across from the motel became a regular part of our routine, with orders containing the works: crispy hash browns, skirt steak, A1 sauce, those perfectly circular pancakes, thin, crispy bacon, maple-syrup-drenched French toast and copious amounts of diner coffee. We got used to American food, the various salad dressings – and, of course, the American cigarettes and beer. When a place feels both new and foreign, every day is a kind of feast for the senses. That was the way it was for us in America in the beginning.

We were very lucky to have made contact with some very caring and conscientious people who were willing to help us when we first arrived. We had a lot of support from the Irish communities in various cities to help put gigs together, including Sligo man and president of the Detroit Gaelic League Chris Murray, West Clare man Mike Keane, who owned the Glendora House ballroom in Chicago, North Clare's Éamonn O'Loghlin in Toronto, and Fr TJ Moloney himself. All four men put on gigs for us to play and hooked us up with other people and places where we could perform. Fr TJ was particularly good to us; he looked out for us and generously took some time off to drive us around. He was a good man whose mission in life was less about preaching and more about looking after people, and he was well loved by the Irish people of Detroit and Chicago. Even though he was a man of the cloth, Fr TJ could party it up as much as the next person. I know this to be true because Gerry, Christy, George and myself spent a lot of time with him in Tom O'Halloran's Tipperary Pub in the Warrendale neighbourhood of Detroit. This was a place where we enjoyed many a good night and made a lot of friends.

The gigs took us everywhere from Cleveland to Canada, and of course to New York, where Maggie lived. Eventually we arrived in the South Side of Chicago. Our biggest booking came from Mike Keane, who owned the Glendora House ballroom. Every March, Mike would host several nights of music and banquet in conjunction with Chicago's Irish Musicians Association and various Irish dance schools. We were booked to be the resident house band for what Mike had called 'Irish Week'. Mike was a very caring and generous man who hosted a lot of social events for the Irish community from Chicago's South Side in his ballroom. A very popular venue, it had one of those specially constructed dance floors with a bit of spring to it, just like the ones in the ballrooms back home that were now closing down. Once a week, Mike would host a night of ballroom dancing with the music provided by an old-fashioned Chicago jazz big-band. It was a throwback to another era and was really something beautiful to see and hear.

Our own week as the in-house band went very successfully. We were playing to 500–600 people each night. The band was tailor-made for this event – it was like playing a big wedding each night. We made a lot of new friends and connections, and managed to secure some new bookings too. Both the Kerrymen and

Cavanmen associations asked us to perform at their annual dinners, and we were also booked for some gigs at the Gaelic Park club. Bookings like those definitely kept us in Chicago, but they were a few weeks away and weren't going to support us financially in the meantime. As I look back on that time, I can't help but think of that jazz-musician joke: 'What did the jazz musician who won the lottery do? He kept gigging until the money ran out!' We weren't really able to make enough money doing this kind of touring, and for us the money was going to run out soon and our tour would be effectively over. We set off walking from our motel looking to find an apartment, as we needed a place to stay until we could at least do the few upcoming gigs. We managed to find a two-bedroom basement apartment just off of 107th Street, gave a cash deposit and moved in the next day.

None of us had a plan for what we were going to do next. I figured we'd keep looking for more gigs and that I might try to get the video business established before returning home. Back in Ireland, Matt and Mahon had produced a demo video of Irish history with a music soundtrack arranged by a friend of mine from college, Pat Cassidy. On my side of the ocean, I set up various meetings with cable-TV companies and immigrant organizations. I flew to New York to speak with people in various relevant sectors, but unfortunately these meetings achieved little success. Gerry, Christy and George, meanwhile, got jobs with Irish construction companies, so it became clear that the touring was well and truly over for now and that we'd have to settle for whatever gigs we could get in Chicago. I remember one day, when the three were out at work, finding myself alone in the sparsely furnished apartment, with no work, no money and no plan. There were only a handful of gigs on the horizon and the video business was showing no signs of getting off the ground any time soon.

To make ends meet, I decided to follow in the footsteps of my flatmates and many other Irish immigrants, and source a job in construction. My leg still hadn't healed fully from the infection from the year before and I had zero construction skills, so overall I wasn't exactly the ideal candidate for a job on a building site, but thankfully Gerry and Christy were able to get me a job in the crew they were working with. They worked for a construction company called Malone and Moloney, the 'Malone' being Éamon Malone from Cavan, and the 'Moloney' being Johnny Moloney from Carrigaholt in County Clare. The houses were all wood-frame construction so there was a lot of nailing to be done. Carpenters on the site wore a nail bag, which comprised a belt with a hook for your hammer and a bag for holding the nails. I got myself the necessary hammer and nail bag and headed off for my first day. I hadn't planned on being a rough carpenter any more than I had planned on selling frozen foods. This was simply where I'd ended up, and in that moment it was the only opportunity I felt I had.

As we got close to the construction site, I was becoming acutely aware of the fact that I had never actually hammered a straight nail in my entire life, and I had this sickly feeling that my skills were not about to miraculously improve just because I was wearing a nail bag. My intuition and fear about my nail-driving capabilities were well founded. I had very little natural aptitude for this work and slowly slipped from carpenter-status to labourer, where my job was to carry lumber all day long. It was tough work, made all the more difficult by the roasting heat of the Chicago summer. For a man more accustomed to the Irish climate of rain, this was like working in a sauna. I worked harder physically that year than I've ever worked before or since. Each evening, I limped off the construction site, my ankle acting up from the weight of carrying the heavy loads of lumber on my shoulder all day. When we'd play an occasional gig, I'd have to do so with bandages on my fingers from where I had splinters.

Construction work didn't pay very much and, to be honest, the only thing that made the experience tolerable was getting home and meeting up with friends for beers. Sometimes we would skip going home and just go straight to the bar instead. No one was admitting it, but we were all a bit homesick. One fast look at the phone bill would confirm that. It was the single biggest bill after the rent. Calling home was a trial in itself. Our house's phone number back in Clare was Feakle 27, and to make a call from Chicago I'd have to first call the operator and ask to be connected to the international operator, who'd then ask for the phone number. I'd reply Feakle 27 in the Republic of Ireland, to which the confused operator would ask if that was a street address. I'd explain it wasn't, after which they would usually just connect me to a Dublin operator, who would then call the Limerick exchange. The Limerick exchange would in turn connect me to the telephone exchange at the post office in Feakle, who would finally dial our home number. It was very important that somebody answer the phone at that point – a busy signal meant you'd have to start all over.

During this time, I wasn't saving any money, nor was I paying any of my debts. Without managing to pay off the interest on my loan, what I owed to the bank was growing, as opposed to reducing. We weren't any closer to making anything happen with the video business and the gigs were an occasional occurrence at best. Nothing was really working out. The construction site reminded me of secondary school. I didn't belong there; it wasn't my tribe. I just kept my head down, did what I had to do, and tried to plot my next move.

With Malone and Moloney's job finished in the autumn, and with the country being on the cusp of winter, the construction work had mostly dried up. However, a Donegal man by the name of Martin McLaughlin was known to keep on going right through the frost and snow, almost up to Christmas. Gerry knew him and when he got a job with his company he managed to get me on board also. Meanwhile, Christy returned to Ireland along with George so, of the original group, just two of us remained. Gerry was living with Maggie by now, and I was sharing that same old basement flat with a new roster of flatmates that kept changing every few months. The work on the construction site in that winter weather was so brutal, it was almost comical. If you left one piece of wood on top of another, they'd quickly freeze together, which meant you'd have to beat them apart with your hammer. I harboured a fantasy notion of constructing a house without nails, imagining it would have been theoretically possible that the house would stand for the winter just by the lumber being frozen together.

One day, a load of pre-constructed roof trusses was dropped at an incorrect location a few hundred yards away. Gerry and I had the job of carrying them to our site. It took every ounce of strength to hold my end as we tried to carry them one by one to the house that we were working on, our feet getting stuck in the snow as we went. Just carrying one nearly finished me, and there was still a whole truckload to be transported. I genuinely didn't know how we were ever going to finish that task. Defeated, I turned to Gerry: 'There must be a better way!' I wasn't even thinking about the immediate task when I said that; I was thinking about life in general. I was aching both physically and mentally. The sentiment clearly resonated with Gerry as he still remembers me saying it to him, and to this day quotes it back to me with a burst of laughter.

AFTER CHRISTMAS 1985, the Irish Musicians Association offered me and Gerry an opportunity to teach music at the Irish American Heritage Center. This was my first time teaching. I knew I could play, I felt I knew good music from bad, but I didn't know if I could teach it. That said, I was pretty confident I had a better chance of teaching music than I'd ever had of driving a straight nail with two blows of a hammer. It was a brief, temporary job, but this first teaching post actually marked the beginning of a process of musical reflection and thought that still continues for me to this day. The construction work was finally shut down for the winter and there wasn't that much money to be made from this teaching effort, but in addition to the tip money that Gerry's girlfriend, Maggie, generously shared with us from her waitressing job, we somehow managed to get through that winter.

One weekend when Fr TJ was in town, he suggested we go to Fox's Pub, where Maggie worked, and that I bring my fiddle along. He was friendly with the owner, Tom Fox, and with the musician George Casey, who had a residency in the pub that month. George was from the Clare village of Mullagh and was part of a duo with guitarist and singer Dennis Cahill. Fr TJ asked if I could join George and Dennis on the stage and play a few tunes to see if Tom Fox might be interested in booking me.

Even though George was unable to sing, due to having developed problems with his voice box some years earlier, he had quite the stage persona. He could read a room and knew just how to keep everyone entertained with witty jokes and anecdotes. His impeccable timing made him a natural raconteur and comedian. Dennis's main role in the duo was primarily that of singer and guitarist. One thing that was obvious to me from the start was that he was a very talented guitar-player. He was also a fine vocalist and would sing everything from The Clancy Brothers to Neil Diamond. He and George complemented each other perfectly. When George was telling a story or delivering a joke, Dennis would quip in with the occasional wisecrack.

Dennis and George played in what is best described as a circuit of Irish cabaret clubs. These included a venue called the Irish Village, which was on the North Side of the city, and Fox's, on the South Side. In both these places you could have an evening dinner and some light entertainment. They also played in venues outside of Chicago, in places like Cape Cod and Omaha. The life that Dennis and George were leading looked very enviable from the position I had now found myself in, as a low man on the totem pole of the construction site.

That first night at Fox's, I was invited up to play a few tunes, but I had a bandage on my finger from the construction work. I decided to play a few straightforward reels in the key of D, tunes I hoped Dennis and George might be able to play with me without too much complication. They weren't that familiar with what I was playing but it still went reasonably well despite this. There were calls for me to play some more, and it was then that Dennis decided to call a bluegrass tune that I really had no idea how to play – I hadn't a clue what I was doing. Things were now not going so well for me up there, but in the end I managed to just about get through the bluegrass tune. Based on this first encounter, there was very little musical chemistry between me and Dennis, and there was nothing to suggest that we would ever share a stage again, never mind have a future partnership and deep friendship that would shape both our lives in huge ways. I decided to hang around afterwards, and as a result ended up chatting with Dennis later that night. It turned out he had been living right across the road from my basement apartment and we knew many of the same people. I found him to be an interesting character with an impressive musical knowledge and a great sense of humour.

For most people, and certainly for me at the time, the irony of moving to a different country is that you find yourself thinking a lot about home. It was often during periods of daydreaming that my mind would wander back across the Atlantic. I would think about simple things, like the times my father and I would listen to the radio music programmes together, afterwards discussing and evaluating people's playing and what tunes we liked, much like we would do with the political programmes and the newspaper articles. I missed those rituals. I missed the ever-present musical energy of the house. I missed my family.

With time, one gradually builds friendships and connections, and the pattern of life becomes familiar and normal. I was settling into the patterns of this new life, but unlike a lot of my contemporaries from Ireland who were now living in Chicago, I still didn't see myself as an immigrant. I continued to hold on to this notion that I was going to be home in Clare in a few months. In reality, those few months just kept rolling on, and before I knew it there was more to keep me in America than there was to lure me home. It was also the mid-eighties, when employment opportunities in Ireland were thin on the ground. This led to people at home offering me advice to stay put, as there were far more opportunities where I was. What I came to realize after a certain length of time is that people at home get on with their lives without you. You're no longer on their wavelength, no longer part of the daily conversation in the way you would have been when you were living there. You're no longer networked into the community you left, and that life you knew just starts to fade. I remember finding it quite painful to feel the disconnect from the fabric of my youth, from that musical environment where I felt so nurtured and where my sense of identity was clear. In my teenage years, I was Martin Hayes, son of PJ Hayes and a recognized musician in my own right by those in the know. In America, I was just Martin, and people didn't recognize me as the carrier of anything particularly valuable or important. The richness of my musical upbringing didn't seem to have any resonance or importance in the America I was living in, and the loss of that identity was quite difficult to come to terms with. The flip side of this situation is that losing one's identity allows you to create a new one. America, the wonderful land of reinvention and rebirth that it is, gave me the chance to start afresh. I didn't know exactly who I wanted to be just yet, but I loved having the psychological freedom to reinvent myself if I wished.

I knew my life wasn't going in the direction I wanted but I also had no idea which direction it should be going in. I had drifted away from the deeper musical passions of my earlier years. Now I was in some kind of holding pattern where day-to-day survival was the most I could hope for in the immediate term.

In 1986, Gerry and I met Paul McHugh, a ballad-singer and guitar-player from Belfast. He had connections in the Irish bar scene in Chicago and proposed the idea of forming a band with myself and Gerry. On the surface, with Paul's contacts on the local scene, there was a good chance the bookings would be on the more frequent side. To start, Paul got us a gig at the Irish Village, playing five nights a week for a month. This job paid us more than we got on the construction site. Compared with the exhausting manual labour of construction in the unbearable summer heat and the brutal wintertime, this type of job was something to be truly grateful for. Paul was skilled at entertaining the room and knew every Irish rebel song in existence, as well as the typical Irish–American songs that were so popular. Paul had grown up in Belfast during the Troubles and sang these songs of revolution and rebellion with a passion. I didn't love this version of Irish music and it was only distantly related to the music I'd grown up with, but for the moment, I was content to play it.

We'd play from around 9 p.m. to almost 1 a.m. from Wednesday to Sunday. The stage was placed against the long back wall, with tables spread out in every direction, where they served dinner and drinks. Our job was to attract people to the venue and somehow keep them there for as long as possible. We played at least three sets each night and engaged with the audience at every opportunity. We needed to form a strong rapport and connection with the customers in order to hold them there spending money on after-dinner beers and cocktails.

Playing these gigs was a temporary dalliance, a stopgap measure while I figured out another path. Playing 'Whiskey in the Jar' was not what I had imagined a life of music might be, but I was grateful it enabled me to afford basic food and shelter during a very uncertain time. The irony that I was now earning my living as a musician, which I'd once regarded as failure in life, was not lost on me. I was all too aware that every other option had led nowhere and that I had now resorted to playing music for a living.

The band I had with Paul and Gerry was doing well around these Chicago bars and cabaret venues but Gerry called it quits before the year was out. He had set up a construction business with another friend and couldn't devote the time required for gigging. Sean Conway, a fine flute-player from Ennis, joined us for a period but eventually left to move to Minnesota. So, Paul and I continued as a duet. I was playing tunes in between the songs, but in a one-dimensional way, basically just playing them as fast as I could – it was what seemed to keep the audiences entertained. I wasn't playing the kind of music I loved or was actually good at. It wasn't music that would be accepted in my childhood kitchen. My initial intuition – that my kind of music didn't have commercial value – was proving correct. Just from seeing what audiences seemed to like, I knew that if I'd decided to play the music of my upbringing in this environment, the music I played on the side of the bathtub, I wouldn't have been able to hold the gig past the first week. There's absolutely nothing wrong with the Irish bar-room ballads, if it's what you genuinely like to do and if those songs mean something to you. There's room for all of it. It made total sense for Paul to sing those songs; he had lived through the political turmoil of Belfast in the seventies so the rebel songs were a fundamental part of his identity. I had lived a very different reality. This was not the music I had grown up with or had any connection with. I just couldn't find an outlet or opportunity to perform or play the music that was dearest to me.

I had literally started doing those gigs to come in from the cold. I was spinning around the clubs and bars of Chicago, having a great time by most standards, but if you're an artist or a musician, you also have to look after your soul and you have to find your place in the world where it feels nurtured. I knew very well that I was dishonouring a kind of sacred bond, that I was untethering from the soul of a tradition and disconnecting from the lifelong desires of my heart. I was chipping away at my own integrity, failing to shoulder and properly carry forth the beautiful tradition I'd been handed. But as long as I had parties and alcohol, I knew I could manage to continue working the bar scene, playing music that didn't have any real meaning for me. Truthfully I felt I had little choice in the matter. I didn't feel I could do anything else at that time, but I also didn't feel as though I could return home either. Apart from the loss of pride in returning to Ireland with my tail between my legs, there was the small problem of the debts that had yet to be paid off: going back home to a faltering economic environment without a college degree meant my job prospects were almost non-existent. Returning to Ireland didn't seem like the best plan of action for paying off my debts. It made more sense to continue playing the Chicago bars for now. At least I'd have some chance of making a dent in the money I owed.

I could not see a way forward from my situation, nor a way back. Even when I slept, my predicament would manifest in the form of nightmares. There was one recurring nightmare that seemed to exactly mirror my situation. In this scenario, I'd find myself halfway up a mountain cliff, at a frightening point where it was impossible to climb back down. The stretch ahead of me was equally precarious. There was no safe choice, no good outcome to be had from either direction. I felt trapped, unable to move, and frozen to the spot where I was standing. This nightmare was obviously connected to my feeling of being unable to move forward with shaping any future, or to return home. I also had this persistent sense of burden from feeling I might never figure out how to properly deliver the musical potential within me, and this left a deep sense of unease in me. Alcohol cushioned it like a temporary salve of sorts, but it was always there. Sometimes I'd think the entire world of my upbringing, the music of my earlier years, was little more than a sentimental memory without any substance – part of an imaginary reality, a delusion rightly deserving to be shattered; the musical world of expression, feeling, soul and emotion from my youth might just have been a nostalgic illusion, an attachment to my family and place.

It's not that I could no longer play music from the heart, it's just that I was no longer sure that the foundations were real. Maybe the value I'd placed in the music was just my expression of the love and pride I felt for my father, a sentimental connection that I'd spun into my own mythology of value and greatness, an untested hypothesis that shattered when actually confronted with the real world – the world I now occupied. When you start losing your past, when you can't seem to create a future, and you don't have a real conscious engagement with the present, you are basically lost and in a dangerously vulnerable position. I felt like I was in some kind of limbo, and to cope I continued to drink more than I should.

Without a green card or an educational qualification, my options in Chicago were very limited. I really was beginning to feel the pain of having frittered away my educational opportunity. I starting thinking about giving college another go, in the US this time, studying law or maybe even architecture. I wanted to stop playing music in the way I was doing it, but first I'd need to get my immigration status sorted out, which had never been properly dealt with. I knew I had to take some sort of action, if only to pacify my inner self-critic, so I found an immigration attorney in the hope that I could begin the process of getting my illegal immigration status remedied once and for all. I can't remember who referred this lawyer to me, but the firm was small – just two people in an office in downtown Chicago. I made an appointment to meet in person to discuss my situation. In the initial phone consultation they had suggested I come in and see them, and informed me I'd need to give them a retainer of \$1,500 if after this meeting I was happy for them to pursue my case. That was a lot of money for me at that point, but I figured that if it enabled me to sort out my immigration status, then it would be money well spent.

I had the meeting and laid out my situation for them. They presented me with a number of options they thought I could take. Like most undocumented people, I didn't have a bank account, so I brought my retainer in cash. It seemed that's how they were expecting it anyway. They told me to call them in two weeks, at which point they'd have a plan in place. I phoned as planned but there was no answer. I kept trying for a few days without luck, so I decided to just call down to their office instead. When I reached the office, there was some other name on the door. I searched the building high and low but couldn't find the two individuals I had been speaking with. They had vanished and taken with them my \$1,500. I was gutted. This experience put a big damper on my hopes of eventually getting my green card. There was nothing I could do except put it behind me and hope another opportunity would present itself.

I continued accompanying Paul's songs and playing a few tunes in between, and once a night I'd play a version of the crowd-pleasing 'Orange Blossom Special' where I'd mimic the sound of a train then gradually build up the speed to as fast as I could possibly play. Another audience favourite was 'The Mason's Apron', a tune that my fifteen-year-old self would have rejected outright but that the drunken pub audience loved, and as I needed to eat and survive, they got whatever tune they wanted. Inside, I felt as though I had nothing but dreams that were dying, or already dead. You'd never really know anything was wrong from the outside – I was always clean-shaven and well dressed, always witty and engaging with the crowd. Even at my worst, I'd manage to hold on to the basic elements of respectability. But despite all the setbacks, I retained an adventuring spirit and I was still constantly on the lookout for the next opportunity, the one that would help propel me towards a happier reality.

I remember when we were playing in Kitty O'Shea's bar in the Hilton Hotel on Chicago's lakefront, I ran into a character by the name of Ryman Flippen, who was working as a director for a futures-trading brokerage firm called Lind-Waldock. Ryman was a banjo-player from Oklahoma. He was a regular at Kitty O'Shea's and a flamboyant character who liked bourbon, cigars and fancy suits. There was a bit of swagger and charm to him. I always had a curiosity about personalities that were different or offbeat. Ryman wasn't exactly offbeat – he seemed a bit more like a milder version of the Michael Douglas character in the movie *Wall Street* – but he was offbeat relative to the people you'd meet around East Clare. I spent some time hanging out drinking with him, so I got to know him quite well. One evening, as we were chatting, he asked if I'd like to try my hand in the commodities future market. He said he could introduce me to the process by having me start out as a runner on the trading floor. My instinct for adventure took over and I didn't think twice about accepting this offer. Just like that, I'd landed a job as a runner on the floor of the futures market at the Chicago Board of Trade. It was a minimally paid job, basically a ground-level entry position, but it was a foot in the door of this world of finance and intrigue, and hopefully a way to unstick myself from the mundane rut in which I had found myself. Chicago was the home of the futures market and the skyscraper, and I was now in the heart of it all, a world that couldn't be more different from the mountainside of my youth.

The trading floor of the Chicago futures market made the *Wall Street* floor look like a church gathering. It was the craziest place I'd ever seen in my life. I turned up on a Monday morning, smartly dressed in my shirt and tie, hoping to blend in as well as possible. For the first couple of days, I had to follow another floor runner until I got the hang of things. What struck me was that the floor wasn't filled only with those with an MBA (Masters of Business Administration). There were doctors, philosophers, gamblers and people from every walk of life. It was completely hectic and off-the-charts wild. It was like an adventure play-ground for anybody with a stomach for gambling, who could process figures fast and make snap decisions. Somebody who was good at playing cards or trading cattle might do very well in this environment. I could have imagined my sister Helen or my brother, Pat, functioning better here than me – they were both great at playing cards, or gambling, as we more accurately referred to it. They were good at calculating risk and strategizing around it. The world is filled with people with lots of natural talent who often never get the real opportunity to prove themselves, but here I was, somehow without any of the natural trading skills or aptitude, and yet right in the middle of the action.

One other little cause for concern was the fact that I was running around that floor without yet having my immigration papers in order. I don't think anyone in the company realized this at the time and I certainly didn't say anything. The job itself was simple enough. There was a desk at the side of the floor where orders were received. The runners waited for a printout of a futures commodity order to either buy or sell. Depending on what the order was, you had in your hand a piece of paper that could potentially drive the entire market for a particular commodity either up or down. My job was to get this piece of paper into the hands of the correct floor trader for this commodity as fast as possible. Time was of the essence, which is precisely why we were called runners. The timing was crucial to whoever had put in the order, as things could change very fast. During my time there the FBI infiltrated the floor in a sting operation. They were trying to flush out the endemic corruption and illegal self-dealing. No one had seen it coming. Thankfully, they weren't looking for people who didn't have their work permits in order. I think I was the only one on the trading floor with that problem.

Meanwhile, I still had my night job playing music six nights a week at Kitty O'Shea's in the Hilton. Early each morning, I would then clock in for my day job on the trading floor, running until the afternoon. It was certainly an exciting, if slightly mad, place to work, with the floor running mostly on a combination of cocaine and adrenaline. I wasn't doing any cocaine, and because I wasn't trading any of my money, I didn't have the adrenaline rush either. I felt like I was in a separate reality to everyone else, like I was out of place. The only thing that kept me going was the allure of the money I might somehow be poised to make if I could figure my way around the bizarre world of trading.

All the while, it was hard to escape the uneasy feeling that, since I likely wouldn't have been good at trading cattle back in Scariff and I already knew I wasn't a good card-player, I wasn't going to be any better at trading futures in Chicago. In truth, I didn't really have the skill set for this work, but on the other hand I was clearly skilled at getting myself into situations I wasn't particularly cut out for. Even if I didn't know what I was doing on the floor of the futures market, I felt some satisfaction from the fact that my adventurous nature seemed to be able to bring me into all kinds of unlikely and exciting situations. My life wasn't panning out the way I'd hoped, but it certainly wasn't boring.

It was October 1987 and I was soon going to have to make a choice; a deadline was fast approaching. Paul and I had a gig booked in Kenneally's Irish Pub in Houston, Texas. The gigs we did were often booked as much as a year ahead, and this one was going to be four nights a week for about four weeks, so I was going to have to decide whether to continue in the futures market or honour this gig in Houston and therefore continue my musical partnership with Paul. I hadn't alerted either side to this potential calamity. I wavered, but in the end I knew if I let Paul down, it'd be a big deal, whereas if I left Lind-Waldock I didn't think anybody would really notice. In truth, as exciting and full of potential as the futures market was, I still knew I wasn't the right kind of person for that environment.

A week later, as I sat in a bar in Houston, no longer delivering soya bean futures trades but instead eating black-eyed peas, the news on a television screen behind the bar was broadcasting scenes of chaos. The infamous 1987 Black Monday stock-market crash was playing out in front of my eyes, as stocks suddenly began to plummet. History books refer to the crash as rapid and severe, and it certainly was. Its impact wasn't limited to America, either; it affected markets all over the globe. My only regret was that I wasn't on the floor to witness the mayhem that must have been taking place that day. I had seen how crazy that place could be during normal trading. It must have reached peak mania on Black Monday.

Working with Paul provided a stable rotation of gigs. I was no longer just financially surviving; I had some pocket money, so to speak, and could finally start enjoying Chicago for the exciting city it was. I got to spend time going to blues clubs, jazz clubs, Serbian clubs and Greek clubs, getting to hear some of this eastern European music up close for the first time and to experience some of their cuisine also. Chicago is one of the most ethnically diverse cities in America, so there was lots to explore. I could afford to occasionally try out Italian restaurants, Indian restaurants and many other restaurants that took my fancy. I would get a buzz from taking a trip down Lake Shore Drive, looking at Chicago's magnificent skyline on one side and the vast Lake Michigan on the other. Even though these vistas were no longer new to me, their novelty was still there as they were all so vastly different from the sights and sounds of my earlier life.

On one level, I was having a fantastic time. I'd had a couple of relationships, plenty of friendships, and was busy loving all that the city had to offer. If you didn't look too closely at it, life was good, and if you didn't think about things too much, it was even better. The reality, however, is that there are always going to be those penetrating quiet moments alone when it's impossible to avoid the larger questions, the moments where you catch a glimpse of your own life, when it becomes difficult to avoid the truth of your situation. To those looking at my life from the outside, I was having a ball. Only I knew that I was stuck, unable to move forward and tortured by the notion that I could see no way of getting to the next level. I felt, and feared, that I might never amount to anything or manage to turn the musical promise of my youth into something I could be proud of. Escape routes such as alcohol and a busy social life all sooner or later led me back to that place of discontent and unhappiness. I knew what I was feeling and fearing, but I had avoided confronting it. The thing is, you can only play the avoidance game for so long. As I would find out for myself, eventually something has to give.

12

MY BREAKING POINT came on 17 March 1988. Normally, St Patrick's Day is memorable for all the right reasons. It's a day when the city of Chicago goes wild. There are two huge parades, the South Side one and the downtown one. The river is dyed green, and all of the city's politicians show up, with most laying claim to some form of Irish heritage. During the week leading up to St Patrick's Day, Paul and I would end up playing a few gigs per day. We could earn more in one week that we'd normally earn in a month. On St Patrick's morning, we had already played on a parade float. I'm not too sure, but I think it might have been the sheriff's float. What I do remember well was the cold. There was a sting in the Chicago wind that day, but it didn't deter the thousands who were there to see and participate in the parade. It's hard to capture the enormity of this parade, but it gave an immediate sense of the impact the Irish had made on the country. Everybody marched – the Polish, the Lithuanians, even the mayor himself, Harold Washington. Everybody could be Irish on St Patrick's Day.

Paul was fundamentally a good guy and someone who'd shown me plenty of kindness over the past few years, but over time fractures began to appear and we weren't getting along too well. I suppose working at such close quarters can often generate some friction but there was also a bit of a power struggle between us. Even if I didn't know it at the time, I was also frustrated with myself, angry at how far I'd fallen from the hopes and dreams I'd started out with. I wasn't getting to play the deeper music of my youth and I was stuck in an environment where it had no meaning. This was a continuously painful reality for me. I've learned over the years that we are rarely angry for the reasons we think. Looking back, I was mistakenly blaming Paul for the choices I'd freely made; I'd become resentful of the songs and music we were making. He was gradually becoming a stand-in for all my own pain and anger, and as a result I was finding it difficult even to hang out with him. He was no more a saint than I was, and he also had his own normal helping of human failings, but when we have pain and anger inside us and are not actually dealing with that, we tend to project outwards and begin to blame others for our own missteps. I still get angry when I bang my head against the kitchen cabinet door when emptying the dishwasher, as if the cabinet door had intentionally injured me. No more than I can blame the kitchen cabinet door, could I blame Paul. I had nobody to blame for all of my past mistakes and choices but myself.

Unfortunately, I didn't have access to that perspective back then. After the parade, Paul and I had a gig in a bar called Tommy Gun's, supposedly an old Chicago gangster hang-out that was at the back of Clancy's Pub on State Street. I'd already had about two shots of whiskey, allegedly to ward off the cold, and while I wasn't drunk, I could feel that I'd had them. I think Paul was annoyed that I'd already had a drink. While we were on the stage plugging in the equipment and getting ready to play, Paul made a comment that somehow felt demeaning to me. It was accompanied by a look that seemed to back up my initial impression. I can't remember exactly what he said but it wasn't sufficient to deserve the response he got from me. I exploded right there and then – all the years of frustrated efforts, all the songs I didn't want to play, the heartfelt music I'd abandoned, the banks I owed money to, the businesses that didn't work out, the college opportunity I'd blown, all condensed into one moment of fury. With a crowd of about 400 people looking on, I took my fiddle and smashed it right over Paul's head. He was obviously stunned, as was I. When I saw the state of the fiddle, I was shocked. I then took the bow and broke it over him too. I managed to pick up all the pieces of my fiddle and bow, packed them into the case, left the stage in rapid time and headed straight out through Clancy's Pub while everybody, including Paul, was left trying to process what had just happened. I had crossed a line that I'd never crossed before, and it wasn't a moment I was proud of. As I reached the front door of the pub, my friend George Nugent happened to be pulling up in his car. I hopped in and said, 'Keep driving.' It looked like a pre-planned getaway scene from a movie, even more so considering the bar was Tommy Gun's. Afterwards I heard from Ann Meenaghan, who was waitressing that day, that by the time the people in the bar could make it to the front door, I had disappeared without a trace and nobody could figure out how, as my car was still in the parking lot.

We went to the Abbey Pub, where my friend Marty Fahey, a

wonderful accordionist and piano-player, was performing with some more friends. The Drovers were playing later, all of whom were friends of mine, as were the pub's owners, Tom and Breege Looney, who looked out for me as if I were family. News of my act of 'violince', as it was now becoming known, had spread ahead of me. When I arrived in the door of the Abbey Pub, everyone seemed to know – an impressive speed for news, considering this was a time before mobile phones. Someone smugly asked me where my fiddle was, to which I remember replying, 'I gave it to McHugh.' For the record, I hold no grievance against Paul. He's a good man. After all, before the fiddle incident occurred, I had been best man at his wedding, and I still consider him and his wife, Mary, as friends. And we have a significant shared history. We all play roles in each other's lives, and in mine Paul helped carry me through some rough and vulnerable times. Likewise, I provided him with as much musical energy and commitment as I could to help make it all work. We still make contact every now and again, and I think it fair to say that neither of us holds any grudge against the other.

I drank a lot in the Abbey Pub that day and ended up sleeping it off back at Marty's place. When I woke up the next morning, the gravity of what had happened began to dawn on me. I was certainly at a crossroads, but I couldn't have woken up in a better house than that of Marty and Patti Fahey. Marty is a fine musician and a sincere, philosophical and kind human being. Our friendship gradually deepened over the years, and he became a very important person in my life. When I returned to my apartment on the South Side the next day, my flatmates George

Nugent, Aidan Hannon and Mike Moore had already put up a donation box accepting contributions for my replacement fiddle. It was just a joke, of course, and I appreciated the humour on a day when the mood was low. But as funny as the box was, it was a stinging reminder of my predicament. To be fair to Paul, he actually phoned me the day afterwards and suggested we put it all behind us and move forward with the remaining gigs, but I just knew I couldn't ever go back to that life, so I told Paul I couldn't do it.

On one level, it's a very humorous story, where nobody was seriously injured – Paul had just a few minor scratches. I was now without a fiddle, and its absence meant I was technically without a job. As I was still without papers, I had no real prospects. The biggest injury was perhaps to my own pride. We have to be careful what we ask for in life; I wanted adventure and I secretly felt I had some permission from my grandfather Quillan to be a bit of a character. But all of this came at a big price. The adventure had brought me to this chaotic moment, and being a character had just brought humiliation and shame.

It is easy to share stories of tragedy that happen to you, but my story was a humiliating one of reckless, foolish behaviour on my own part. I had really fallen. I felt like a failure. I never really wanted to talk to anyone about dropping out of college, breaking my shinbone in a silly accident, selling frozen food or smashing my fiddle over someone's head – it was all too inexplicable and I felt it would just make me look ridiculous and undermine my own credibility. At that moment in my life I felt like a fool whose life since secondary school had consisted of little more than a string of self-inflicted failures and mistakes. With every passing month and year there seemed to be more and more that had to be redeemed. I could only hope that Shakespeare had it right when he said, 'The fool doth think he is wise, but the wise man knows himself to be a fool.' I knew for sure I was a fool. I was really hoping that, underneath all of this, I at least had some wisdom. From the archetypal Jungian perspective, the fool still has something valuable to offer.

What's more, this wasn't just any fiddle that I'd broken; it was the instrument my father had taken down from the ledge above our doorway entrance and given to me as my first full-size fiddle. After several years of wandering aimlessly from one misadventure to another, I had shattered the last sacred piece of home, the physical connection to my years of imagination and dreams. My father's fiddle lay broken to bits in its case. I no longer even possessed the tools of my trade. I could laugh at the situation but internally I was broken and ashamed.

I left the fiddle in the case for a few days. I was unable to bring myself to open it. After a couple of days, I took my fiddle to the only fiddle-repair man I trusted, Gerry Field. He explained that the situation was so dire, it might not be worth the enormous effort needed to put the instrument back together. I told him I didn't care what it cost or how long it would take, it just had to be done. The fractured and broken parts of the fiddle mirrored all that was broken inside of me. For me, this was about putting my life back together, about healing the years of not listening to my own heart. I needed to redeem myself from my own foolishness. Gerry agreed to embark on the painstaking job of reconstructing my fiddle, and I would set about the even bigger task of putting my life back together, once and for all. On a musical level I made a commitment to myself that, from then on, every musical and career choice was going to be about something that was real, something that was meaningful to me. I wanted to stop being governed by fear. I wanted to start living with more faith and courage. In the meantime, Tom Gibbons, who was from Mayo and a regular patron of the Abbey Pub, gave me a replacement fiddle to use so I could continue working. Gerry eventually finished the gargantuan reconstruction effort, producing a truly remarkable result – my fiddle was actually better than it had been before the incident. The lifelong lesson I took from this experience was that I could not indefinitely continue to ignore my own emotional needs. I thought I could avoid my feelings, drink them away, and just plough ahead. I had become used to responding in that way, but now that I had experienced this breaking point, that approach was no longer tenable.

I didn't know what my next move should be. I had no idea where to start or how, but I knew I needed to choose more wisely, and I needed to finally start getting things right. A few days after the breaking of the fiddle, I was walking along the kind of street where nobody is ever really meant to walk. It was in the barren urban landscape around the suburb of Chicago Ridge, where I lived. I was aimlessly walking past gas stations, diners, used-car lots, drug stores and run-down motels. This was the kind of location where it was particularly difficult to find meaning or hope when in the depths of a really bad day. I was feeling lost and very unsure about how to proceed; I genuinely had no idea what to do next. Anybody watching me walk that day would have been able to tell a lot from my posture alone. My head was down. I was clearly defeated. I wasn't looking at the horizon – I had no reason to: I couldn't see any future. I was walking along, just watching my feet, when it occurred to me that I could only take one step at a time. Maybe I'd always been looking too far ahead at distant and unclear dreams and I wasn't being fully present in the moment, where the future is actually being made. We never really know for sure where we're headed, and as much as we can try, we really can't predict the future. We don't have control over the world out there in the way we'd like to think but we do have control over each step we take. I didn't really know where I was headed from this point, but I surmised that just maybe, if from now on every choice I made and step I took was taken with courage, integrity and trust, there was perhaps a chance that I would chart a way out of this confusing maze and eventually find my way to a more meaningful life.

13

I HAD NOW been making my living from music for a few years. Though this was initially intended as a temporary measure, the reality was that I was now in fact a full-time musician. If I was going to continue as a professional musician, I now knew I needed to do so in a way that was more meaningful and nourishing to me. It was time to get serious, but I was still firmly convinced that there were no career opportunities in playing the more subtle music of my younger life. All the trends in traditional music at the time were leaning much more towards the high-energy and high-speed playing. I could never find much more than a handful of friends and musicians who seemed to really appreciate this music the way I preferred to play it. Traditional music was marginal, and I'd always known that my style within that genre was even more marginal again. From a performance perspective I couldn't imagine more than twenty people who'd want to hear my version of traditional music. I felt I needed to steer away from my subtle, nuanced music and instead find some other kind of authentic musical vehicle, some kind of new sound that could still ignite some feeling of excitement and possibility within me even if it wasn't the music most deeply lodged in my soul. I didn't know what shape this might take; I was just guessing. The only real plan I had was to take it one step at a time with as much integrity and faith as I could muster.

However, I still needed to play traditional music, the music I loved most, even if I only did so on the side while I pursued some other creative hybrid version as a music career. Playing sessions at the Abbey Pub in Chicago was one way to renew that connection. Tom and Breege, the owners, had carried out major renovations on the place with a view to making it a central location for Irish music in the city. Chicago was in many ways already a major centre for traditional music in its own right. It was the city where, at the end of the nineteenth century, music enthusiast Francis O'Neill, also the city's chief of police, had put together the most influential collection ever of traditional music transcriptions. Chicago has always had a significant community of traditional musicians living there. When I arrived in the city, the Irish Musicians Association, whose mission it was to preserve and promote traditional music in the area, was still going strong. They functioned as a kind of social hub that kept the musicians of the city socially connected with each other. The organization had a long list of notable musicians on its roster, such as the fiddler Johnny McGreevy, flute- and uilleann pipe-player Kevin Henry, flute-player Tom Masterson, concertina-player Terence 'Cuz' Teehan and accordion-players Pat Cloonan, Jim Thornton and Jimmy Coyle. Most of the musicians in the association were of my father's generation and reminded me very much of my own experience growing up around the Tulla Céilí Band. They were a fantastic group of people and it was heart-warming to see how much they loved the music and how enormously proud of it they were. They were like a really big céilí band and played for many of the social events of the Irish community in Chicago. They would have been paid some small fee for these performances, but in reality this was a labour of love and not in any sense a professional endeavour; everyone involved had day jobs too.

The impact of the Irish Musicians Association on the culture of traditional music in the city was obvious given the number of very fine traditional musicians of my generation who were living and playing there at the time I moved there. Among them was Liz Carroll, who was and still is regarded as one of the finest fiddlers in traditional music, Michael Flatley, a world-famous dancer as well as a flute-player, Jimmy Keane, who is regarded as a pioneer of the piano accordion in traditional music, John Williams, a first-class accordion- and concertina-player, my pianist friend and a wonderful accordionist Marty Fahey, and Seán Cleland, a fine fiddler and now prominent music teacher in Chicago. These are just a few of the many great musicians the city was lucky to have living there.

When Tom Looney asked me to help organize some informal music sessions at the Abbey, I didn't hesitate. This was a chance to reconnect with my music again and I was really excited by the idea. Once the sessions at the Abbey were underway, there was a big supply of musicians on the North Side of the city who were more than eager to come and join in just for the enjoyment and love of the music. I was being paid a nominal fee to host these sessions, to make sure they ran smoothly and to be a reliable musical presence and anchor with whom other musicians would enjoy coming to play a few tunes.

As traditional musicians, we take it for granted that everyone understands what a session actually is. A session is not a stage performance, it's a social gathering of musicians coming together to enjoy playing some tunes collectively. People who like to listen come along just to be around the music and enjoy the ambience and atmosphere that the session generates. Even if you have witnessed a session, you may not fully understand its purpose and how it all comes together. A session is a loose, informal gathering of musicians, usually in a pub, playing selections of melodies both in unison and in sequence, where the musicians play extended sets of up to four or five tunes, switching from one melody to the next without stopping. Often there is no discernible leader and sometimes the next melody in a set can be led by whichever musician gets to the punch first, usually by giving a nodding gesture. There is often a moment of musical chaos, a loss of momentum in this transition while the other musicians try to identify and jump on board this new tune as fast as they can. Sometimes there are widely known sequences of melodies from popular recordings, some of which may go all the way back to old 78rpm recordings. Many musicians will know those selections and so these changes tend to be quite smooth. Other times, there may be sequences of tunes that are part of a local tradition. In these selections, a nod of the head is all that's needed for a graceful and coordinated switch of melodies. Sometimes there might be two or three musicians calling all the shots, with everyone else just following along. There's plenty of ambiguity and variety around these procedures. In theory it shouldn't function at all, but somehow it does, even if the result is often an uncoordinated and ragged version of the music that is less than the sum of its parts. To those on the outside looking in for the first time, the idea of gathering together a group of musicians to play single lines of melody in unison might seem like a very basic, redundant and unnecessary duplication of musical effort, and a recipe for melodic and harmonic clashes, but powerful moments of music also occur. Sometimes the session just lumbers along, but every now and then, as if out of nowhere, a critical mass of consensus around the rhythm and phrasing of the tune starts to form among a small grouping within the session, which then slowly begins to spread. The rhythm gradually starts to become locked, and an instinctive agreement on the shape and expression of the melodic phrases of the tune gradually takes over. Then the energy of all the musicians becomes united in a powerful flow that sweeps everyone along, musician and listener alike. In these moments, players find themselves transported to a higher order of playing; the combined energy and unified will of all the musicians lifting every player beyond their normal abilities. In those moments, we players are often afforded a personal glimpse of our own unrealized musical potential, and it's a very powerful feeling. It would be nice to think that these elevated moments happen all the time, but they don't; yet they happen just enough for any musician who has experienced this moment, even just once, to be willing to take his or her instrument and head to the session over and over again in the hope that tonight they will once again experience this powerful flow.

The modern pub session is a relatively new phenomenon, only gradually becoming popular over the past fifty years, and has a lot of inherent dysfunction. Sometimes the musicians are at very different standards of playing; sometimes they don't even get to know each other. Very often you'll find an alpha personality attempting to dominate the whole thing. These were the factors I needed to address when organizing sessions at the Abbey. It was important that everyone got a chance to choose a tune, that everyone felt welcome and that they could all get to know each other socially. One of the musicians who regularly took part was a Mayo man named Francie Campbell. Francie worked on a construction site and when he arrived at the session you could tell he'd been waiting for this moment all week. He would turn up at the pub with his red Paolo Soprani accordion and his sleeves rolled up, ready to get things started. I couldn't even guess his age but he probably wasn't as old as his beard and demeanour suggested. Francie had a few selections of well-known favourites he liked to lead off the session with when it was his turn, but only after he had ordered his pint of Guinness. Francie had no pretensions towards being a great musician. He was, however, a solidly good player whose satisfaction and pleasure was clear to see when his pint was in place and his accordion was on his lap. This was his coming-home moment. It seemed as though the music had found just the right place in his life – he truly loved to play. Watching him absorb and relish the whole experience of the night always did me some good in a way I can't really put into words.

At the Abbey, we ran two sessions every week, one on Wednesday nights and one on Sundays. Right from the start, there was a sense of a real community coming together. On session nights, we'd gather in a circle near the piano and fan out from there. I would do my best to make sure that everyone got the opportunity to pick a tune and felt included. The social aspect of the sessions was every bit as central to the night as the music. The better the camaraderie, the stronger the session and the more enjoyable the whole experience would be. The Abbey had some amazing sessions, attended by a mix of people from Chicago's folk-music world, old emigrants from Ireland and those who had arrived relatively recently. Plenty of visiting musicians would drop by for a tune or two, and before we knew it the Abbey had a reputation as the place to go if you were in Chicago and loved traditional music.

Though I had the sessions and other small gigs in bars, it wasn't enough to keep me going financially. I needed either to form a band or find one to join if I was going to make enough income to survive. Whichever it was going to be, it had to be a project that would excite me musically and also give me some financial stability. By then, having played bars all over the city for some years, I was relatively well known within the Irish community in Chicago and had a little bit of following that would be helpful in putting something together and getting it off the ground. I was adamant, however, that from this point forward I would only play gigs that would challenge me musically and feel musically rewarding on some level. I desperately wanted to avoid a repeat of past mistakes. I had no desire to return to playing everything and anything just to keep the money coming in. That utilitarian engagement with music had hurt me enough already.

By this point, I had been hanging out a good bit with guitarist Dennis Cahill. A friendship between us had grown during the time we were both playing the cabaret scene. Back then we would often meet up for drinks in one of the late-night bars with other people from the circuit, like the singers Pat O'Brien, Kieran Conway and Seamus Ó Kane and guitarist Jimmy Moore, when we'd all complain about the club owners and the music we felt compelled to perform to keep the audience happy. Dennis and I were fed up with playing music that was uninteresting to us. People went to those kinds of venue just to have a fun night of food, drink and some light musical entertainment; subtle, refined and nuanced music had no place there. The rarefied world of great music had seemed sealed off in some other existence of which I knew nothing. I couldn't even imagine the world of the musicians whose recordings I was becoming familiar with, such as Bill Frisell, Jan Garbarek and John McLaughlin. It was as if we were living in a different universe – a gritty underworld of music that had no links or pathways to this other musical world. People who play music in bar-rooms rarely make it out of there. We personally didn't know anybody who'd escaped the gravitational pull of the bar scene. Once you were a bar-room musician, you didn't have credibility outside that scene.

In the mid-eighties, Dennis was making a comfortable income from playing the Irish dinner club circuit. He was definitely over-qualified for this scene, but it allowed him the luxury of a good car and a nice apartment of his own. Even though the financial side was stable, Dennis felt agitated and angry because he knew he wasn't living out his true musical potential. On this front we both had a lot in common – neither of us at that point could see a way forward from the cabaret scene, at least not one that didn't involve an immediate cut in pay and a jump into a very uncertain situation. The music each of us had separately played in Fox's or the Irish Village wasn't feeding our souls, unlike the jazz guys we knew, who were digging deep at least a few nights a week. We envied them, though they in turn envied our more lucrative set-up – most of the jazz musicians we knew in the city could barely afford to put food on the table. There didn't seem to be any way to access that happy medium where you could earn a good wage without having to sacrifice your soul and peace of mind. Today there are so many more opportunities, but back in the late eighties prospects were thin on the ground. Dennis eventually left his comfortable cabaret scene behind, and with bass-guitar player Erwin Yasukawa began working the more regular bar-room scene, where he had much more freedom to play music close to the style he wanted. Dennis was playing the less lucrative bar scene while I was playing sessions at the Abbey. We were both now beginning to live on jazz musicians' wages but still hadn't yet figured out how to properly feed our souls.

Seán Cleland, a Chicago-born fiddler who'd come up under the tutelage of County Offaly flute-player Noel Rice, was just a year older than me and had been to the very same fleadh cheoils (Irish traditional music festivals) as I. He was already familiar with my music and style of playing, and knew where I was coming from. I first saw him doing a performance at the Glendora House ballroom with the band Baal Tinne. Over time we started hanging out, discussing music, and eventually did a few gigs together. Seán had formed a band called The Drovers a year or two previously and had just taken on two new lead singers from Ireland, Brendan O'Shea and Liam Moore. They were writing their own material and making their own music, but they also covered songs from the then very popular *Fisherman's Blues* album by The Waterboys. There was a bit of a buzz about them around Chicago. Their performances started to draw crowds, and it wasn't long before they started to get real citywide attention. Their guitarist, Mike Kirkpatrick, was a very

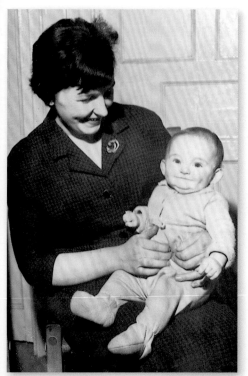

Above left: Me as a baby with my mother Peggy, 1963.

Above right: Dad, me and Mam. *Front*: Anna Marie, Pat and Helen.

Left: The house where I grew up, with my mother's flowers all around.

Right: Helen and Anna Marie.

Left: *Back*: My father PJ and Uncle Liam. *Front*: Grandmother Maggie, Grandfather Martin (Quillan) and Aunt Philomena.

Above: Joe Cooley.

Left: The Tulla Céilí Band in the early 1950s.

Below left: Tommy Potts.

Below right: PJ Hayes and Paddy Canny on a street in Dublin in the late 1940s.

Left: The Tulla Céilí Band at the back of Pepper's Bar in Feakle in 1996, when they made a recording to celebrate fifty years together. *Back row:* Jim Corry, Jennifer Lenihan, Mark Donnellan, Sean Donnelly, Michael McKee. *Front row:* Francie Donnellan, PJ Hayes, JJ Conway, Mick Flanagan.

Right: Playing with PJ Hayes and Francie Donnellan.

Left: Me at fourteen or fifteen.

Left: Playing with my father, PJ Hayes, in the kitchen.

Right: Midnight Court. Erwin Yasukawa, me, Dennis Cahill and Dave Simone.

Left: Playing with Dennis in the 1990s.

Left: With Paddy
Canny in his kitchen
in Kiltannon, Tulla,
County Clare.

Right: April 2014. On
stage with Paul Simon
at the National Concert
Hall, Dublin, performing
at the memorial concert
for Seamus Heaney.

Left: Brooklyn Rider. Me,
Michael Nicolas, Johnny
Gandelsman, Colin
Jacobsen *(standing)* and
Nicholas Cords.

Left: Triur. Caoimhín Ó Raghallaigh, me and Peadar Ó Ríada.

Right: The Teetotallers. Kevin Crawford, me and John Doyle.

Below: The Martin Hayes Quartet. Left to right: me, Liz Knowles, Doug Wieselman and Dennis Cahill.

The Gloaming. *Left to right*: Thomas Bartlett, Iarla Ó Lionáird, me, Dennis Cahill and Caoimhín Ó Raghallaigh.

The Common Ground Ensemble. *Clockwise*: me, Cormac McCarthy, Kate Ellis, Kyle Sanna and Brian Donnellan.

Oct 2014. Receiving the Spirit of Ireland Award from The Irish Arts Center, New York. *Left to right*: Gabriel Byrne, Liam Neeson, me and Sting.

Above: Lina and me on our wedding day, September 2011.

Left: St Patrick's Day, 2011, after playing for President Obama. *Left to right*: Taoiseach Enda Kenny, me, President Obama, Dennis Cahill and US Speaker of the House, John Boehner.

Right: Being conferred with an Honorary Doctorate of Music from National University of Ireland Galway, November 2018. With Lina, my mother Peggy, and siblings Anna Marie, Pat and Helen.

interesting musician who was adept at creating a hypnotic rhythm. He was the John Lennon of the band and even looked a bit like him. Jackie Moran played percussion and the bodhrán (traditional hand-held drum), Kathleen Keane played fiddle and tin whistle, and the bass was the responsibility of Dave ('The Rave') Callaghan. Seán asked if I'd consider joining the band and maybe getting an apartment with him in one of the hip neighbourhoods closer to Lake Michigan, maybe near Wrigley Field baseball park. It felt like it would be a real lifestyle change and there was a lot about this plan that appealed to me. I'd never been hip in my entire life. Maybe now was my chance. This was a ready-made, truly urban, bohemian scene, and here was an invitation to just glide right into it.

As I was mulling over Seán's suggestion, Dennis proposed that I join up with him and his music partner, Erwin. He had the idea that together we could really try to push some boundaries with traditional music and create some kind of jazz–rock fusion, The more I thought about it, the more I found this idea strangely interesting and adventurous. I knew Dennis had studied classical music for a number of years and could also improvise with some fluency – certainly better than I could at the time – but he had no background in traditional music. Also, they were using a drum machine instead of a drummer and performing covers rather than using their own material, all of which to me was a problem, at least in terms of how we'd be initially perceived. They were, in some ways, everything The Drovers weren't. The guys in The Drovers, meanwhile, had the whole vibe and ambience thing figured out. The band had done more than just establish an image; they had generated a presence, and one that was hip, too. Dennis and Erwin didn't have this.

When Dennis and I would speak on the phone about his idea, the conversation could run for hours. He was basically pitching to me what could be achieved musically if we worked together. I knew Dennis and Erwin were the less trendy, more challenging option, but this choice also afforded me the opportunity to create something brand new, whereas with The Drovers I'd have to merge my playing style with something that was already well established. One strict condition accompanied my decision to join Dennis and Erwin: they had to lose that drum machine. They agreed, and began searching for a drummer to take its place.

Tom Looney was renting out the ground floor of a house on St Louis Avenue that was across the road from the Abbey Pub. Dennis and I swiftly made the move to what would now be our new apartment. The move was a huge convenience for me as prior to this I had been living about thirty miles away. Now, we lived in an apartment in a long, narrow house in the north-west of the city. It was sparsely furnished with tasteful pieces of furniture that Dennis owned. Inside the front door there was a staircase that led to an upstairs apartment, and a door to the left that brought you into our living room. We also had a dining room, where we never ate any food, not even once. Instead, Dennis had turned it into a makeshift studio with his studio speakers, amps and microphones. This was where we'd work on music.

Tom had taken it upon himself to promote our band at every opportunity and gave us all the bookings that he could conceivably drum up. We ended up playing in the Abbey two or three times a month with the band, in addition to the two informal sessions that I ran each week. I still maintain today that without Tom, his wife

Breege and the Abbey Pub, we might literally have gone hungry. Their support of the band kept us afloat. They didn't dictate any musical preference; they gave us full freedom to do what we wanted. But while there was a consensus in the Irish community that we were all skilful musicians, there was something about our combination of songs and tunes that just left audiences confused. We still hadn't found a drummer and those listening couldn't really understand where we were going with our performances. I could understand why they felt like that. It didn't make a lot of sense to jump from a Van Morrison song to a BoDeans song and then to Erwin and Dennis jamming along while I played some tunes. For now, I was content with this situation because I felt the future was still wide open and the possibility of what we might create was limitless. I suppose we can generally cope with any situation as long as it also contains hope and possibility.

Eventually, Dennis and Erwin, who knew a lot of drummers around town, found a drummer named Randy Harrah, and we set up a first rehearsal in the house for the band I had named Midnight Court. This rehearsal with Randy should really have been an audition, but instead of asking him to try out, Dennis and Erwin had immediately asked him to join the band. I didn't know anything about him or what kind of music he played. Still, the plan was fairly straightforward. Although not explicitly stated, it was understood that this was going to be an egalitarian band without any actual boss; every musical idea and contribution had equal validity. We would find some collective way to achieve musical unanimity. It seemed like a positive strategy but proved far easier in theory than in execution.

For the rehearsal, Erwin brought his electric bass and amp, and Dennis had his electric guitar and amp. I was on fiddle and glad to have an amp also, and Randy of course was on drums. Randy hadn't ever heard a note of Irish music in his life; Dennis and Erwin hadn't heard much more. We had no idea where to start so basically I picked a tune with the intention that we just let everyone play and respond in any way that they thought might make sense. Another idea that seemed great in theory. The whole thing was louder than I could possibly describe. The word cacophony is utterly inadequate in describing the musical mayhem that ensued. I couldn't make head or tail of what I was hearing. Irish music had finally met American jazz–rock fusion drumming, and it was a truly bizarre mix. I genuinely thought the lads were playing a practical joke on me, that they'd set up Randy to bombard and shock me with completely over-the-top drumming. Sadly, it was no joke. This was, instead, my first taste of just how differently we each saw the world of music and how differently we can each perceive things musically.

For Randy this was a moment to explore every polyrhythmic and fusion idea he could think of. Polyrhythm is the use of two or more rhythms at once, and it would later turn out to confuse audiences to the point where they could neither clap along nor tap their feet to our music. Musically, not much came from that first rehearsal, but it was clear that the challenge would be to somehow organize all this frenetic energy into something coherent and stage-worthy. As daunting as this all seemed, I still felt invigorated by it; if we could pull together all these threads, there might be something there. Gradually we made arrangements of some of the tunes

I played, and held on to the most artistically interesting cover songs, just so we'd have enough material to get through a gig.

Though we were managing to secure gigs, mainly inside the Irish and Irish-American communities in Chicago where we had contacts, the audiences were still a bit thin, which wasn't surprising as they didn't fully understand what we were all about – it wasn't exactly Irish music in any form that they were familiar with. There was plenty of good will coming our way from fans of our previous musical incarnations – people wanted to like our music; they just couldn't get a toehold. The kind of music we were making obviously had an Irish component but it was a blend of polyrhythms, tunes and fusion riffs that was too weird to make sense in the environments that we were playing, where people might still have been just as happy to hear a version of 'Whiskey in the Jar'. We hoped that at some point we'd find our audience, but for now we were just trying out stuff, feeling our way through and trying to make a living. The band was extremely loud, and I struggled to make the fiddle heard. My good friend Brian O'Malley (a huge fan of British folk–rock band Fairport Convention), who lived just the other side of the Abbey, attended most of our gigs and had noticed I was struggling to be heard. He then surprised me with the generous gift of a Zeta electric violin, the same kind used by Fairport Convention and by the esteemed French jazz violinist Jean-Luc Ponty. Brian knew I couldn't afford such an instrument at that time, and he was genuinely every bit as committed to the band as the band members were and really wanted to see us succeed.

When the apartment above ours became available, Randy moved in. Now we had a real band house, with loud music both upstairs and downstairs. Meanwhile, looking out my back window, I could see across to the apartment where the banjo-player Pauline Conneely lived with her boyfriend Colin; my friend Timmy O'Sullivan, a singer known locally as 'The Bard', lived over the Abbey Pub; and Christy Barry, the great Clare flute-player, lived in another apartment in the Abbey building for a while. It was a scene, a moment in time, that was rich in music, fun and community.

Most of these people could be found walking in and out of our apartment at any hour of the day. It reminded me a bit of Jerry's apartment in the TV show *Seinfeld*. If our house was like *Seinfeld*, then the Abbey Pub was undoubtedly some Irish version of the bar in the sitcom *Cheers*. Some of the happiest days of my life were spent in that house. There were some moments of pain but they were blended with moments of clarity; moments of struggle that were blended with deep realizations. This was the place where I would finally begin the job of rebuilding my life.

This was a time of musical discovery and experimentation, of spiritual and philosophical reflection. I had conversations with friends and acquaintances that went on for hours, whether in the living room of our apartment or late at night standing outside the Abbey Pub and other bars where we'd played music, and sometimes continuing into the early hours in one of the late-night diners close by. There was plenty of debate and opposing ideas; the assemblage of friends included people of different ages and backgrounds, but they were all passionate and serious thinkers. It was a moment of my life when everything was up for questioning. Cultural identity, creativity, tradition, music, philosophy, the future of the music, what's wrong with it right now, what is good music, who is playing good music, should Irish music merge or blend into some new hybrid, what about commercialism in music, what about the beauty of the older life or the shallowness of our materialist consumerist world: these were the kind of things we talked about all the time. These discussions and debates were very important to me, for while it's easy to formulate ideas and opinions, it's another matter defending them. I would sound out my opinions and thoughts in these discussions and see how they'd fare.

Timmy O'Sullivan came from a farming background in County Kerry. He loved the old ways of life back at home, he loved poetry, storytelling and sean nós singing. He wrote poetry and sang, and I suppose, a bit like myself, didn't really fit in anywhere. The new clever 'sophisticated' world of fashionable tastes and opinions that was disregarding the old wisdom back in Ireland drove him crazy. Instead he lived an uncompromisingly poetic life. Chicago provided him with the distance and mental space to reconstruct the Ireland of his imagination – his own version of Padraig Pearse's West of Ireland vision, a vision once capable of fuelling a revolution. His bible was Robin Flower's translation of the Blasket Islands' native Tomás O'Crohan's *The Islander*, from which Timmy could freely quote large sections from memory at the drop of a hat. The Blaskets had lost their final inhabitants in the early fifties, and these islands represented to Timmy a glimpse into an older Irish consciousness and set of values. He didn't just read books, he slowly digested and memorized them, and absorbed them in a way that made them part of him. Timmy had internalized the values of that time, the values of the Blasket Islands and those of his own, gentle father, who Timmy often talked about and who also seemed to uphold many of the old ways. Timmy brought these values and perspective to every single conversation and debate we'd have.

Despite being raised in Chicago, Dennis Cahill was in some respects born into a more culturally Irish family than either Timmy or me. Both Dennis's parents were native Irish-speakers from Baile na nGall (Ballydavid) on the Dingle Peninsula. His mother was related to the famous Irish revolutionary Thomas Ashe. His father still had relatives back west of Dingle who were all known by the Irish version of their name, Ó Cahallan. Dennis was as American as you could possibly be and regarded himself as such, but he was somehow always surrounded by Irish people, always existing inside an Irish community. Dennis was a very grounded realist who could dissect every musical idea into a logical construction of scales and modes, whereas I seemed more concerned with the intangibles and feeling-expression of each tune. For Dennis, the world was perfectly logical; there was no fuzzy idealism. He was also endlessly practical. At the same time, he was – and still is – a very sensitive person and an extremely sensitive musician.

Timmy would visit our apartment most days, the three of us often sitting around chatting about music, politics or history, which would often lead to an argument. Dennis and Timmy at the time were only in each other's company because they were both friends of mine; it's almost certain that in normal circumstances they would have avoided each other, believing that they had nothing in common. I could empathize with the points of view they were both making while also enjoying the dichotomy – Timmy's romanticism and Dennis's rationality. Once, I remember Timmy began to wax lyrical about the native culture in America. He imagined the reality of the Native Americans, their lives in the days before the white man had arrived, their previously utopian existence, comparing it to the life on the Blasket Islands. These poetic worlds of his imagination, the idealism of these romanticized lives, had sustaining value for him. Dennis, however, was adamant that this kind of utopian thinking wasn't grounded in reality. He responded to Timmy's Native American utopia by saying he was sure every tribe had at least one asshole, someone who could make life miserable for everyone and fuck up the consensus. In fact, why couldn't there be many assholes in a tribe? Dennis didn't buy Timmy's utopian vision. He was becoming a kind of John Wayne, shooting holes in Timmy's Native American bubble. This kind of argument never abated. I found it endlessly entertaining but it was a challenge for me to find a path through this where both truths could exist simultaneously and harmoniously, where peace between them could be achieved.

When Dennis and Timmy were together in our living room, it didn't matter what the subject was, the battle was always the same: romanticized idealism versus rational empiricism. These were competing viewpoints that I instinctively knew I needed to keep in equilibrium within myself. I had come to believe that if you have two opposing truths, there must be a larger truth that contains them both, a broader philosophical viewpoint where the contradicting truths could harmoniously exist. As the years passed and my reading expanded, as I searched for this broader truth, I would attempt to maintain a balanced diet of reading material that included food for the soul and food for the rational mind, from the Hindu Upanishads or poetry of Rumi to layman's books on physics, science, the arts and politics.

After my Wednesday and Sunday night music sessions at the Abbey, a group of people such as Timmy, Brian O'Malley, Jimmy Keane, Marty Fahey, Seán Cleland and Noel Rice would stand around outside continuing the conversation about the future of traditional music. Noel Rice had a lot of opinions on this matter. He played a silver flute rather than the wooden flute more commonly used in Irish music. He wasn't sentimentally attached to the old sound and instead preferred the accuracy and the extra range of notes that were available using this more modern instrument. Though he had a successful career as an executive headhunter, his main passion was teaching music. He founded an Irish music academy and had a band called Baal Tinne that was mainly made up of his students – it was his laboratory of sorts. He had cut his own path separate from the Irish Musicians Association, which was more about preserving the tradition and fostering a community of musicians where people at different levels of accomplishment could be included. Noel didn't have much patience for simply preserving tradition – he challenged their orthodoxy and didn't really care how anybody felt about it. He believed that Irish people living in America should open up their thinking and shed their old ways. He was interested in new possibilities for the music and wanted lots more experimentation. When we'd get tired of standing around outside the pub, we'd take the conversation to some nearby late-night diner. When Noel and Timmy would both end up in the diner, the debate would resume, the raw, elemental music of the peasant soul now doing battle with the enlightened, modern and rational mind. Was there a place for all of it?

Noel believed in the power of critical thinking and was

unsentimental in his views. I certainly had a lot of sentimental attachment to my childhood of old whistle- and concertina-players, and wondered if this world could withstand such scrutiny. There is a kind of valid, subjective, intangible truth in the sentimental experience of the heart and there is also the truth that objective analysis can provide. There was a danger with all of the ruthless inquiry that if I shone too harsh a light on this music, I might come out empty-handed, but I'd have to take that risk. At some level I knew that I had to examine and challenge the traditional music of my childhood, and to do this I would need to separate the music from the cloudiness of my own sentimentality. Were my experiences back home in our kitchen real music experiences of value, or just sentimentality? Could this music exist as a music of real value outside its social context and be rationally measured against the larger world of music? If my investigation told me that the music didn't have real value, I'd have to accept the result and continue with my efforts towards some hybrid, cross-pollinated version of the music that challenged the tradition head on. I was now attempting to objectively investigate the roots of my traditional music while at the same time developing a band that challenged everything I'd known about this music, growing up. If the traditional music of my early years survived this kind of honest scrutiny and challenge then my teenage commitment to the music would be fully vindicated. Rebuilding myself and my music meant challenging all the previously unquestioned orthodoxies of my life. There were many stimulating nights of conversation and debate that went on around the issues of music, identity and culture that were vital to helping me figure out how to proceed with my music and with my career.

14

WE STARTED SECURING more bookings for the band around the city and found ourselves a manager, Colby Krauss, who helped get us gigs in some of the hipper clubs and street festivals around the North Side of the city, though our bread-and-butter gigs were still in the Irish bars. One of our regular bookings was in a pub called Vaughan's. The Vaughan family, who owned and ran the pub, were salt-of-the-earth people who had moved to Chicago from Cork some years previously. Their bar was mostly popular with the new wave of Irish immigrants. Each evening, it would be filled with lads who had popped in 'for one' on their way home from the construction sites. We got a regular Friday-night gig there but, unfortunately for us, it wasn't set up for music. There was an area in the corner where we could arrange the amplification, but before we could even do that we'd have to move the pool table. Getting all the speakers, amps and microphones into the right place involved a great degree of man-oeuvring on our part. People often assume that bands just hop in their cars, arrive at the venue, unpack a few bits and start playing, but the reality is that moving gear and setting up is a whole day's work in itself. We'd usually start by loading Dennis's jeep. This meant hauling everything out of the basement, up the stairs, down the front steps and into the back of the vehicle. This process required a bit of the same knack I'd developed as a kid for packing the car for the Tulla Céilí Band. Some of this stuff was really heavy, so by the time you'd get to the jeep, your lack of fitness would really start to show. We'd unload the equipment at the pub, move the pool table, set up the gear, and then do it all over again in reverse once the gig was finished.

Vaughan's paid us $120 each and it was $120 we certainly welcomed. We were skirting very close to the edge at this time, and a regular gig like this helped keep food on the table. We would play reels and jigs, merging them with riffs that resembled lines you might hear from bands like Weather Report or the Southern rock band the Dixie Dregs. We turned obscure covers into pieces that could make room for my kind of fiddle-playing. Everything was played with maximum intensity, volume and speed, as if our very lives depended on pushing everything to the limit. Dennis was able to grind out some very powerful grooves with his electric guitar and Erwin, with his five-string bass, was able to create menacing-sounding low, rumbling bass lines, and all the while the drums were driving at full rock 'n' roll velocity. We didn't want some soft-pop, tame version of rock music mixed with Irish music, we wanted it to have a real rock band's aggressive bite. That was certainly the intensity I felt we achieved on many nights. Years later, people who had been to those nights at Vaughan's told me how much they had enjoyed the music. I always find these remarks funny because, when I look back, we had no idea what the audience thought of it. I just assumed that most of the people there were on their way home from work, so it seemed to me they would be there regardless of whether or not we were playing. There was usually very little response from the audience, no applause. I eventually understood that everybody had a drink in their hands and had no way of letting us know what they thought of the music. I remember, one night, looking at a fella in a pair of work boots slumped on a bar seat at the counter, his head hanging down. We clearly weren't having much of an impact on him. He'd probably been drinking since the early evening. It was at this point that somebody had the bright idea to suddenly spin the bar stool on which he was hunched. After it stopped spinning, the man stood up, dizzy and clearly about to vomit. He made his best effort to get to the men's room, Since I was positioned near the door to the toilet, I could see him bolting in my direction, and right in the middle of a tune he puked all over my feet and the effects pedals for my amp. I continued playing. That incident gave me a perspective that has stayed with me all the way from that night to the Royal Albert Hall and the Sydney Opera House. If ever there was a moment that kept my feet on the ground, it was certainly that one.

One face that kept showing up at Vaughan's was the writer Tim O'Grady. Tim had left his home in Chicago in 1973 to move to Ireland but was now paying visits to see his elderly dad. Tim had that writer's curiosity for the backstory in any situation. He liked to understand the deeper strata of events underlying any scenario, and always had the most pertinent question on the tip of his tongue. We ended up on his radar after a few of his friends brought him to Vaughan's one evening. He hadn't been around the Irish bar scene growing up, so when in Vaughan's he was surprised to hear our band's kind of music. Instantly, he wanted to understand what was going on with this band: why were we in the corner of this bar, playing this very weird blend of traditional music with rock 'n' roll intensity? There was an incongruity to this scene that I think was interesting to him. We got chatting after the gig, and straight away I knew he was an interesting character and a wonderful conversationalist. If we were as good as he felt we were, then it didn't make sense to him that we were performing in this situation. He wanted to know what sustained us to play those gigs with every ounce of conviction. I wanted answers to those questions myself, and in attempting to answer them I was also getting a bit more clarity about my own situation. I explained to Tim that we played with such intensity because frankly it's easier to play when you give it everything you have, no matter the situation. Even if the environment isn't conducive to your highest ideal, there is still the best that the situation allows, and I always wanted to go for that. These gigs were all opportunities to stretch and push ourselves.

Tim and I spent many nights talking about the search that goes on, both as a writer and a musician, to find one's authentic voice. His excitement about language and expression, and the joys of breaking through and finding a flow, could keep us talking for hours; it was inspiring to me and gave me hope. Tim seemed to sense in me a deeper musicality that was searching to come out, and I found this faith in me empowering. The quest to find the clearest, most direct artistic expression with the greatest economy, devoid of pretentiousness and unnecessary clutter, was a goal we both shared. Just having conversations about these thoughts provided fuel for the journey ahead. Tim and I have remained good friends ever since.

Years after Tim and I first met, we embarked on a book tour, with esteemed actors Stephen Rea and Mick Lally reading excerpts from Tim's novel *I Could Read the Sky*. Myself, Dennis Cahill and the Galway accordionist Máirtín O'Connor sometimes played music at these readings from this book, while singers Iarla Ó Lionáird and Sinéad O'Connor occasionally contributed too. Tim now lives in Poland, and whenever he phones, my wife will hand me the phone before automatically proceeding to make a cup of tea and put together a plate of biscuits for the long chat she knows we're about to have. We still love these conversations that go right to the heart of the creative process. I find that interdisciplinary conversations in the arts are hugely helpful and offer insights that are often difficult to spot when we just stay inside our own artistic worlds. This is why I love to chat with my painter friends Helen O'Toole, Helen O'Leary and Mick O'Dea, or my architect friends John Tuomey and Sheila O'Donnell, about their creative processes. I learn a lot from how people in these other disciplines do their thing. My friend the poet Paul Muldoon rightly says that on some level we are all doing the same thing. The creative process is an open engagement with one's discipline where unbidden, accidental and synchronous insights can become welcome elements to be woven into our artistic efforts. It is important for all artists and creators to find and cultivate a free and playful space where this can happen.

Tuesday nights were an opportunity to explore with freedom: a few of us would play at a bar called the Augenblick. This regular

Tuesday night had something of a goth-like subculture going on – lots of piercings and black finger nails and black clothing. But mixed throughout this scene on these Tuesday nights were some Irish people who'd come for the music. The event consisted of a loose gathering of musicians on a small stage, playing acoustically. Fiddler Seán Cleland and guitarist Mike Kirkpatrick from The Drovers were always there, as was accordion-player John Williams. This wasn't a gig in the standard sense – I think we only got $15 each and a couple of drinks – but there was a refreshing freedom to it. We didn't have to entertain an audience, we just had to connect with the vibe of the place. (There was a continuous hushed chatter and the room was very dimly lit.) We could play whatever we wanted, whichever way we liked, so it was worth the low pay just to have that freedom. We played long, extended sets of tunes, improvising and jamming with a freedom that no other gig could really offer us. It was a unique opportunity and one that allowed us to explore and discover new musical possibilities, where accidental elements could freely weave their way into the music. We could call for silence at any moment and have Timmy (The Bard) O'Sullivan get up on the stage to sing a song, recite a poem or tell a story. Cork bodhrán-player Neiley Collins was another stage regular who would give us an occasional song. I remember there was a very nice older Irish-American man who occasionally liked to come up and sing a few. Given that he shared a famous-sounding moniker, I always got a kick out of welcoming him to the stage and asking the audience to give a very warm welcome to Mr Bob Dillon. Those Tuesday nights were very special – just the perfect blend of people and the right atmosphere in which to experience some musical abandon.

The only place where Midnight Court managed to create a real following was in the Half-Time Rec in St Paul, Minnesota, a venue I had played with singer-guitarist Paul McHugh many times before. When we played there with the band I'd have some musician friends sub for me at the Abbey Pub. The Half-Time Rec was located on a quiet, remote street. It had a U-shaped bar that divided the room into a regular bar at the front and a back-room space with a stage. It wasn't a pretentious place – no airs or graces. In fact, some of the lettering that made up the words 'Half-Time Rec' on the outside had fallen off, and in all the years I played there, they were never replaced. The guy who ran the place was called Louis Walsh – and no, not the famous band manager from Mayo. This Louis was a big, strong man, almost as broad as he was tall, who reminded me of Bluto from the Popeye cartoon. His presence automatically kept order in the place.

The back room consisted of an assortment of tables and chairs mostly facing a small stage with a black curtain at the back. It was all very plain in the light of day, but at night, once that stage spotlight was turned on, the room had a kind of warm atmosphere. You felt you could really make of that space what you wished. In the basement there was a court for bocce ball, which is a type of Italian bowling. On Wednesdays, the local Mensa club would meet there before our gig and stay on for our show – clear evidence, if ever any were needed, that our music was meant for the super-intelligent! On Thursdays, a squadron of bodhrán-players would bring their instruments and play along with the band from their seats in the audience. It must have been tricky for them to match Randy's polyrhythms, but I didn't ever know for sure as we were so loud, we never actually heard them.

Our music was attracting the interests of a wide variety of people, but we all noticed there was something about our band that seemed to appeal to the pagan community. There was always a generous helping of witches and tarot-readers in attendance at our gigs. Between them, the bodhrán-players and Mensa, they made an unusual blend to say the least. There were a number of audience members I still remember well – some with great fondness, others with some unanswered curiosity. There was a couple who would attend at least once a week and sit at a table with a mannequin seated beside them. Curiosity always got the better of me, so during the break I would sometimes sit with them for a chat, hoping they would voluntarily shed some light on why their doll friend was accompanying them. They were nice, normal people, always very friendly and engaging, but whenever we chatted they would never make any remark about the mannequin sitting in the chair beside them. It was almost as if they were pretending it wasn't there. I could never bring myself to ask them about it. There was another guy, who used to turn up with a ferret on his shoulder. Dennis found this even more bizarre. Apart from these occurrences, it was just a regular gig. We'd play there four nights a week for a month at a time, and we might do this two or three times a year. When Janet, a lovely lady from Kilkenny, took to organizing posters and publicity for the band, more and more people started turning up. I still savour those wild nights of music. I formed some great friendships in the Twin Cities area, so much so that at different points I thought about moving there. My friend Mark Stillman and his wife Mary Ann became close friends of mine. Mark is a musician who did a tremendous amount to encourage me to push on with my musical dreams. Childrens' book author Jim Latimer, musician Sherry Ladig and her husband Don were also part of a circle of friends who were incredibly supportive. I got a grounding in the politics of social justice and human rights while staying at the house of Mike Whelan and his housemate Teresa Puff, both of whom were committed political activists.

St Paul was a partying town; there was always a party to hit every night after the gig. We were really living the life back then. There was so much fun to be had, and admittedly maybe a bit too much pot and alcohol consumed by me. I hadn't quite reached that part of my awakening where alcohol served no purpose. I still enjoyed its presence in my life, and at this point had no desire to quit.

After a relatively short period of time, Randy decided to leave the band. I think it wasn't developing into the kind of band he had hoped it would become. I liked him a lot, but Dennis and Erwin felt he was pushing into musical territory that didn't suit the band. The next drummer was a very nice African-American guy called Charlie Johnson. By day, Charlie worked as a sound engineer. Again, there was no audition, but I suppose for Dennis and Erwin it would have been difficult to audition people they'd already known and worked with. I remember when Charlie first hit the drums, I was just about immobilized by the volume – I could barely begin to play my fiddle. Charlie somehow managed to be even louder than Randy. He had a style that was perfectly designed for an arena performance, which was fantastic except for the fact that we were still playing small clubs and I was standing about two feet away. After we finished the first tune on the first gig we did with Charlie, I leaned towards Dennis and whispered, 'This is not going to work.' But this was how he played, and although he'd try to tone it down and had successfully done so in rehearsal, over the next few gigs he'd inevitably get louder whenever the music got more intense. Charlie was good-humoured about it and just understood this wasn't a good match. The next drummer was Dave Simmone. He was one of the most humorous, permanently smiling, good-natured individuals you could ever meet. We were now a bit like Spinal Tap, moving through drummers at a rapid pace, but we felt we were on to a good one with Dave. Right from the start, he knew his mission was to not play too loudly.

All throughout this period, I continued to drink. I was actually starting to drink a little too heavily. I found it difficult to contain this impulse in the environments that I was finding myself in. I didn't play when drunk – I didn't need drink in order to perform – but I did like to party afterwards, and to get prepared I'd loosen up with a couple of drinks towards the end of the performance. I'd hang around afterwards having drinks before maybe going on to a late-night bar with friends and musicians. Given that we were performing in a pub, it usually meant that we didn't have to pay for the drinks. This advantage, combined with not having to get up in the morning, proved a dangerous formula. I had thought that as long as I was alert, attentive and focused for my gigs, I could basically do whatever

I wanted in the time in between. As my drinking progressed, I would achieve some level of drunkenness most nights of the week. I may have moved on from doing gigs purely for money, opened my mind up to all kinds of musical possibilities, but I had yet to make deeper changes in my life. The partying was starting to veer out of control, and I knew it.

One day around this time, a startling and vivid image appeared in my mind. I saw a fork in the road that seemed to suggest I had a choice to make, an opportunity that might not present itself again. There was a sense that this was an important moment and that I needed to immediately make some changes. To begin with I ignored this omen and continued on as usual for another few weeks without knowing how to address that moment. At the time, I had a girlfriend named Martha. We were walking along a street on the far North Side of the city when we decided to visit a bookstore that was owned by the mother of a mutual friend. I felt compelled to buy a book to show my support for the place. I wasn't looking for anything in particular but I noticed a book called *The Crack in the Cosmic Egg*, which I presumed from the cover might be humorous and light. I was literally judging the book by the cover; it somehow reminded me of *The Hitchhiker's Guide to the Galaxy* – maybe it was just the word 'cosmic' that got me making that connection. As we left the bookstore, I turned to Martha with the book in my hand and, in reference to its grandiose title, jokingly said, 'This will change my life!'

Once home, I left the book beside my bed, and there it remained unopened for a few days. When I finally picked it up, I was about a page or two in when I concluded the book made zero sense. I just couldn't process the concepts being presented, so I put it down, leaving it on the floor beside my bed. I went on about my business over the next few days, but I found that whenever I returned to my room, the book would bother me. I was annoyed that I had a book beside my bed that I couldn't understand. It injured my pride a little too much, made me feel a little stupid, so I decided I wasn't going to be defeated by it. I picked it back up again, this time determined to grasp what it was all about. As I read it this time, I began to realize that I was being introduced to a world of thought that questioned the fundamental nature of reality as I had understood it up to this point. It weaved between science, culture, spirituality, imagination and creativity. It questioned everything, and in essence was a perfect book for me at that moment of my life, when I'd just begun to question so many things myself. The book referenced thinkers and authors such as Bertrand Russell, Jean Piaget, Descartes, Carl Jung, David Bohm and Pierre Teilhard de Chardin, and it provided me with a road map to worlds of thought that I'd hadn't explored before.

I was ripe for change. This book provided an organic continuation from my days in school where I enjoyed metaphysical poetry and the writings of Edmund Burke and Francis Bacon. That curious part of my soul had not received even a modicum of nourishment in years, and it was hungering to be satiated once again. While the wisdom contained within this book resonated with me, it would remain in my subconscious for a little longer before I began to implement the change in my everyday life that it was pointing me towards. It played a part in a significant decision I was about to make about cigarettes and alcohol. Before I tackled the drink, I quit smoking. I had been a ridiculously heavy smoker. I knew cigarettes were a bad idea and now I would act on it. I ditched them. No weaning myself off them, just a swift cut from my life. It was freeing – I was no longer in their grip.

One Tuesday night after performing at the Augenblick, I stayed on drinking before heading to another bar. I was with my friend Timmy O'Sullivan but I was flying solo on the partying front as Timmy didn't drink any alcohol. He didn't need it. He always had a good time just hanging out and having a chat and a laugh. Later that night, Timmy drove us both back to my apartment. En route, I nodded off, falling into a deep, alcohol-induced sleep that not even Timmy could wake me from. I slept that night in the car, waking up in the unbearable heat of a Chicago summer morning.

Making my way into the house, I realized Timmy was still there. He had slept on the couch. I took a seat next to him. 'This is it. I'm done with the drink. I quit, here and now.' Prophetic words I had uttered a few times before but never with the same intent as on this occasion. I really meant it this time. I was beginning to realize that I needed to be sober, not just for the gigs, but so I could finally move my whole life forward in a new direction. I needed to change lots of things. I was just halfway through *The Crack in the Cosmic Egg*, and even though this book couldn't answer all my questions, it did open the door to new ways of looking at the world, which was hugely important for me in that moment when I quit drinking.

15

CHANGES IN LIFE sometimes fall in such a way that they seem like a disaster as they're happening, but when viewed with the clarity of hindsight, a beautiful synchrony can become apparent. The moment you are on the right path, it is not just the future that feels assured; the past suddenly comes into focus as though it were a series of experiences designed precisely to guide you to this very moment of change and transformation. In the moments when I'd gain this perspective, my regrets no longer had meaning, as if life had been shepherding me towards this moment; the pain, misadventure and heartbreak I'd endured was simply a measure of my resistance to following my deeper truth. I was beginning to find my way, but there was plenty of work ahead.

Quitting alcohol, while significant, wasn't going to do much for me unless I made more fundamental changes. I had some tough questions to ask of myself. Why was I drinking? What was I covering up? Who did I want to become? In some ways I was grateful for the drink problem; it forced my hand and drove me to make fundamental life-changes. It created a crisis that gave me an opportunity to start over. America is the land of reinvention

and redemption – it's stitched into the very DNA and consciousness of the country. I was glad to be there while I embarked on
my slow process of finally becoming who I am. All the questions
I'd been unable to ask myself when I was younger, the questions
that had remained unexamined for these many years of misadventure, could no longer be left unexplored. *The Crack in the
Cosmic Egg* had opened me up to a line of inquiry that I felt I
needed to follow into every area of my life. The questions that
barman posed to me in that bar in Limerick years earlier were
finally on the table: where did my happiness lie and what was my
purpose in life?

When I look back on the partying period of my life, I can see
the ways in which that chapter had to end in order for a new one
to begin. Martha was also leaving Chicago for Utah, but I couldn't
leave my world of music for the desert. In either case, she hadn't
invited me and neither had I tried to stop her going. We had hit
that moment when a relationship must move to the next phase
or finish. Years later, when I met Martha again, she saw all the
changes I had made and she said I had somehow become more
'me'. I reminded her of that moment when I held that copy of
The Crack in the Cosmic Egg at the door of the bookshop, when
everything did in fact begin to change

In the same way that I was surrounded in my early years by all
the music, musicians and inspiration necessary for my musical
grounding, I was now surrounded by the people and opportunities that would help shape me into the person I needed to
become. Being sober meant I was also free from the grip of hang-
overs and so I started getting up earlier. It was like I was looking

at life through a different lens. I started wandering and exploring other areas of the city, going to wherever my creativity felt awakened and inspired. Often I would head towards the Wrigleyville area of the city. This was known as a more vibrant part of town, with nice coffee shops, second-hand bookstores and healthier restaurants. I had become curious about the spiritual and philosophical side of things – the side that had been ignored for most of my life. I read books on Hinduism, Buddhism, Sufism, physics; I read music biographies, books on the psychology of performance and so on. I also began tracking down worlds of previously unexplored music and spending time discovering the paintings at the wonderful Art Institute of Chicago.

Thanks to Randy's influence during the mornings we'd spent drinking coffee and having an occasional hit of pot, I had developed a real interest and curiosity for jazz music. On our initial meeting, I couldn't have envisaged Randy and I having any shared musical interests, but as I got to know him, I started to get a sense of his musical world. We listened to lots of jazz fusion music, including Tony Williams, one of Randy's heroes, and I finally began to understand that first rehearsal when I thought Randy was going mad on the drums. The opening track on Tony Williams's compilation album *Ultimate Tony Williams* is called 'Some Hip Drum Shit'. This was really who Randy was; these were the ideas he had attempted to introduce to the band, and he had as much right to those as I did to the music of my mountainside.

My friend fiddle-player Seán Cleland introduced me to a live recording called *Shakti with John McLaughlin*. This fusion of jazz and Indian music blew my mind – a perfect balance of virtuoso playing and soulfulness. Dennis, meanwhile, had given me a mix tape with music by Miles Davis, American guitarist Michael Hedges and American fiddle-player Darol Anger. I devoured it all. Most of the music I was now hearing was something I hadn't heard on the radio back home; it wasn't the kind of thing that you'd easily stumble on around East Clare. I was beginning to fall in love with America. There is an enormous cultural richness to the country. The amount of new musical ideas created there over such a short period is staggering – blues, jazz, rock 'n' roll, country music, bluegrass music, Cajun music, Old-Timey music and hip-hop are just some examples.

I bought an album called *Vision* by L. Shankar, the fiddler on the Shakti album Seán had introduced me to. I was trying to find the recording that Seán had played me but this was the only one with L. Shankar that I could find in the record shops around Wrigleyville. I had just bought a Sony Discman and this was my first CD. It wasn't anything like the recording that Seán had played me so I was a bit disappointed at first, but then it grew on me. It became the backdrop to my morning coffee and night-time reading for the next couple of months. L. Shankar was on the fiddle, Jan Garbarek played his saxophone and Denmark's Palle Mikkelborg the trumpet. The music had an almost contemplative and spiritual quality, a mixture of Indian sounds and Scandinavian-influenced minimalist, spacious jazz. The overall sound veered towards that of New Age music except there was something deeper and more real contained within this music. My mind at the time needed musical therapy, and this album was it. There was one track called 'Psychic Elephant' that would come around every morning. It had a saxophone mimicking elephant sounds. It drove everyone mad. Dennis didn't really enjoy having to listen to a frenzied safari in the morning, and even Randy in the apartment above complained that the noise of my Indian elephant was also making its way through the floorboards into his apartment.

On the CD sleeve of the recording, I noted the record label: ECM. They were a small, independent company, but I figured if they produced this type of recording, they would surely have others in a similar vein. This led to a discovery of all kinds of music and all kinds of other labels, and over the years I ended up with literally thousands of recordings in my collection, many of them from ECM but also lots of music from the Blue Note catalogue and labels such as Nonesuch. Initially through the ECM catalogue, I also began discovering lots of great jazz and began listening more closely to forms of classical music that had never received my proper attention before. I stumbled upon the work of the great Estonian composer Arvo Pärt, whose music travelled as deeply into my heart as anything I'd heard growing up. Listening to his music was like a spiritual experience for me – it was meditative and blissful. To me, Arvo Pärt's music was a distillation of music to its deepest, simplest and clearest form. There was no pretension in it, nothing trendy, intellectual or unnecessarily complex. My first recording of his music was appropriately called *Tabula Rasa*, a Latin phrase for 'blank slate'. I was a blank slate, and as I listened to Pärt's music with intensity, I allowed each and every note to enter and mould my mood in whatever way was meant to be.

There was no doubting that I still deeply loved Irish traditional music and the way in which it reached deep inside me; it was lodged deeper within me than anything else. However, I became convinced that my professional musical future existed somewhere in a new mix of music, some of which I was just beginning to discover. This music was filling my imagination and my soul, opening my mind to all sorts of possibilities, musical and otherwise. This was all edging me towards the idea of creating some kind of more universal musical voice for myself.

It's no coincidence that it was around this time that I began reading Buddhist texts and the Indian Upanishads. The Upanishads are some of the oldest spiritual texts in the world, rich with spiritual and philosophical insights. Absorbing this material also expanded my mind and exposed me for the first time ever to a whole new world of non-Western spiritual thought. I felt as if I were answering some deep unacknowledged yearning that I'd been carrying my whole life. I didn't turn into a saint or mystic from all of this, but my mind was definitely altered in a way that made my previous way of being and thinking no longer possible. Old patterns and habits no longer served me, and so I welcomed and embraced change in a way I had never done before. I felt as though I should ride the wave and change as many things as possible while I had the chance. I was still carrying a lot of baggage, not to mention nursing a few sore wounds. I had plenty of unresolved issues – I still do, only now I'm no longer trying to solve them in a world that is meaningless to me, nor do I head to the pub in search of a solution.

From my Buddhist readings, I became more aware of

respecting all living creatures and not harming them. I always loved animals, but I was brought up in a farming environment where natural progressions involved the often untimely deaths of some animals. Growing up, I witnessed pigs being killed, bled and butchered in our farmyard, chickens' necks being swiftly snapped, and cattle being raised and sold for slaughter. These were all just a standard part of the farm life I had grown up with. Now, I was trying to remove spiders and other multi-legged creatures from the bathtub without frightening, injuring or harming them, the one exception being mosquitos. There was no one moment where I consciously elected to change in this regard; it was just something I started to do instinctively, as if the Eastern philosophy was seeping into my consciousness and filtering into my everyday actions.

My attempts to not harm any living thing seemed a tad hypocritical, however, considering I was still eating meat. Vegetarianism was my next adventure. I was somewhat on the fence about whether or not this would be a lifestyle change I could really commit to, so one day I decided to just boil some potatoes and vegetables. It was my first intentional vegetarian meal, and to my surprise I didn't miss the meat. I was relieved and happy to have made this move, as if I'd freed myself from some gnawing guilt that was beginning to arise. Bit by bit, I was growing into this new person. A new life was starting to take shape.

The other concept that was presenting itself to me was meditation. The Buddhist teachings kept referencing it over and over, so I started to feel like I was missing out on something essential, something that was necessary for this deeper understanding I longed for. I didn't have any particular kind of meditation in mind, as I hadn't realized there were different approaches. I assumed it was all the same. In fact there are many different types and different approaches, but they are all working to serve the same purpose.

I signed up for a week of meditation instruction at a local Transcendental Meditation centre. The technique is based on ancient Indian meditation methods and part of a movement that was founded by Maharishi Mahesh Yogi. The Beatles visited him in India some years previously, when they were on their own voyage of discovery. It's not a religion but rather a technique for accessing the deeper and calmer levels of your mind. To reap the full benefits, consistency is a necessity, so I started meditating twice a day.

In just a few short months, I had quit drinking, smoking and eating meat. I had started to meditate and was exploring philosophical and spiritual thought-processes from around the world. My plan of making my best effort in each step along the way had already guided me towards a profound change. I had adopted a new way of living and thinking, and for a brief moment I really thought I might have solved all my problems. In some ways I was only just beginning to tackle many of the issues that I needed to deal with, but the idealist in me was nourished by the possibility that my problems and stresses in life could be eradicated through Eastern philosophy and meditation. Fantastical as that idea was, I was finding a perspective from which it was at least possible to begin to see my problems for what they really were. This newfound outlook afforded me some glimpses of my new potential.

For now, I was sure I had made the correct choice at the fork in the road.

At one point in the middle of this transformation, I experienced a two-and-a-half-day-long episode of what I could only describe as some kind of spiritual enchantment and flow. It was an entirely natural occurrence, a short visit to the state of mind to which I would always yearn to return. This state didn't seem dependent on any particular belief or theology; it simply felt like an extended moment of grace, a glimpse of a potentially joyous way to live, a different way of engaging with the world. During those two and a half days, I felt I was on the correct path, or 'The Way' as it's also known in the Chinese Taoist tradition. I was deeply engaged with everything and everybody, interacting with them in a way that was outwardly normal while inwardly I was experiencing a peace and calm that allowed all the events and troubles of the world to flow past without disturbing this tranquillity. I was able to be fully present and capable of interacting with everybody and everything in a truly mindful way. It was as if my normal, chattering brain had temporarily paused. I was suddenly able to avoid the conversation habits that normally got me entangled in ways that pulled me away from my centre. For this short period, I took full refuge from the weight of everyday stresses and just felt the present moment in which I was living.

This beautiful feeling passed and I gradually slipped back to my regular up-and-down normality, but the experience, though fleeting, provided me with an awareness of the deep happiness and contentment that potentially exists within us. I have faith in a deeper reality beyond the rational, scientific construct of man's intellectual knowledge – a realm that may never be touched by a scientific instrument, or even be fully understood by the great scientific minds, but yet a reality that could ignite an imperturbable happiness within anyone who might access it. It is perhaps the reality in which our souls actually live but from which we are normally cut off by our own agendas and disconnection.

Though I was on a bit of a spiritual odyssey at the time, I also had a genuine interest in the tangible, real things of this world. I find the worlds of science and physics to also be a source of wonder and inspiration. Though I love the world of spiritual inquiry and discovery, I had also become a secular humanist in my political world view. I believe that secularism and freedom of thought are essential foundations for society. I personally try hard to keep a balanced view between the inward and outward paths of discovery and insight. Freedom to think as we wish, and the societal tolerance that makes space for this, are essential to both society's and our personal well-being. In my way of seeing the world, the search for truth and knowledge that the sages undertake is an inward journey through the layers of our consciousness, while scientists explore outwardly through a measurable conscious reality. The scientists produce concrete, verifiable results while the sages access the direct experience of truth within.

I cannot pretend to have attained any personal deep wisdom or insight myself. If anything, I have been mostly unsuccessful in my own spiritual efforts. What I have found, though, is that this path I have taken has given me possession of the necessary tools and insights to help me cope with the ups and downs of life. I now have a place of security, residual hope and happiness that I am able to access whenever I become lost and am really in need of it. I have learned to trust the flow of life without too much fear or insecurity.

During the time I was making these changes, I spotted a poster announcement that Rory Gallagher, one of the world's great rock and blues guitarists, from Cork, was set to play the Park West, a popular large venue in Chicago. My friend Andrew Mac-Namara from Tulla was a huge Rory Gallagher fan and had invested a great deal of effort in helping me understand and appreciate his music when I was a teenager. I never fully got it but I knew there was something important in his music. I had never seen him play live, and with all the tickets for his Park West gig sold out, it didn't look like that was about to change any time soon. I decided to go along anyway; I had a feeling that, nonetheless, it was somehow my destiny to see Rory Gallagher that night.

When I got there, the ticket situation was still the same, but I just stood there, close to the ticket-booth window, confident in the belief that if I remained patient, willing and trusting of good fortune, there'd be some way in which I'd get to see Rory play – that this destiny I was feeling would be fulfilled. After a while, I saw a couple leave, so I went up to the window and explained that I now knew the venue was no longer completely full. The person behind the window explained that they really couldn't do anything because there were physically no tickets available that they could sell me. I stepped away from the window but didn't leave. I hoped that perhaps my unrelenting patience might wear them down. It was then that another thought came to me. I went to the window again, visibly holding some cash in my hand, and said, 'Maybe someone could deliver this personally to Rory?' They took the money and let me in. I was actually genuine when I offered that money to go directly to Rory, but I suppose it might have worked as a bribe, even if I hadn't intended it that way.

The atmosphere inside the venue was intoxicating. Rory was in full flight on the stage. It was awe-inspiring to witness this rock and blues player from Cork just burning it up in the great blues town of Chicago. I was proud of him. Just watching him onstage, giving 100 per cent, holding absolutely nothing back, and unreservedly revealing himself, was totally inspiring to me. I knew right then that to perform well I'd have to be willing to freely open myself emotionally to the audience and freely give with the same level of trust that Rory did that night.

16

DESPITE HAVING SPENT my teenage years playing to audiences with the Tulla Céilí Band, I still felt as though I didn't possess a fully developed attitude to the stage. I already knew how to communicate with relatively small crowds, audiences at competitions, local concerts in Feakle and so on. When starting off as a teenager, I was able to disregard the audience and go inside myself to find feeling and emotion; I didn't care what the overall crowd thought, as long as I had at least one or two people to reach out to in the audience. In Chicago, however, I learned how to do the opposite. I disregarded my inner self and played whatever the audience wanted. This is a true example of the distorting impact of using music solely as a means to entertain and to meet the needs of an audience. I questioned whether Irish traditional music should even be performance music at all. On one level I felt like the essence of it was so deep and pure that all performance was potentially a corruption of the music itself. With Midnight Court, however, I was attempting to pursue some hybrid version of traditional music rather than subject my purer, more subtle form of the music to the potentially distorting impact of performing it onstage.

Through Timmy O'Sullivan, I met a man called Norman. Norman was a kind of mentor to Timmy in his poetry endeavours. I didn't know him very well, but he struck me as someone with some wisdom and a deeper understanding of matters. One evening, as we were chatting, I posed to him my performance dilemma. His response was simple: 'The stage is a sacred space.' He then went on to say that I should only play what I liked and what held deep meaning for me. He stressed that this approach would only work if I expressed my music with a deep intention of sharing and connecting; it needed to be offered to the listener with an attitude of giving. He reminded me that when the audience sit in front of a performer, they are offering their trust and there is therefore an obligation on the performer to respect this trust by being transparent and giving. That one thought-provoking conversation with Norman gave me a framework that has guided my approach to performance ever since.

While I was discovering new worlds of music, books and art, I was also rediscovering the roots of my own music. There was one singer in Chicago who I got to know very well. Her name was Ann Meenaghan and she was a sean nós singer from Connemara, in the heart of the Gaeltacht (Irish-speaking area), where Irish is still the first language. Timmy was a huge fan of Ann and it was through him that I first became aware of her. Ann was waitressing at Clancy's Pub on State Street, where Midnight Court often played, doing our strange mix of music. One night, I called Ann up to sing. Sean nós singing can be either horribly boring or powerfully transporting – everything depends on how deeply connected the singer is to the song, how real the feeling is, and how present and musical the singer is. Ann had it all and more. She sang the very roots of our music and culture in a powerful yet quiet and connected way.

Years later, when I would ask Connemara natives or any of the people with a deep sean nós knowledge if they had ever heard of this great Ann Meenaghan, no one seemed to know her. It turned out she wasn't known to locals as Ann but rather by the Irish version, Áine, and she didn't grow up with the surname Meenaghan. That was the name she took when she married Seán, a man from County Mayo. Once I discovered her maiden name, I returned to the same people and asked them if they were aware of the singer Áine Ní Dhonncha. It was a different story this time: she was well known and admired. In her earlier life, before her journey to America, she was a winner of the Corn Uí Ríada Oireachtas singing competition, the holy grail for sean nós singers. She was going to make a recording before she left for America, with another great sean nós singer, Darach Ó Catháin, but for some reason it didn't come to fruition. Instead, she disappeared to America, where nobody knew her or the treasure she carried within. She became Ann Meenaghan, her other reality just a memory to her and to the people back at home. When Ann sang, her longing for home and the feeling of never being heard seemed to fuel her singing with a passion that gave it a real depth of emotion. It was powerful and touched a raw nerve in me. I could hear in her singing the echo of my own loneliness and my own wish to be heard. Maybe the deeper music within me might never find an outlet either.

Every night in Chicago was a music night of some kind. One night I was in the house of musician Gerry McKee and his wife

Jocelyn, chatting at length about one topic or another. It was getting late, and they suggested I take the couch. Before they headed off to bed, Gerry pointed to some records and said I could play them quietly if I wasn't ready to sleep. I was still very much on a fervent mission to find new music and expose myself to as many new discoveries as possible, so I chose to rummage through Gerry's records rather than turn in. As I started sifting through them, I came across the *Liffey Banks* LP recording by Tommy Potts. I hadn't seen or heard him since the evenings many years ago when he played in our kitchen in Maghera. With music so easily accessible these days, it's easy to forget just how difficult it was to find back then. I didn't have this record in America and I hadn't heard Potts since my childhood. I put it on and sat quietly listening in a house I didn't really know in a city thousands of miles away from the place where I'd last heard him. Suddenly every twist and variation that might once have gone over my head was now going straight into my heart. I was profoundly struck, moved to tears, even. Here, by pure chance, was a call of truth across the years and miles to remind me of my roots and who I was. The music transported me right back into the cosy kitchen of my home in Maghera, connecting me to the deepest musical yearning of my heart.

Tommy's music kept weaving in and out of my life from then on. I got a copy of the *Liffey Banks* recording for myself and even had a copy on a cassette. I remember on a car journey through the wide open landscape of North Dakota listening to the recording as I drove along. I pulled in to take a look at the vista and left the car door open as I stepped outside, letting Tommy's music mingle with the breeze of the big open plains. His music made sense wherever I was, no matter what I heard or listened to in the wider world of music. His playing always held up; it never stopped being deeply meaningful to me. Years later, when I was collaborating with the great American quartet Brooklyn Rider, the lead violinist, Colin Jacobsen, wrote a piece based on Tommy's tune 'The Butterfly' – in fact, the five of us made a full album together called *The Butterfly*. Colin's composition for this tune perfectly captures the whimsical and light movement of a butterfly while delicately intertwining some of Tommy's signature motifs. Apart from being amazing musicians, Brooklyn Rider are a true joy to be around. It's a privilege to make music with them and a delight to have been able to introduce such fine musicians to the music of Tommy Potts.

As I sought more ways to consciously reconnect with home and with my own music, I found that one of the best ways to do so was through teaching – passing on the knowledge I myself had acquired from musicians such as my father, Martin Rochford and Joe Bane. The first student I had was a young girl named Emily who had a basic knowledge of both traditional and classical music and was maybe around eleven or twelve years old when she started coming to me for lessons. Her parents, both successful professionals, lived in the prosperous north-western suburbs. On the morning Emily and her mother, Kathleen, were due to arrive for her first class, it just so happened that I'd had some people from Minnesota staying over. They were all sleeping on the couches and on the floor, their stuff strewn all over the room, and I desperately needed them to leave so I could make the place presentable. This was tricky because on the one hand I wanted to be hospitable to my guests and not make them feel rushed or unwelcome, yet on the other hand I was feeling compelled to bundle them out so they wouldn't be in the way while I cleaned up the place.

My Minnesota friends from the Half-Time Rec, with their

dyed-black hair, black nail polish and head-to-toe black every-thing, continued to lounge around, almost steadfast in their determination to smoke their morning pot before they would even entertain the idea of heading out and facing the world. Time was ticking by too fast for my liking. I could feel we were approaching a deeply awkward scenario where two very different worlds would collide. Finally, the pot was finished and the friends seemed ready to leave. Slowly, the relief began to dilute my anx-iety as I accompanied them to the door. This optimism proved premature. As my friends paraded out the front door and down the steps to the street, a strong scent of marijuana smoke trailing in their wake, Kathleen and Emily were making their way up. I saw Kathleen's expression change as she scrunched up her nose at the lingering smell of pot. I could only imagine what was going through her mind. To make matters worse, I had decided to start growing my hair some months earlier, so it, too, was looking a bit wild that morning. The hair decision was my attempt to fit in with a more hip, urban world while at the same time shedding the look of an East Clare farmer. Frankly, I think Kathleen would have been much happier if an East Clare farmer had answered the door. Rather than apologize for the situation, I just smiled and welcomed them inside, behaving as if what they had just witnessed hadn't happened at all. Despite her concerns at leaving her young daughter in this situation, Kathleen didn't cancel the class there and then. Gradually, I earned her trust, and in the end Emily made great progress with her music. By the time she was on her last lesson with me, I was actually good friends with her and Kathleen.

One of the great things about teaching, apart from the number of wonderful people it introduced me to, was its therapeutic aspect. Teaching became a way for me to make logical sense of the music that I'd absorbed through my pores since I was a child. I started teaching to make a little bit of extra income but it served a larger picture. It enabled me to unpack and lay out my cluttered and disordered world of intuitive musical knowledge in a way that allowed me to see it more clearly than ever before.

Rob Adams was another student who came regularly, and our lessons quickly began to feel a bit like the book *Tuesdays with Morrie,* where Morrie offers deep philosophical advice to the author. I may have been the fiddle teacher, but in fact Rob was Morrie. Rob was a fascinating man who'd been a rare-book dealer and now owned an art gallery. We would play tunes, have a cup of tea, talk about music, and I would attempt to show him some of the things I was doing on the fiddle. I really looked forward to our get-togethers. Every time I'd manage to clearly convey an idea, he'd respond by providing me with an analogy somewhere else in the world of art or just in life. He said that the knowledge gained in one area of life often has a resonance and meaning in other areas. Being a rare-book dealer had taught him a lot about unearthing and discovering things that others may have overlooked, and this resonated with me musically. His art gallery was focused on bringing to life the hidden and unknown artwork of the African-American community. It was difficult to persuade people to acknowledge deep artistic value in African-American art, just as it was in Ireland for the educated class to see artistic value in the music of the peasant class. We had great chats about this kind of thing and these conversations provided an invaluable source of insight for me. My friend, and wonderful painter, Helen O'Toole also came by for a few fiddle classes. I think I was getting more from these teaching experiences that I was giving. The classes weren't really classes, they were deeply engaging conversations that delved into the very nature of art, music and creativity.

Meanwhile, our band Midnight Court wasn't really progressing in the way I'd hoped. We were trapped between two different worlds. We were playing what was needed in order to hold on to our club gigs in Chicago, while at the same time trying to push into more adventurous musical territory that might help us escape the gravitational pull of those same clubs. We couldn't make up our minds which direction to take. We constantly questioned whether we could really go all the way and develop some new hybrid music. What had once seemed like an exciting challenge had evolved into a persistent doubt. The other guys wanted to make a record but I just didn't feel like we had reached anything close to our potential, so I was against that idea. A meeting was called to sort this out, to be held at one of those Greek diners that seemed to be on every block of the city. When I got there I kind of knew there had been a meeting before the meeting, that they had reached a consensus to move forward with a recording and just needed to get me on board. They were happy with the music we were making, but I wasn't. I was also coming to the conclusion that we weren't ever going to make the push to go beyond this point. Making a record would have been tacit acceptance of the level we'd reached. I told them to count me out, and if they wanted to use someone else, I'd be OK with that. That was effectively the end of the band for me. I played the rest of the summer gigs with them and remember one particular street festival we played where we really hit our stride. On that night the band was powerful and connected, the place was rocking, and we all knew that this was the last moment. It was bittersweet – I was both tasting the band's unrealized potential and giving up the dreams that the band had held for me. The band never did make a record.

Around this time, when Midnight Court was winding down, I started playing John D. McGurk's pub in St Louis, Missouri, with the highly respected Offaly accordion-player Paddy O'Brien and the Dublin-born singer and bouzouki-player Pat Broaders. McGurk's was a famous venue in the world of traditional music and was one of the few bars in the US to have actual traditional music five nights a week. We'd perform three sets a night, five nights a week, for a month at a time. It was a convenient set-up, because for the duration of our visit we stayed next door in a single-storey house owned by the pub. The house had been nick-named 'The Palace', primarily because it was anything but. All the bedrooms were in a single row, with the bathroom at one end and my room – which was only the width of my bed – at the other. If I wanted go to the bathroom, I had to walk through every other room in the house to get there. Overall, The Palace was a ramshackle place, but despite this we were very happy and content there. It actually felt like a home to us. We could pop in and out and have a cup of tea between sets. It was kind of like living in a backstage area.

Playing onstage in McGurk's was a very relaxed experience. Some of the audience listened, some chatted amongst themselves. We could play without the requirement to entertain the whole audience. Those who wanted to listen did so in their own way. We were always aware of these people. The nice thing was that one didn't have to overtly play for them. It was very similar to the way many jazz musicians perform in cocktail lounges, with some people listening and others just chatting and hanging out. We could go as deeply into any obscure version of any tune we liked at whatever tempo suited us. In some ways, it's an ideal space for the very serious musician who just wants to play real music without the pressure of being some kind of slick performer.

Throughout this part of my musical journey, Paddy O'Brien became a very important figure in my life. He really helped to reground me, and I ended up learning a lot of tunes and variations from him. Paddy, much like myself, revered the old players. He was an encyclopaedia of melodies, tune-settings and stories from many older musicians I'd never had a chance to know. He would also regale me with stories from the time he spent with musicians like Tommy Potts, Sonny Brogan and James Kelly.

I loved chatting with Paddy about music, and our conversations would often run on for hours. In a way, it reminded me of being a fourteen-year-old boy playing tunes in the living room and listening to Tony McMahon's brother Brendan playing beautiful and unusual settings of tunes for me on his accordion. Paddy was a few years older than our bandmate Pat Broaders and me, and had lived in Dublin when the big folk revival was kicking off. He was the kind of player who didn't care about what others thought, nor did he care too much about building a career. Paddy just loved the tunes and wanted nothing more than to spend all the hours of the day playing them.

Life at this stage was pretty good. I felt I was moving in the right direction. On a personal level I still had plenty of work to do but I was definitely more content than I'd been at any point since my early childhood.

Some time later that year, 1989, another good friend, banjo-player Seán O'Driscoll, from Cork, organized a week-long gig for us at The Plough and the Stars Pub in San Francisco, along with a couple of other gigs that he'd asked a Seattle-based booking agent named Helen Bommarito to organize for us in both Seattle and in Portland, Oregon. Seán was living in the middle of the Mississippi River, on Nicollet Island between St Paul and Minneapolis, with his wife, Mary, who was also a fine fiddle-player. I'd never been out west before and looked forward to seeing the place.

People on the East Coast and in the Midwest like to make fun of California and its hippie consciousness. I loved San Francisco from the very first minute I arrived. I loved the hills, the bridges, the light – it was a whole new America. I could sense freedom and spaciousness; it was just a breath of fresh air. San Francisco was the place the late, great Joe Cooley had returned from and perhaps the place where he'd left the biggest impression, where the memory of him and his soulful accordion-playing was freshest. I had the feeling that the place that had once welcomed Cooley was also the place where my music, too, might find a friendly reception.

The Plough and the Stars was run by Seán Heaney. Seán was a man of few words who'd always keep you guessing about what was going on in his mind. Behind the stern look was a generous and thoughtful person, and one who really adored the music. Playing at this pub was a bit like playing in McGurk's in St Louis, with the same relaxed, casual and free atmosphere, where you could be yourself musically. I spent my week in San Francisco exploring the city and attempting to invoke the musical spirit of Cooley in my playing.

I was eager to connect with people familiar with the music of Cooley and his accordion-playing sidekick, Kevin Keegan. I met Patricia Kennelly, who learned from Joe Cooley and could play almost just like him, and Gloria Greg, who was more familiar with Keegan. Gloria has become a close friend over the years. She is a psychologist who plays traditional music and is very interested in the creative personality and the act of musical performance from a Jungian perspective. She understood where I was coming from musically and fully appreciated the soulfulness I was seeking out. Over the years, we have had many powerful conversations about music culture and performance. She has continued to encourage and guide me, from her Jungian point of view, towards deepening, and understanding, my own performance skills.

After San Francisco, we headed to Seattle, where Helen Bommarito had arranged a gig for us in Murphy's Pub. For this leg of the trip, we stayed at Helen's house as she lived in the city. When we arrived, I noticed Helen was wearing a badge on the lapel of her coat. The familiarity of the design caught my eye. I realized that what I was looking at was a miniature of the cover artwork for an album I loved very much, by the band Montreux. The amazing fiddle-player Darol Anger, whose music Dennis had introduced me to, was in this band. I mentioned this to Helen and she explained that she knew all these people and had worked with them. It turned out that Helen played some fiddle herself, as well as the mandolin. She was also friendly with Mícheál Ó Dhomhnaill and Kevin Burke, who were living down the coast in Portland, Oregon. Straight away we had a lot we could talk about musically.

During our trip, Helen had another guest in the house, a friend visiting from Scotland named Shona McMillan. Shona guessed there was a spark between Helen and me, and decided to take on the role of matchmaker. Her efforts were successful! Helen had organized another gig for us in Portland, Oregon, and we chatted non-stop for the entire journey there and back. I loved the Northwest. It had a lot of San Francisco about it, except it was bathed in green, with cedar and fir trees everywhere. There seemed always to be a beautiful soft mist falling, and when the clouds cleared, it was possible to see tall, snow-capped mountain ranges in the distance.

I was living in Chicago but I knew I would return to Seattle. Helen, however, wasn't confident she'd ever hear from me again. Truthfully, I felt a connection to Helen, to Seattle, and to the progressive mindset that seemed so prevalent there. I was starting to become a member of that same tribe of meditating granola-eaters. Despite Helen's doubts, we maintained a long-distance relationship for about a year and a half after that. In those days, after I'd stopped drinking, I relied a lot on her help and support to get through some of the difficult times. She'd travel to Chicago, and I, likewise, to Seattle. We racked up a lot of phone bills and frequent-flyer miles.

In her role as an agent, Helen offered to help me advance my career and get me some traction outside of bars in Chicago. She arranged for me to be part of an event at Boston College that was being organized by the well-known pianist Mícheál Ó Súilleabháin and renowned fiddler Séamus Connolly. They were going to record the most prominent Irish fiddlers in the US, all on one album. I suppose I needed to have been ranked as being worthy of inclusion on this recording to even begin to have a career as a fiddler in North America. The album was named after the tune 'My Love is in America', but was also often referred to as 'The Boston College fiddle recording'. For my contribution, I reverted to my core, elemental truth and played the music that had been inspired by my father and people like Joe Bane. It was a decision to plant my flag and return to the truths that were becoming once again certain for me. If this music wasn't going to be good enough for me, then there was no journey to be had. I couldn't really envision a career playing this music, but I was also becoming impatient at the idea of doing anything else other than this. I would sooner or later have to just follow my heart's desire, even if I couldn't see any logical way forward. Bit by bit, I was returning to my roots.

18

In 1989, I learned that my father was ill. He had been losing weight and his energy levels were low. It was discovered he was suffering with undiagnosed Addison's disease, an adrenal disease that can be regulated with cortisone medication. He almost died before they identified the problem, and just as fast was almost miraculously cured with one injection. Medication would now be a daily necessity for the rest of his life. Even though he was very ill, I had a gut feeling that it wasn't his time to go. Being without a proper visa, I couldn't travel freely back and forth between America and Ireland, so I decided to wait it out, and shortly after he'd recovered I took the chance and headed for home. I arrived at Shannon Airport, and as I walked out the main doors I savoured the brisk, moist breeze of County Clare on my face for the first time in years.

When we arrived at the house, I got out of the car to the sound of the stream, the rustling of leaves and birdsong as I'd never heard them before. The previously barely-noticed aural backdrop from my earlier life was suddenly in the foreground. Most of my time in America was spent in urban environments, and now I was able to hear and feel in a much deeper way the beauty that had always surrounded my childhood home.

I was visibly shocked when my two younger sisters, Anna Marie and Helen, appeared from the house. I'd only known them as children, and now here they were, both young women. It really hit me there and then just how significant a part of their growing-up years I had missed out on. My mother, too, had changed a little, but my father was thin in a way I had never seen before. I was used to seeing him as a strong, robust man, and even though I knew he was very ill, I don't think I was quite prepared to see him looking so frail. When I got inside, the big kitchen of my childhood suddenly looked tiny. The whole experience of returning made me feel like I was in some kind of waking dream.

My mother and brother had kept me in the loop on my father's brush with his mortality. He was getting older, and time was moving faster now for both of us. We knew that we should record some music together; we needed to document and acknowledge our musical relationship. My friend Matt Purcell had started a recording studio with Pat Talty, a local veterinary practitioner with a deep love of music, in Pat's house near Tulla. I asked him if he'd be up for making a recording of my father and myself. There was no planning, no set list, just all the tunes I could remember playing with him during my childhood. On a technical level, my father possessed a very powerful rhythmic sense and was in love with the vigorous pulse and syncopation required to satisfy the best dancers. This was the main heartbeat of the recording. He also adored a well-constructed melody and had a very good ear for finding great tunes. In traditional music, the very first act is to simply choose a strong melody. If you don't have a good ear for that, then it will always be difficult to make good music. People sometimes choose melodies that challenge them, suit their playing style, satisfy their technical curiosity, make them look technically competent or satisfy their intellectual curiosity. There's nothing wrong with any of that, but if those things are the only criteria you use, then you will likely fail to see the simple treasures that are sometimes more emotionally rich and beautiful.

For the recording with my father, we played straight through, mostly recording each track in the first take without ever going back over it or repeating anything. Guitarist Mark Gregory, who lived locally, provided guitar accompaniment. We simply wanted to document ourselves playing together and that's exactly what we did. We finished the recording session when my father had to go to play for a dance – his friend and band colleague Francie Donnellan was coming by to pick him up. What we'd recorded came to just about thirty-five minutes long and was released as a cassette tape. About 500–600 copies were made and mostly sold locally. Some years later we would add a few more tracks, with my father and myself accompanied by Dennis Cahill in order to make it into a proper, full-length recording that became available on CD. There was nothing manicured about this record; this was just how my father and I might have sounded playing together any evening in our kitchen.

When I first left for America, I was just out of college and sinking in debts accumulated from failed businesses. Soon after this visit home from America, at thirty years of age, I finally made that last repayment. I had spent my years in the desert feeling broken and dejected, mentally punishing myself for all the things that had gone wrong, but slowly I had begun to put myself back together. Making that final repayment felt like closure on that time in my life.

In 1992, I finally got my immigration status through a visa lottery. Being relieved of the worrisome burden of being illegal was definitely a milestone worth celebrating. That year, I was back home again to appear on an RTÉ television programme being produced by renowned accordion-player Tony McMahon – my first in many years – and to teach at the famous Willie Clancy Summer School in Miltown Malbay. The summer school is one of the most significant events each year, where the luminaries of traditional music gather, where those with a fervent love and understanding of this music convene. The TV appearance and my week-long engagement at the summer school was all organized by Tony. I can't say with any great certainty, but maybe the recording I made with my father, or the track on 'The Boston College fiddle recording', had come to his attention. Whatever the reason, it felt wonderful to somehow be invited back into the fold. The TV programme, hosted by fiddler Paddy Glackin, went smoothly, and from there I went on to reconnect with the world of traditional music in Miltown Malbay.

I had dropped off the radar as far as this world of traditional music was concerned – it was as if I'd never been there before. I was somebody new. But I had been there as a teenager with my father and now I was back as an adult with a lot of experience under my belt. At the summer school, I enjoyed meeting with musicians I hadn't seen in years. Many of them couldn't quite remember the quiet teenager with the shirt and tie who had always accompanied his father.

Along with a daily routine of music classes, the summer school puts on a series of instrument-specific recitals and I was to take part in the fiddle recital. I'd only have to play for seven or eight minutes as there was a long line of fiddlers to perform, including some of the best players in the country – Bobby Casey, John Kelly, Junior Crehan, Joe Ryan and Tommy Peoples, to name just a few. As I stood at the side of the stage waiting to go on, the memories of all my years of humbling misadventure, playing the wild rover in Chicago bars, having broken the very fiddle I was now holding in my hand, were all now condensing into one emotional homecoming moment. I performed my adaptation of fiddler Ed Reavey's reel 'The Whistler from Rosslea' and 'O'Connor Dunn's' reel. I played unimpeded from my heart, out from my depth, remembering the performance advice I'd received from Norman back in Chicago about playing with an attitude of sharing and giving. As I hit that final note, the room exploded into applause that quickly turned into a standing ovation and calls for more. This was a response I had not attempted to make happen; I could not in my wildest dreams even have anticipated this reaction. This was not music of high energy or obvious excitement; this was moderate-tempo music – but it was coming from my heart. The world of imagination and soul that I'd lost contact with, that I thought might just have been an illusion, suddenly seemed very real once again in that moment in the hall in Miltown Malbay. I felt I had been welcomed back to the sanctum of the traditional music world. As I left the hall that night, people shook my hand and kept asking why they'd never heard of me before. Everyone seemed to want a recording. In the past, I was always on the fence about whether or not people would want to hear me play. That one performance changed my mindset completely. I once heard the singer Maura O'Connell say that she had spent her life becoming an overnight success. I hadn't yet been very successful, but it had taken a whole lifetime of experience to make that one moment.

I returned to Chicago at the end of the summer, but I knew my time there was approaching its natural end. Helen and I had talked about living together in Seattle, so it seemed like the right time to make that change. Between playing in McGurk's with Paddy and Pat, and some house concerts out west, where various local folk societies would put on small recitals for up to fifty or sixty people in the house of someone with a space big enough and willing to host it, I found myself spending less and less time in Chicago, and slowly my attachment to the place began to loosen. I will always be indebted to Chicago, that windy City of the Big Shoulders that had taken care of me over many years, indebted to the collection of wonderful friends there who enriched my life so much, who supported me and carried me through most of my twenties. It was my hometown in a way that no other city ever will be again. I have loved other places, but I have never put down the same kind of roots as I did in Chicago. I was closing a very important chapter in my life and beginning a new, adventurous phase.

I had no idea if I'd be able to actually have a career in Seattle, however. I was also a little nervous about moving in with Helen and leaving all that I'd known behind. But in the autumn of '92, it was time to make the big move. I decided to take the train so I could get a better sense of the distance between Chicago and Seattle. The morning I was to leave, I crossed over to the Abbey Pub to say goodbye to Tom and Breege, who'd looked out for me for many years. They were like parents to me, and it was heartbreaking to bid them farewell. The taxi to take me to the train arrived and I loaded my two suitcases that contained all my belongings. As the car pulled away, I looked out the back window. My two dear friends, Timmy and Dennis, were waving goodbye as the taxi set off. I felt a genuine sadness in that parting.

It's about a two-day journey by train from Chicago to Seattle, but I needed that time just to begin letting go and transitioning to the next phase of my life. The train I was on went up through Wisconsin and Minnesota, where the fall colours were at their most radiant, an endless array of orange, red and yellow shades flying past in a blur. Then came North Dakota, that vast open space where children's author Jim Latimer and I had once driven from school to school to tell the children about his book *The Irish Piper*, a pied piper from County Clare. I would play all the tunes of the piper for the children as they listened intently, captivated by the beautiful blend of story and music. The panoramic views of North Dakota remained open and beautiful all the way into Montana. Here we passed through Butte, a city that was once filled with Irish miners, after which we passed through the mountains of Idaho and Washington. Next stop was Seattle. As the train approached Seattle, the clouds were low and the ocean matched the greyish-blue of the sky above it. Seattle was the city from which my career as we now know it actually started.

Helen was the person who first introduced me to her friend Randal Bays, a wonderful guitarist and fiddle-player who I'd already done some gigs with over the previous year. Randal would visit Seattle regularly, and he and I would just sit around playing for hours – it was a joy playing with him. By this stage, I had resolved to make a recording. There was no doubt in my mind that Randal would be the guitar-player – we loved playing together. Helen, who had been persistently encouraging me to record, reached out to Green Linnet Records and managed to get me a contract and organize a recording session.

I loved the sonic quality of the recordings that guitarist Mícheál Ó Domhnaill and fiddler Billy Oskay were making in their studio in Portland, Oregon. I felt this would be a good place to make the recording. Billy was also the engineer and I trusted him implicitly to get me the best fiddle sound possible. I didn't really prepare for this moment specifically, but in reality I'd been preparing for it my whole life. This was a moment to bring it all together.

I'd already been playing some house concerts with Randal, so by the time it came to recording, we were familiar with each other's style. Those house concerts also helped us to pull together a selection of tunes. After arriving in Portland, Helen and I stayed with Randal, who was living there. There's a soft, natural beauty in the Northwest – it's a soulful place that invites me into a more contemplative reality. It was November at that time and there were lots of heavy clouds, with mist and fog falling on the cedars, all of which seemed to beckon me inside to a more reflective space. This was the atmosphere that surrounded the making of this recording.

When we arrived at Billy's studio in the morning, he had an array of herbal teas laid out as a welcoming gesture. There was one called 'Tension Tamer' – I went straight for that. The studio was very comfortable, and Billy was a talented engineer who could hear the smallest of details and follow the music very closely. Randal and I started to play without much fuss. I was putting the medleys of tunes together in the studio. I'd pick a couple of tunes that I felt worked well together and run it by Randal, and then we'd just go and record them. This didn't give Randal much time to prepare, but he didn't need any time. His playing was perfectly in sync with how I liked to play; we could sense each other musically, and there was an empathic connection between us. Playing with my father and with concertina-player Mary MacNamara was where I had first experienced this kind of musical connection. There is a synchronicity and communication that can happen between people who are making music together that goes beyond the obvious, technical elements. For this recording I just summoned up all of the musical experience of my youth and was met by Randal with the most beautiful and evocative chording. The entire process of making this recording was carefree and relaxed; there was no attempt to do anything other than play the tunes we loved playing in the way that had the most meaning and offered us the most joy. There was no other agenda.

Randal was my new musical partner, with whom I could so

easily connect. He was already familiar with the recordings of my father and Paddy Canny, and as an accomplished fiddler himself he could also play all those tunes on the fiddle. If I wanted a guitarist who could support my efforts at pulling together all the music of my youth, I couldn't do better than Randal.

I didn't mind if the recording generated criticism; I didn't care if anyone liked it, beyond the handful of musicians I'd dedicated it to. What was more important to me was that it was a true and genuine expression of the music I'd grown up with. Before I went anywhere else musically, I felt it important to plant the foundations solidly and clearly. This recording was the very core of my playing; it was the statement of something fundamental and true for me. Green Linnet wanted the recording to be very simply titled as *Martin Hayes*. I was sorry that Randal's name wasn't on the front cover of that recording – it should have been, and I should have pushed harder for that.

The finished mixed and mastered recording finally showed up in the spring of 1993. We put it on the stereo and listened. This was the moment that I knew I'd finally managed to shoulder the gift I'd been handed. I had found my way back from the wilderness. I knew that my father, Martin Rochford, Junior Crehan, and all the people I'd dedicated the recording to, would be able to understand and connect to this music. This was a crescendo moment in my musical life. I had no idea if a career was possible as I faced the world with nothing but this recording, my fiddle, the tunes I'd always known, the wisdom of the old players, and whatever else I'd been able to add to that myself. Now, whenever an opportunity to perform would arise, I would just play with all the passion and sincerity I had, and see where that would take me. I continued performing at McGurk's in St Louis with Paddy O'Brien and Pat Broaders, while also playing some house concerts with Randal.

My CD was launched at the Willie Clancy week in July, and much to my surprise it began to get attention from the media in a way that I hadn't expected. Green Linnet were working with Amy Garvey, who was then a freelance publicist. She had only recently started promoting traditional music. She worked in the Dublin media scene and didn't see any reason why traditional music shouldn't be heard on more general radio programmes and written about in more mainstream media. Her work over the years was instrumental in connecting my music to the broader musical and media world in Ireland; she later became my agent and looked after the booking of all my concerts in Ireland. Amy liked the recording, as did her close friend, the music writer Bill Graham. They both took every opportunity to promote it where they could. It was time to organize a tour of Ireland.

Amy was still just doing PR at this point, so the booking agent Madeleine Seiler had been brought on board to put the tour together. It was a difficult job, given that just about nobody knew me, which is probably why it was just a three-gig tour. The first gig was in a bar in Sligo with guitarist Francie Lenehan. This particular venue consisted of a front bar and a back bar where the gig was taking place. They'd tried to sell tickets but only managed to sell a handful so they let the locals who were drinking on the other side of the bar in for free. The whole thing was a shambles. People started to talk and the music was simply fading into the background. I don't mind fading into the background but not on a stage when it's meant to be a sit-down listening concert. I asked the audience to keep it down, telling them this was their music and that I just wanted to play for them. After I said my piece, the crowd did quieten a bit but there wasn't a great atmosphere after that. Certainly not the most promising start to my Irish touring career.

The day after the Sligo gig, I was scheduled to do an afternoon gig at the Galway International Arts Festival. Maureen Hughes, who was on the programming committee for traditional music for the festival, really liked the recording so she booked me for a midday slot in the small Taibhdhearc Theatre right in the centre of the city. I was approaching this performance with some apprehension. If there wasn't an audience in a bar the night before, how on earth was there going to be an audience in the middle of the day? I was to do this gig with the bouzouki player Pat Marsh. It was set to be an acoustic gig, without any amplification or technical set-up, but I got there about two hours ahead anyway, in the hopes of having a chance to rehearse with Pat, as I'd never played with him before.

When I went inside the venue, there were a few stagehands at work. The place didn't seem like one that was about to host an event. I asked one of the guys if they knew about the gig and he responded, 'Is there something on here today?' If the people working in the venue hadn't heard about the gig, it didn't seem like anybody else would be aware of it either. I went to the dressing room and started putting together a set list, all the while knowing that I would very likely be facing a humiliatingly empty room. Pat turned up shortly after and together we ran through the tunes. Happily, we instantly clicked. He sounded just perfect for the gig. Then we just sat in the silence of the backstage area, waiting for the nod to go on. It's not a big theatre, but when I walked on to the stage, I was nonetheless stunned to see the place was packed. I had prepared myself for empty seats.

Pat and I had a really great gig that day. I got to play all the tunes from the album exactly the way I liked to play them, and the audience responded with a swell of enthusiasm. The next gig on my grand, three-gig tour was the upstairs music room of a bar in Athlone in County Westmeath. Pat was to play this venue with me also. It was nicely set up with tables and low lighting. There were maybe forty people there, so it was looking OK again. We started playing but there was one table of people that kept talking loudly while others around them strained to hear the music over their animated voices. After the first set, I asked if they'd be willing to keep it down. It seemed to do the job, but sadly the fix was just a temporary one – after a while, the talk built right back up again. I stopped mid-tune and offered them their money back. They were pretty indignant about the whole thing, arguing by some strange logic that since they had paid their money to be there, they were therefore entitled to talk. I insisted that they get their money back so that they wouldn't feel entitled to talk, gently encouraging them to leave and waiting while they did so, after which the gig resumed. It actually turned out to be a great night.

The stand-off was an important gesture for me. I had now established in my mind that if I was going to perform this music, it was going to be on my terms. I didn't care if I was playing to only two people, so long as the experience was meaningful. Just knowing this inside myself somehow produced an energy that from then on conveyed to people that I'd be prepared to put my fiddle in the case and walk away with a smile if the situation wasn't right. I've never had to offer anyone their money back again. There would be occasions after that where I might have to begin playing in loud, noisy situations in either a festival or a club, but I knew in my soul that these moments could be transformed without compromising the music. The very first note played must be serious and from the heart; it must be expressed with deliberate intention and confidence, projected out into the room, not necessarily with volume but with focus: *I must go to the space that I want others to enter, go as deep as possible and trust that the invitation is powerful enough for others to come along.* The most challenging moment has often been the one with the strongest reward, like one night in The Plough and the Stars when the crowded room of people standing around chatting with drinks in their hands became so silent that I could play with a whisper, even to the point of silence. There is a special energy in those moments, the best note of any night potentially being that note of silence in between, where the silence itself becomes music. And the sweetest sound of all – as Fionn mac Cumhail once said in an Irish legend – is the music of what happens.

19

BACK IN THE US, I started exploring smaller gigs and house
concerts up and down the West Coast, from Alaska to California. I wasn't really making any money, just about covering
costs and returning home with something to help pay the bills
and maybe a bit of pocket change to buy a few second-hand
books and CDs. I was out there playing and there wasn't much of
a sense that it was building to anything or going anywhere in
terms of a career. I would have to learn to be content in the present moment and not be anxious about the uncertain future.

My meditation and evolving spiritual outlook was very helpful
to me for letting go and just moving freely with the music. I had
heard the story of Irish monks in the early Middle Ages climbing
into boats, raising a sail without a destination in mind and just
letting God's will take them to a destination of His choosing. My
boat was my fiddle and the music in my heart. I'd simply have to
trust that this would all land me somewhere.

Bit by bit, opportunities would come my way. Musician and
producer Eddie Stack invited me to play at the 1993 Celtic Music
and Arts Festival at Fisherman's Wharf in San Francisco. I was
to perform with singer Seán Tyrrell and uilleann piper Davy

Spillane. It was a huge room, an old warehouse where up to 10,000 people could fit, and there may have been 5,000–6,000 people in front of us. As we were going onstage, Davy offered me a piece of chewing gum. I was puzzled by the timing of this offering, to which he explained that if I chewed gum, it'd look like I didn't give a damn. It would help hide any nervousness I had, and maybe even make me look cool. If I had known that looking cool was as simple as chewing gum, I'd have been doing it my whole life. Davy was a naturally cool character, with or without gum.

This was really Seán and Davy's gig, but I was happy to blend into their music. The gig was a boost for me – I was playing with two very accomplished musicians who were much further along in their careers than I was. Davy, Seán and I went on to play The Plough and the Stars later that week. On one of those nights, I ran into a fellow called Seamus Finneran from County Offaly. Seamus was living in San Francisco but was about to move to Australia, having already spent time there. During our conversation, he asked me if I'd like to do a tour in Australia. I said yes there and then. Seamus was a bodhrán-player and clearly a good networker, but he had never booked a tour before so I just thought I'd wait and see. I had nothing to lose. In the weeks and months that followed, Seamus got to work on organizing the tour, taking what had been a random idea and seeing it right through to fruition

Right from the start, the plan had been to tour with Randal. However, as it got closer to the time, Randal backed out. He felt we wouldn't make any money from the tour. I didn't want to let

Seamus down, but I explained to him my dilemma in the hope that he would know of a suitable replacement. Seamus suggested an Australian-born guitarist and banjo-player called Tony O'Rourke. I didn't know anybody in Australia, so I had to place full faith in Seamus on this one.

It was early March 1994 when I first arrived Down Under, my first time to the southern hemisphere. The place was on one level immediately familiar – Melbourne had tall buildings downtown, similar to cities in Canada or the US – but on some deeper level I could feel it was truly foreign and different. It starts with the sun in the north, with the Big Dipper of the night sky being replaced by the Southern Cross. The thoughts of the Aboriginal culture of Australia, which had existed for over 50,000 years, were on my mind a lot. I wondered often about their Dreamtime and the magic of their landscape. For our first few days we stayed with Seamus's friends Gerry and Stefan in the St Kilda neighbourhood of Melbourne. The morning after I arrived, I had my first-ever 'flat white' coffee, something you could only find in Australia at that time.

Later that day, we met up with Tony O'Rourke to try out some tunes together. He had diligently learned all of Randal's guitar chording, even though Tony played with a different guitar tuning from the one Randal had used on our recording. He still managed to pull it off. Any worries I'd had about performing with Tony, who'd been previously unknown to me, were certainly eased when I realized how diligent he was. I remember noticing on one tune there was a chord being repeated that didn't sound quite right. It was then that I remembered right back to the studio, when Randal said he'd made a mistake and wanted to go back and do it again. I had reassured him at the time that it wasn't worth it for such a tiny mistake. I was certain nobody would notice. I was wrong – Tony had noticed but assumed that if it was on the recording, it was surely meant to be there. That alone showed me how much work he had put into preparing for this tour.

With Seamus being a bodhrán-player the plan was to do the tour as a trio. We performed our first gig at the Daniel O'Connell Hotel in Melbourne. We seemed to gel together pretty well. Green Linnet Records had a publicist working in Australia, Gaynor Crawford, who did a lot of PR work for the tour, generating a great deal of media attention for it and for the recording. There was a good buzz around our music and people were really taking notice.

We were scheduled to play the Port Fairy Folk Festival, which I assumed would be a run-of-the-mill event, nothing too out of the ordinary. When we arrived, however, I took one look at the big tents with seating for thousands of people and realized just how wrong I had been. This was a far bigger deal than I had imagined. I remember being surprised at seeing my name displayed so prominently on the festival posters. It was sitting right alongside the famous blues singer John Hammond and English folk singer Martin Carthy. I later discovered that Jamie McHugh, who ran the festival, had really liked my recording, and booked me, with a good billing, based on the CD alone. Seamus and Tony were slated as support musicians.

The music I was playing was not the kind you can just blast

out from the stage, taking control of the room; it would have to be powerful in a different way, it would have to be invitational. I was going to have to dig deep to make my music work in this environment. This was on a much larger scale than I was used to, and I wondered if I could play at moderate tempos, and with subtlety and feeling, in this setting. I decided I would at least attempt to do it.

One approach I decided to use was to start out quietly, almost as an invitation for everyone else to be quiet. I'd warned the sound engineers not to counteract this by turning me up; I would control the dynamics in the tent myself. I was OK playing very quietly, even if lots of people couldn't hear very well. If people want to talk, they'll just talk louder if you get louder. If I could make a real connection and create a critical mass of attention and engagement close to the stage, a ripple effect would hopefully occur, spreading back into the audience space and out towards the sides of the tent. To execute this plan well, I put together a medley of tunes that would start out quietly and then crescendo through to some piece of fiery and dexterous playing. This fiery playing was there to serve as a musical release of energy and also as a message to the audience that I could also deliver high-energy music with virtuosity. For the remainder of the gig people would now at least know that when I played very simply and slowly it wasn't out of necessity, it was intentional. I would attempt to build a trust with the audience by vulnerably presenting very delicate and sensitive pieces of music, pieces that ran a very big risk of me losing the audience entirely, but a risk worth taking nonetheless. I would hold the audience engaged by using dynamics, key changes and time-signature changes, leaving them wondering at which moment this whole thing might explode again. I didn't want them to be able to anticipate the direction it was going to take next. This was the rudimentary stage-craft I'd put together to make the gig work; it was a plan that at the same time gave me the possibility to deliver tunes in the way that had most meaning for me. This approach worked, and our various performances at the festival were well received.

I have come to believe that the art of performance is a separate art from that of simply playing music. It is an art form that is central in the world of theatre but almost never mentioned in the world of traditional music. In the same way that an actor must walk on to a stage and confidently become the character, a musician must walk on to a stage and confidently become the music. Your interior reality determines what happens in the performance and you have to strive not to be pulled away from your centre, no matter how challenging the environment.

The Australian tour was a big success. We travelled to Sydney and played a lot of smaller gigs there, then performed at festivals all over New South Wales and Victoria. I got to visit some beautiful sites and even made a night visit to a nature reserve with Seamus, Gerry and Stefan to see the rich diversity of nocturnal marsupials such as koalas and wombats. I left Australia a more confident performer and with a love for the country and the people I had met there.

Back in Ireland, interest in the CD was still growing. I did some tours of smaller venues there, but it mostly wasn't financially feasible to bring Randal with me from the States – I couldn't afford to fly him over and pay him. He did, however, make one trip with me when he came to the Willie Clancy Summer School. He made a lot of friends and connections there, many of whom are still good friends of his to this day.

Despite the success of the tours and the increasing success of the CD, I was still barely making enough money to survive. Randal had a day job as a cartographer back in Portland and would travel around America with me when he could. At one point we even made a trip to France together to play at a festival outside Paris. I couldn't make it worth his while to travel but he was willing to do it for little pay if he'd get a few free days to explore Paris. Mostly, though, I was having to pick up other guitarists as I travelled to gigs in small bars, little coffee-house-type venues and some very small arts centres. It was wonderful to play with new musicians so often but also stressful, because until you met them and played together you never knew for sure if it was going to work. I played with John McGann, David Surette and Tony Cuffe in the New England states of the East Coast and with Gerry O'Beirne and Pat Marsh in Ireland. The money wasn't great, but I was happy because I was getting to play the music I loved.

A few months later, Randal and I were invited to play to the San Francisco Celtic festival. Our quiet, intimate music was not common in such a large space, so everything I had learned from playing the big festivals in Australia would really pay off here. I was coming to realize that the speakers, microphones and the reverberation in the room were as much a part of the final sound as how the bow touched the string. I started to view the space and the amplification as an extension of my fiddle, and would respond and interact with the space, working out how the amplification could help with that. Today, I never just play my fiddle with disregard to the space that I'm in or the amplification I'm playing through. I adjust my playing to the room and to the sound I hear coming from the speakers. At the festival, I began to sense the acoustics of the room and played the tunes in slightly broader strokes, emphasizing the beauty of the melodic lines, abandoning non-communicable intricacies and playing at a tempo that would work in those acoustics. Being responsive to the space and being musically flexible was a critical factor in making those gigs work and has remained an important part of how I perform to this day. That San Francisco performance was a success, and I was invited back every year after that.

A day after the Celtic festival, Helen and I had to go to the Irish Arts Office to pick up the cheque for the gig. Helen was my agent but also my partner. I can't remember what had set off an argument between us that day. Sometimes after the intensity of a gig like that festival, I'm running on empty, as if all of my energy has been used up. I was in a bit of a huff and decided to go for a walk in the city on my own, without any real plan. I was rambling around aimlessly without a destination in mind, so I decided on a little experiment. At every street intersection I'd follow my first impulse and turn left, right or go straight ahead just to see where I would end up. In my mind, this was a small version of the monk aimlessly sailing away in his boat. I walked and took turns based on my first hunch, and after about thirty minutes I found myself on a street just randomly standing in front of a door.

A man opened the door, and after some pleasantries he welcomed me inside. It almost felt as though my arrival was expected. We sat on two chairs facing each other. He asked me a few questions about myself and what I do, so I gave him a synopsis of my life and career. He had assumed a kind of elder brother/guru-type posture in our conversation. I felt I was a student, and he was going to impart some wisdom to my benefit. Normally, I'm very sceptical of any cult-like guru figure and would usually avoid them like the plague, except in this situation it was my own inner guide that had landed me in the room, so I felt I needed to listen.

We spoke for a couple of hours, during which he told me that if I wanted to know the soul of this country, I would need to see the wilderness, spend time in its natural beauty and splendour. He told me I was very lucky to have my music but stressed the point that my life wasn't, and shouldn't, be only about my music. He suggested that music was just my way in the world, that I could simply follow the music, offering it as a gift while trusting it to look after me. He also emphasized that music was not who I was, that there is a deeper journey in life beneath our life of outward activity. He put me through a guided meditation where he asked me to listen to and identify all the sounds around me, to hear them all and slowly expand to hear further off into the city.

At another point during this encounter, he did another kind of exercise, where he asked me questions and I had to answer without using the words 'I', 'me' or 'my'. Every time I slipped and accidentally used one of those pronouns, he thumped the side of my leg good and hard, reminding me of just how egocentric my reality was. This whole encounter was directing me to trust my own instincts, to trust the music, to realize that music was central in my life but not who I was and not the most important thing in life. He was teaching me to listen more intently and to be more aware of the world around me, reminding me that I needed to be in nature for some periods of time and that I needed to work on my own egocentricity.

I left the house some time later, feeling reassured that the encounter had left me in a better place mentally. The next time I returned to San Francisco, I searched along that street for the house I had visited but could never find it again. I still can't believe I never got the man's name. Strangely, I can't recall having felt compelled to even ask his name. The experience certainly felt surreal in hindsight, yet there was something strangely calming about it. It suggested to me that the strange, anonymous world out there is a place we can trust if we ourselves can face the world with trust.

20

THERE ARE SOME musicians you can play with who always take you into new musical places and make you aware of musical capacities you didn't know you had. My musician friends over in Ennis, flute-player Kevin Crawford, accordion-player PJ King and my old friend Matt Purcell, proposed that I do a gig with Steve Cooney, the Australian-born musician who'd moved to Ireland in the early eighties and played bass with the band Stockton's Wing. Steve had in more recent times been playing a nylon-stringed acoustic guitar with the accordion-player and singer Séamus Begley, creating the most exciting and dynamic pairing in Irish music at that time, an explosive and energetic distillation of West Kerry polkas and slides intermixed with some of the most soulful and angelic singing that one could imagine.

Steve had the rhythm and pulse of the Kerry set-dancers' feet right there in his hands. He would get so carried away that bits of his guitar would fly off; he would wear holes in the surface where his pick would repeatedly hit the wood in the frenzy of rhythm he was creating. It was completely wild. I don't really know what people thought might happen if Steve and I played together. I don't think I myself knew what would happen, but I would soon find out. A gig was organized in the Greengrove lounge bar just outside Ennis. Steve was a better-known musician than I, so playing with him would be a boost to my career, of which I was very appreciative.

Steve had listened to the CD I had made with Randal, and prior to the gig he and I ran through some tunes that weren't on the album – just basic information about chords and keys that would be a guide for Steve during the gig. He'd map out the tunes using his own notation system, which was circular in nature. It looked beautiful and was a complete rethinking of how we can potentially interact with notated music. He would later receive a doctorate degree for this work.

We had a set list of tunes but still had very little idea of what it might actually sound like. Would it be subtle and subdued, or would there be bits of Steve's guitar flying off? Neither of us knew what to expect. A crowd of about 120 people had gathered for the gig. This was the single largest audience I'd been able to attract in Ireland. It turns out that a lot of those in attendance were there because they were curious about this perceived big clash of styles. It became clear very soon that Steve is an intuitive musician who is completely awake and in the present moment. The very slightest twist of every note I played was responded to, his chording beautiful, his rhythm powerful. All of the emotional phrases I wanted to express were underpinned with chords that only further amplified every feeling. In return, I was able to respond emotionally to the colour of his chords and the pulse of rhythm he was making. When two musicians playing together can each allow the other to influence their playing, then another thing begins to happen: music is created that neither of you had imagined, as the cycle of mutual response leads us to previously unknown musical territory. Steve and I both played tunes that night in ways that we'd never played before and yet we managed to do so without losing our connection to the feeling of the music. The audience loved it and no parts of Steve's guitar came flying off.

I played again with Steve later that year, this time at the Feakle Festival, after which we embarked on a tour of Ireland that took us from Cork to Dublin and up to Armagh and Derry. There were a few memorable occasions on that tour – I remember finding the Stray Leaf Folk Club in Mullaghbane, County Armagh and driving into what looked like a farmyard. The club didn't look very promising, and things didn't dramatically improve once I got inside. It was a bit like a used-furniture warehouse, with different chairs at every table, before that kind of idea had become hip. But once people began to trickle in and the place filled up, a vibrant atmosphere began to take hold. We were introduced by Mick Quinn, a great storyteller who was really more of a comedian, with exceptional timing.

Despite our initial misgivings about the place, Steve and I had a fantastic gig at the Stray Leaf Club, and in the end we wished that all venues could be just as atmospheric. Lots of people brought tape recorders with them that night to record the show, and afterwards the bootlegs started to circulate. I even got one myself recently!

Steve and I arrived for the Derry gig of our tour on a very interesting night. It was the evening of the first IRA ceasefire, and it was my first time visiting the Bogside area of the city. While we were onstage, I noticed a kid with blond hair sitting in the front row with his parents. I'd seen him with his parents at a few of our gigs that week already. I wanted to say hello to these ardent fans so that their enthusiasm didn't go unrecognized. The boy in question was twelve-year-old Thomas Bartlett. His parents told me they were from America, on vacation in Ireland. We chatted for a bit, and after I returned to the stage I assumed I would never see them again. Little did I know that very same twelve-year-old would later go on to be the piano-player in our future band The Gloaming and the producer of our albums!

The tour was a wonderful success, and in Steve I felt I had found a new musical soulmate. Steve approaches traditional music with a deep respect and understanding. His recording of ancient harp music that he adapted for guitar on the album *Ceol Ársa Cláirsí* brings the music to life in a beautiful and soulful manner. I think his knowledge of the natural phrasing of sean nós singing, which weaved its way into his playing while working with Séamus Begley, was hugely important in these interpretations.

In 1994 I recorded my album *Under the Moon* in the studio of my old friend Matt Purcell in Ennis. The album was a slightly more elaborate recording, featuring more musicians than on my first recording with Randal Bays. Randal joined me again, but this time my father also came and played with me on a track. What was an easy process of letting go in the first recording seemed to require a much greater effort this time – the dreaded second recording, where you could easily mess up what you'd already achieved and make your past success look like a fluke. There was a modest and finite budget, and at the end of the short week we'd scheduled for it there had to be a finished recording. I had the flu but we had to proceed anyway – Randal and John were flying in, studios were booked and plans were made, so I had to soldier on no matter how sick I was feeling. This musical life feels like one long continuous call to throw caution to the wind. I was having a hard time pulling it all together in the short week that we'd scheduled for this recording. But when you have the flu and you play music by going all in, body and soul, your symptoms disappear in the process. I've experienced this many times sitting at the side of a stage towards the end of a tour, exhausted and sniffling with a cold or sore throat, just wishing I was in bed instead of having to face the gig ahead, but ten minutes after it starts, the exhaustion, the sore throat and sniffles disappear and I have a fantastic time. It was the same in the studio for this recording. I was able to let go and really play the tunes, with my flu temporarily on hold. During the mixing of the recording, however, I was back to feeling terrible and felt unsure right then if there was such a thing as good music. My friend Matt kept assuring me that we were getting good stuff, but I'd lost perspective and was hoping I'd never have to make a record again.

When the CD was released, the following year, it actually sounded good. There was even more media attention for it than for the previous one. For the day of its launch, Amy Garvey had set up lots of radio and print-media interviews, including one with Ireland's most famous broadcaster, Gay Byrne, on his morning radio show. The CDs were supposed to be available the morning I was to do the radio programme, but because of some delay, they weren't ready. This meant I had to go to the radio studio without the recording I was promoting. It wasn't ideal but I figured I would make it work. When I arrived, I told the receptionist I was there to do the Gay Byrne show. After she contacted the production team to let them know, I was told to take a seat and that somebody from the show would come and get me when they were ready. I waited there for what seemed like an age, watching the clock and wondering if they had in fact forgotten about my interview. Eventually someone came to get me in what seemed like some massive last-minute rush. Apparently, whoever was originally supposed to come for me had messed up, and now it just appeared to Gay Byrne that I had arrived late. As I headed into the studio, I stopped at the engineer's desk to give him some suggestions regarding my fiddle sound as I was going to be playing live in the studio. 'It's too late for that now!' came the reply. It wasn't a great start, and it wasn't about to get any better. I took my seat in front of Gay, who was looking down at his notes. Without lifting his head, he asked for the CD. I explained I didn't have one and before I could elaborate on why, he replied, 'Well, this isn't very professional, is it?' I felt like I had turned up late for school without my homework and Gay Byrne was the impatient headmaster.

We could hardly have gotten off to a worse start, but I had learned from my gigging experiences that no matter how bad the situation, there is always a best possible approach that can be adopted, that it's important never to give up looking for the best you can do in that moment. I decided to let go of focusing on whatever attitude I thought Gay might be harbouring; I was clearly making a very bad first impression but I'd have to let go of that, along with my own long-standing judgement that Gay didn't really like or understand traditional music. In all likelihood he'd never had a chance to really get a proper sense of this music; it can be a confusing and incomprehensible art form for many who've not grown up with it or had a decent exposure to it. In some ways this was part of my overall mission: I wanted to make the core of this music comprehensible to a wider world. I knew Gay was a jazz fan, and I too loved jazz, so I figured if I could establish that musical common ground with him and use jazz as a metaphor to explain my thoughts on traditional music, then we might get somewhere. We ended up having a great chat that went on much longer than the allotted time. By the end of it, I felt like we had made a genuine human connection. He had let go of his initial judgement and I had let go of mine. I left the studio feeling as though I'd been heard and understood, certainly not the outcome I originally would have predicted. Soon afterwards, Gay invited me on to his iconic television chat show, *The Late Late Show*, which I would return to on a number of occasions after that. One time he even brought on the Tulla Céilí Band.

To watch Gay presenting his TV or radio programme was to be in the presence of a consummate professional. He was completely present and in the moment, attentive to everyone and to every detail. Gay was very much an open-minded, kind-hearted person. I feel that he cared genuinely about people and this was one of the reasons he had such a tremendous connection with the public.

Amy Garvey continued to do lots of work promoting the latest recording, and she and her music journalist friend Bill Graham were giving copies to every influential journalist and musician they met. Bono, Sinéad O'Connor, Gavin Friday . . . they all got one! I thought my first recording was the definitive one, but it turns out that this recording was where a broader section of the public started to become familiar with my music. It did well enough for me to receive a national entertainment award from a broad jury of Irish panellists from across the music and media world, with Gay Byrne himself apparently one of my strongest advocates. Suddenly my music was beginning to reach beyond the world of traditional music. Certainly, things were moving up a notch, but even with all the PR and attention, it was still hand-to-mouth living. People think that if they frequently see you on TV or read about you in the newspapers and magazines, this somehow equates to you making plenty of money. This was not the case – and to be totally honest it's still not the case. I'm lucky, however, in that I never associated money with success. I still don't. I make a living doing the one thing I am most passionate about, the thing that fires up the excitement within me.

Sometimes the real success of a recording isn't necessarily what happens at a career level. For me, making an album was an opportunity to clear the deck, to realize a musical vision, document it and then put it behind me. Usually people create in the studio and then tour; I was doing it in reverse. I tended to discover things musically as I performed and toured, and when I'd discovered enough possibilities, I could then record them. With this second recording I was closing a chapter in which I presented the musical foundations of my earlier life. Now that I had achieved this goal of laying out my musical foundations, the deck was clear and some new path needed to be charted.

21

ACK IN THE States, I continued for now with my usual touring, taking both small gigs and festivals, and basically going
anywhere I was asked. One day, we got an email from a fan asking
if we had any plans to play in Vermont in the near future. Helen
replied saying that we had no plans or bookings there, but that if
the fan had any suggestions of where we might play, we'd be happy
to pursue it. A few weeks later we received a response with a date
and a venue. He was going to put the gig on himself. Helen agreed
a fee, so the booking was confirmed. As we got a little closer to the
date, Helen emailed again, trying to sort out some of the logistical
details. She had asked whether we could be picked up from some
train station or airport, to which the response was, 'I'll have to ask
my mom.' We began to suspect that this was not a regular pro-
moter, so we looked into it and realized the booker was none other
than the now thirteen-year-old Thomas Bartlett, the same kid I'd
met in Derry and my future musical partner in The Gloaming.

We went to Vermont as planned, played to a full house, and
overall had a fantastic gig. Afterwards, we hung out with Thomas
and his friend and music partner Sam Amidon. We played some
music together, and even then Thomas was showing signs of

being a great pianist. We were staying in the Bartletts' family home, situated in the beautiful Vermont countryside. His parents were lovely people, warm and welcoming with a refreshingly progressive approach to life. I remember having a chat with Thomas's mom about the house, during which she mentioned that she had built it. I naturally took this to mean that she paid a contractor. She hadn't – she had built the house with her own hands. I was both flabbergasted and impressed.

I remained in loose contact with Thomas in the following years, and to this day I can still remember an email I received from him where he excitedly outlined his plans to move to New York. He wasn't the first person to think about having a musical career in New York. It's not easy to break in and not everybody succeeds. But it wasn't long until I heard of Thomas doing gigs with people like Yoko Ono, Martha Wainwright, David Byrne and Laurie Anderson. I knew then that he was doing just fine.

With my second album out there, it was time to think about my next move. I had been touring and picking up accompanists in different locations, which was very enjoyable on one level, as each musician interacted with me in new ways and brought out something different in the music. The only problem with this set-up was that it was fundamentally difficult to advance. With each new musician came the necessity to start again from the beginning. I needed to choose a musical partner with whom I could work on a permanent basis, developing musical ideas and continuously building on them. Randal, though a wonderful guitarist, was growing disenchanted with his role. He preferred to play fiddle and ultimately chose to mostly do that. Steve

Cooney was a non-runner as he was already in a very successful duo with Séamus Begley and living in Ireland.

I thought about asking my old friend Dennis Cahill, but this posed a few concerns. Dennis and I had only ever really played a kind of experimental rocked-out version of the music, whereas I was now playing in a very different style from the music we had played in the band. Dennis also had almost no direct experience of playing traditional music in the conventional sense. Even though we'd been playing together for years, we never just sat around playing tunes with a fiddle and guitar. On the plus side, Dennis had a very wide range of technical ability. He could play different styles of music and had a great theoretical understanding of it. We were also good friends and had spent a lot of time talking about music and dreaming up new possibilities. In the end I concluded that Dennis's lack of experience in accompanying traditional music could actually prove advantageous. It meant that we could start from scratch and build a whole new approach. I decided to give him a call and invited him to come to Europe with me for a summer tour in 1995. Immediately he cancelled all his bar gigs and packed his bags. He told me later that he'd always imagined I'd come back after my first album and record with him. I had originally vaguely suggested that idea but when I'd gone ahead and recorded *Under the Moon* without him, he presumed I wouldn't ever return. I think he felt that we'd really missed an artistic opportunity with the band, so he was eager to take on this second attempt at making music together. He was ready to experiment and was up for trying anything.

In the fledgling stage of a music career it often feels like one wrong move might result in the world of music critics, record labels and promoters making a judgement call that could finish your career. Choosing to work with Dennis at this point was an act of faith, a hope that we could achieve the unrealized potential that we instinctively felt was there. I felt under pressure: I was now no longer the unknown fiddle-player in a quiet bar somewhere; people in the traditional music world were now familiar with my work and were watching closely. Dennis, meanwhile, would have to dive into a genre that he didn't actually know that much about, with the veteran guitarists of the Irish music world looking on. It was an intimidating and difficult situation for him, but he handled it fearlessly.

That July, we went to Norway as we'd been invited to the Førde Traditional and World Music Festival. As we were on tour, there wasn't time for Dennis to turn into a standard traditional Irish-music guitarist overnight. He willingly engaged with me as we began looking for ways in which his guitar-playing could be integrated with my interpretation of the tunes. Maybe, instead of becoming a traditional guitarist in a generic sense, there was a way in which he could see the tunes less as idiomatic pieces of music but rather as universal melodic ideas. I encouraged him to look at these tunes in the way one might imagine a Bach partita or a Beatles song. This way he could engage with the tunes using his current skill set and background of knowledge. The harmonic and chordal side of traditional music is not clearly defined and I always felt there was a lot of unexplored possibilities in that area. We talked about how each tune would be approached harmonically and rhythmically, and how the chording and rhythm could highlight the natural beauty and power of each melody. We would have loved the chance to explore that beautiful part of

Norway, but we were only there for four or five days so we used every waking hour to work on the music. For the entirety of the stay, we would pop in and out of each other's hotel rooms constantly testing out new ideas for tunes and chordings. It felt like we had made a lot of progress and had found a way of working together in that time, which in itself was reassuring.

Dennis has a unique set of guitar skills, having been a folk guitarist who studied classical music, as well as played a little bit of jazz with Howard Levy of Béla Fleck and The Flecktones fame. When I'd been living in Chicago I'd become familiar with the term 'jobbing musician' – someone who could be hired by different band leaders to play in a wedding band one day or a Top 40 band the next. Dennis had worked as a jobbing musician, covering everything from country to disco music. It would take the two of us working very closely together throughout that summer to find ways to integrate his full range of skills into the music. After all, the guitar was a relatively new instrument in traditional music, only really becoming popular in the sixties and seventies. I was already rethinking the music from the ground up, so it made total sense that a new guitar accompaniment could be developed from the ground up also. My approach to playing was basically to be in service to the melody itself – my ethos was simply to do whatever was necessary to make the beauty of the tune more transparent and obvious. Often this would involve doing something very simple, where there would be no obvious display of musical skill. It wasn't about my playing; my playing was there just to deliver the tune.

I asked Dennis to join me in that effort to be in service to the melody. That way he wasn't just following me; we'd both be following the tune. Traditional music is fundamentally a line of melody, and Irish melodies are unique in terms of structure, pulse and the techniques we use to play them. The core of the music is melody that has a potential for universal resonance, where it can be fully experienced independently as a line of pure melody that doesn't require the listener to have a pre-existing knowledge of the music or its cultural background. I didn't feel we would transgress the essential nature of this music so long as we were only seeking to reveal the innate beauty of the melodies themselves. We would just search out guitar chords by trial and error until we found something that matched and amplified the mood of the first phrase of the tune. This would give us a start and Dennis would be in his element figuring out the remaining chords. I kept my musical antenna tuned for whether the chords were indeed amplifying the feeling of the melody and highlighting the tune's natural beauty. There is a profound beauty in these melodies and there are particular notes in the tunes that carry more weight than others. I would point out the parts of the melody that I felt required the strongest and most powerful underlining with guitar chords. We approached each tune as a unique piece to be interpreted without applying any formula, starting afresh in our exploration of each individual tune.

We also avoided cluttering the tune with ornamentation. This minimalist approach required every note to really count, for every chord to contain only the most necessary and meaningful notes, not just the ones that were most convenient. This approach often pushed Dennis into creating some very demanding and taxing finger patterns and chord progressions. Though his playing sounded beautiful and disarmingly simple, in reality his musical constructions were incredibly complex, and playing them would have pushed any guitar-player I knew to the very limits of their ability.

In previous generations, it would sometimes be down to a lone fiddler without accompaniment to generate the pulse and rhythm required for the dancers at a house dance. Through the influence of my father and my years playing for set-dancers, this pulse and rhythm had worked its way into how I played. It was, however, becoming common in traditional music to have a guitarist or bodhrán-player take care of the rhythm while the melody-player went straight ahead without much rhythmic inflection themselves. I wanted to incorporate the set-dancing rhythms of my own playing, however; I wanted both Dennis and me to be co-creators of the groove, coming together in this older rhythmic pulse of the music. I had noticed that bands with good rhythm had everyone on stage being active participants in making that rhythm. To help us achieve this pulse, I gave Dennis a tape recording I had made, in the family kitchen in Maghera a year or two previously, of the great set-dancer Willie Keane dancing to my fiddle-playing. Willie was staying overnight in our house after an event in Feakle. He and I stayed up late chatting and at one point he asked me to get out my fiddle and play a few tunes so he could dance. Willie was one of the best set-dancers ever, so I decided to tape-record the performance. I gave this tape to Dennis and suggested that he ignore all other approaches to rhythm, that in my opinion this recording of Willie's set-dancing was the most natural and organic rhythmic response to this music. We needed to think about the rhythm from this perspective. Dennis worked very hard to get this rhythm into his playing. The combination of chording and rhythms that he was coming up with pushed him each night to produce music that required incredible chordal and rhythmic acrobatics. We had come up with a way of playing tunes where both instruments were interlocked yet interdependent in creating the rhythm. When this pulse was achieved between us there was a kind of subtle subversive power to it that could bring an audience along with us.

The next thing we worked on was the process of performance itself. We used the image of a piano-player, both hands often carrying out two separate functions but working together as one. Our aim was for the two of us to be as integrated in the playing of the tune as the two hands of a piano-player. It was a bit of a tall order, but when it happened it had a beautiful flow to it.

After Norway and a few more gigs in between, we came back to play at the Feakle Festival, where we received a fantastic reception from the audience. We had received the local blessing.

Our summer tour never concluded; we just kept on gigging together from then on. We started by touring all around the States, Australia and the UK. We also made it back to Ireland at least twice a year. When you don't have a very big following, as was the case for us at that point, you just have to play a lot of small gigs. This tends to involve lengthy drives, red-eye flights, lack of sleep, airport queues, shuttle buses, rental-car desks, check-in times, check-out times, sound-check times, lugging instruments and suitcases through airports and up and down the stairs of guest houses. What time we would need to be on the road the next morning was the last question to be answered at the end of every day. This kind of routine can be very challenging to cope with it unless the music itself is working well. Dennis and I both adapted to this tiring lifestyle but truthfully it was the music that sustained us.

We drove thousands of miles all over the US, the UK, Australia, Ireland, Holland, Italy, Japan – the list is long. Our car journeys were spent discussing politics, music and more casual topics, like the latest renovations Dennis was having carried out on his house or the last thing he'd had changed in his vintage Mercedes (which, in the end, was basically everything). Dennis and I had a conversational style where we didn't really delve too deeply. We'd often reminisce about the old days in the bars of Chicago, marvelling at how we'd made it out, how unlikely it was that we'd even gotten to where we were now, and how we were blessed to be doing real gigs with people listening and appreciating what we had to offer. Equally so, we were both OK with long stretches of silence where an hour or two might pass by without either of us saying a word, perhaps both lost in our daydreams as the car's comforting hum took us where we needed to be, whether we were on the motorways of England or in the wide-open deserts of America.

There's certainly a magic to the open road in America. One's imagination can roam freely as distant mountain ranges creep closer and the desert passes by in a blur. We'd often fly to some hub like San Francisco, Washington DC or Phoenix to do three or four gigs within driving distance of each other. I always felt a sense of excitement as we'd get in the car and leave the airport. Dennis was the map reader; it wasn't his favourite task, as directions were not his thing, but the only alternative was for me to be a passenger with Dennis driving, and that was absolutely not going to happen. Dennis is not a great driver and I'm a horrible passenger. I have tracked this passenger-unease of mine back to the days of my father's infamous driving. There were a few accidents that had occurred on the way home from céilís, and even though he was not to blame for any of them, it didn't help ease the tension that I felt whenever I had to be a passenger in a car.

As we toured more and more, and our musical arrangements gradually evolved and became more refined, we realized we were getting close to the time when we needed to make a record together. When I visited the uilleann piper Davy Spillane at his home near Doolin in north-west Clare, he showed me his recording studio and mentioned that his record company's advance payments to record and produce his own recording had been in the form of the equipment in the studio. Davy's contract was with Sony, but I wondered if I could do a similar deal with Green Linnet Records, as I was still contracted to them at the time. They could pay me in advance for the record, and instead of renting studios and paying engineers, I'd buy the equipment then record and mix the album myself.

By the time I'd paid all the expenses for the first two records, there had been nothing left for me, and the records were then owned by the record company. If they agreed to this plan, however, it would mean I'd still have my money's worth in recording equipment after the record was made and the means to make more records thereafter. There wasn't a lot of money available, so the equipment I would be able to afford wouldn't be top of the range. Unlike Davy's state-of-the-art studio, this was going to be a more modest affair.

I decided to set up my studio in the basement of Helen's house, where she and I lived. Some construction work was required in order to make a discreet space in the basement – a partition had to be built and the walls around the basement needed to be dry-walled. Meanwhile, as Green Linnet began planning the release of the next album, they started asking me for its title. Here they were, looking for album titles, while Dennis and I were painting the studio as if to avoid making the actual recording – the typical artist-procrastination that every writer, painter and musician knows only too well.

It was the recording process itself that was causing most of the procrastination: I had never recorded or mixed an album before. The most I'd ever done prior to this was press play-record on a tape recorder. At a certain point there was no need for any further decorating, so we moved from that phase of making the recording to the manual-reading phase. The record company were eager to know how it was all going, and how much we had recorded so far – there was a deadline in place – but we were still trying to figure out how to format tapes for the ADAT recorders. Our efforts at creating our debut duet recording, which would be called *The Lonesome Touch*, had only so far produced some painted basement walls. I didn't know anything about recording technology or techniques, but I did know how I wanted the record to sound, so I took my seat and committed to staying at it day and night until I'd figured out how to achieve the result I had envisioned.

During the time we were setting up the studio, Dennis and I were both listening to Pat Metheny and Charlie Haden's *Beyond the Missouri Sky*. This was a laid-back, uncluttered duet of guitar and bass that had a lovely relaxed mood. Their approach definitely crept into our recording, as if it had given us the confidence to make a record that was more open and reflective in nature. For some reason, Dennis and I both felt compelled to record at night. It seemed to have a calming influence on how we played, as if the stillness of the world in the early-morning hours was the perfect atmosphere for the record we wanted to make. Some of the tracks were recorded in one take, such as the long, twelve-minute medley track 'The Pol Ha'penny Selection' and also 'The Lament for Limerick'. The first tune of the album is a composition by Paddy Fahey, and all I knew of the tune when we started recording was the first part. It just kept coming into my head, and I thought it'd be a nice tune for the recording if I knew how to play the second part of it also. I phoned up Debbie, an old girlfriend of Dennis's who knew the tune well, and asked her to lilt it to me over the phone. That became the opening track.

We took a few risks with some tunes, where we abandoned the standard approach and created new elements of our own. We chose a very non-traditional approach to 'Toss the Feathers', 'Rolling in the Barrel' and 'The Morning Dew' where we bent and improvised these tunes in ways that were not standard for this music. The latter two were tunes my father and Paddy Canny had played on their recording from 1959 and were deeply embedded in me in their most traditional form. We were now crossing a line that I hadn't crossed on any of the previous recordings; I was doing things that would have been confusing to the old players back in Clare. My father would not have cared for how I was now playing 'Rolling in the Barrel' and particularly 'The Morning Dew', a standard of the musical canon since the recordings of the great Sligo fiddler Michael Coleman. This troubled me and it took me some time to come to terms with the choice I had made. Of course, I wanted the older musicians' approval, but I had also come to the view that respecting and understanding them and their approach to music was what was most essential; seeking their approval was not what was important. Musically I didn't want to be held hostage by the fear of their rejection. They may not have liked all the things I was doing, but they also knew that deep down I really respected and understood them and their music. My experimentation was in no way a rejection of older ways of playing, it was in addition to the older ways. Integrity for a musician or any other artist is a complicated thing. There isn't all that much integrity in playing something the same way as previous generations if we do it out of fear of being rejected or out of the need for acceptance by the tribe. Tommy Potts was essentially rejected during his lifetime. The very nature of integrity and authenticity had gradually become a different thing for me – it was now personal. It involved courage and fearlessness, and my loyalty was now to the sincerity and truth of the musical expression itself. I wanted the music to function for me as an unhindered universal communication of joy and beauty. I was very well aware of the melodic treasure that is Irish music. I just wanted to be free to explore every possible avenue of expression in the music, even ones that hadn't yet been explored. I had begun to regard my musical mission in a much broader scope; it was now music in the universal sense first, and Irish music second. I wanted my music-making to be relevant and alive; I wanted to express it as a universal and soulful language.

When I was a teenager playing tunes at home, it was difficult for me to believe these tunes might be universally understood, but I often wondered what kind of harmonic possibilities might exist behind these tunes. I never imagined I'd find someone like Dennis, who would so thoroughly explore those possibilities alongside me. At this point, our friendship is much more than just a musical one. After all the years of touring together, we're not just friends, we're more like brothers. Dennis is a caring, sensitive human being; a very kind and loyal person whose life is dedicated to music. Our differences and shortcomings complement each other. Dennis has a theoretical knowledge of music that I don't have, whereas I have a particular grounding in the tradition and insight into its possibilities. Dennis is deliberate and analytical, whereas I'm more spontaneous, developing everything out of feeling. His analytical approach really comes to the fore whenever he slowly stitches together his guitar parts. Many times, he has played me the progression of chords on their own that he has come up with, and they've been beautiful compositions in their own right. The introduction to the tune 'Pol Ha'penny' that we perform on *The Lonesome Touch* is just a run-through of the chords Dennis had distilled to play behind the tune. The two later albums that we recorded as a duet are permeated throughout with Dennis's beautifully distilled minimalist chording and subtle rhythm.

Even though I have new musical projects with other collaborators every year, the biggest bulk of my performing life has comprised just Dennis and me travelling the world together. There's an almost telepathic connection when we play. We can play selections of tunes together as part of medleys that might extend for a half-hour. I never know how many times I'm going to repeat any of these individual tunes before I transition straight into the next one. I'll usually give a nod to Dennis before the change, but he'll have somehow picked up the signal almost as soon as I've mentally made the decision to move into the next tune. On a few occasions, I have made the choice in my mind to move to the next tune, but just before it has been time to signal Dennis, I'll make a snap decision to continue without changing. I've watched Dennis switch to the next tune anyway, having somehow picked up on my plan just by hearing the intention in my playing, which I have communicated to him without even realizing it myself. That's how closely we are synced.

There are, of course, quirks about each other that we don't always find tolerable. I'm very intense when it comes to performing; it's as if I expect to constantly exceed all previous performances, with every single occasion an opportunity to reach a new, higher level. Dennis, on the other hand, is much more easy-going than me. He has a tolerance and acceptance of an OK gig, whereas I kick myself if it's not 110 per cent every night. There were times when we were exhausted, when the gigs weren't going as well as we'd have liked, and my intensity would become just too much for Dennis to bear. He would always forgive me on the basis that any angst between us was always about music and my desire to get it to the highest level. He knew it wasn't personal. We both trusted our underlying bond of friendship. I would never have been able to replace Dennis and I don't think he could have replaced me that easily either. The uniqueness of what we shared was too precious for either of us to walk away from. This was a collaborative artistic opportunity that seemed tailor-made for the both of us. Just like the bond of two brothers, it would have been impossible to replicate it with anyone else.

2 2

Despite my father's ill-health, he somehow managed to stay playing with the Tulla Céilí Band and going to music sessions right up until a couple of months before his death. On top of his Addison's disease, my father had also been struggling with Parkinson's. Whenever he would play with the band or attend the weekly session in Pepper's Bar, the band members or friends at the session would be there to support him. They knew he was really struggling to play but they also knew he still wanted to be part of it, so they all worked to make it as comfortable as possible for him.

In the first few months of 2001, his condition became more serious. Dennis and I were scheduled to tour Holland that spring, but I was able to make some time either side of the tour so I could fly home. My father was by then just resting quietly in his bed, tended to constantly by my mother, who was his primary caregiver. We knew he might remain this way for some months, so at the beginning of May I returned to the States. I had just arrived back when I received a call asking me to return home immediately. I got the first flight from Seattle to Shannon and made it home just in time. It soon started to sink in that my father, my friend, and my constant support, was about to leave my life for ever.

I stayed up with him that night I arrived and started thinking back to my childhood, all the nights of music and all the places we'd gone together with the band. I thought about the times he used to make us all say the rosary in unison as we made our way home from a gig. I thought about the days I spent out on the land with him saving hay and herding cattle, the endless hours in the bog footing turf and fighting midges. I went back through years of memories in my head, replaying them on a loop as I watched him resting peacefully. The image of the frail man in the bed was completely at odds with that of the strong, full-bodied man in my memories.

The following morning, I watched my father take his final breath and said goodbye to him one last time. When my father passed away, I began to see the totality of his life, with memories of the younger, stronger man, the more vibrant musician, the farmer, equally present alongside the images of the older, more frail man – all of him suddenly just a collection of memories and feelings within me. He and I had enjoyed a very close relationship and understanding, and his loss left me with a big emptiness inside, and yet there was some beauty in the whole experience also. It was a beautiful, sunny May morning. There were birds singing and I could hear a gentle breeze in the trees. I was comforted knowing that his life had been well lived, that above all he had been a good man, a kind and generous man, a gentle soul. Death is not the tragedy; the tragedy is not having lived well. In the end, money, wealth and status are less valuable than a sincere and kind heart. I put his tie on him after he'd been laid out in the room where he died. We waked him for the next two nights. There was a feeling of love and warmth in the house, and though we missed him deeply there was something sweet and beautiful in his transition.

When I got back to my apartment in Seattle, I felt an emptiness and loss. I was a bit rattled. When someone close dies, a part of us dies also. I was saying goodbye to a very important part of my life, and letting go of a huge support. I was acutely aware that I needed to steady myself and work through what I was feeling. I needed to grieve this loss. Soon after this, I started having some very vivid dreams. I would be in the middle of some situation and suddenly my father would be there, and his presence felt very real. The two of us would talk in the dream and acknowledge that his death and funeral had taken place, but we'd joyfully marvel in this dream about how death was not the end at all, that he had survived, that nothing had really happened, he was still with me. I found these dreams comforting, as if death could be met head-on and transcended.

I had been living in my own place in the Ballard district of Seattle for almost a year, since my relationship with Helen had finished. I had recently started seeing Liz Roth, who I had been working with for a couple of years. She had a booking agency in Seattle and had taken on Dennis and myself, booking concerts for us in performing-arts venues around the States. My apartment in Ballard was just off a lovely bike trail that ran along the edge of Lake Union on an old rail track that goes all the way along the north shore of the lake. I would cycle that trail most days and spend most evenings with Liz and her young daughter, Danielle. Just as with Helen I seemed to be choosing relationships with women with children who were either divorced or separated, as if I was unconsciously avoiding relationships that might involve a commitment to start a family. It seemed I was willing to sacrifice that possibility; my deepest commitment was always to music and I didn't want any other commitment to have to compete with that. Relationships were, in truth, essential to my existence as a musician. That need to return to the safety and warmth of a loving relationship was what made being out in the world actually possible for me. In the times when I would run out of ideas and was lacking in either confidence or inspiration, a loving relationship was a ballast that helped me get through those rough periods. I could never have flourished as a musician without the support and help that both Helen and Liz gave me at different stages of my life. On-the-road musicians know only too well what a rarity it is to find someone who understands our line of work and the commitment it requires. It takes a special kind of person to make a relationship work with a musician. For one thing, a deep trust must be there. It's not easy for either person when one spends so much time away touring. Compassion and empathy must also exist on both sides.

Eventually, Liz and I moved to Connecticut, where she was originally from. Her parents and sister were still living there, and she was keen to move closer to them, so we relocated to the East Coast, where we remained together for five years. My summers were normally spent in Ireland and Liz would travel there with me. One year, Francis Humphrys, the director of the arts organization West Cork Music and his then-partner Ruud Kuper, approached me about starting a festival of traditional music in Bantry, where West Cork Music is based. I'd never thought about being a festival curator or artistic director, but it seemed like an interesting challenge. They explained that West Cork Music would do all the administration and I could just dream up the kind of festival I'd like. I agreed and we set about putting a festival in place for the summer of 2002.

By then, traditional music was becoming more popular and was being accepted into mainstream society; a lot had changed in that respect since I was a teenager. The country seemed to be full of traditional music festivals, so I had to think about what we could add to the mix. I imagined that with all of this newfound popularity there might actually now be enough of an audience for a festival that wanted to delve deeper into the core of the music. If the West Cork Chamber Music Festival, which was (and still is) run by Francis, could present chamber music in a respectful manner that honoured the subtlety and refinement of that music, maybe we could do the same with traditional music. We often hear traditional music in loud and noisy environments, but here was an opportunity to present it in a way that might allow its subtlety of feeling and expression to be more easily heard and experienced. I wanted people to be able to hear the masters of this music up close in a relaxed and intimate atmosphere.

I normally structure my own concerts by using the tunes to paint a picture, to create a logical narrative for a performance with a beginning, middle and end. I try to achieve this by giving each tune its best placement and opportunity. Some tunes are best experienced after having heard others; some tunes are most effective when they stand out in contrast to the one previously heard – they each have an optimum placement in the performance. I used these very same ideas, along with my experience of shaping concerts with Dennis, to curate and structure evenings of music of other musicians. I try to place musicians and their music at just the right moment of the evening for the right amount of time. I'd try to create a balance of feeling and mood that all fitted together to form a coherent evening of music that also gave every musician the space and opportunity to be fully who they are. For the audience, this would be an opportunity to experience the tradition in a way that was both in-depth and comprehensive. Traditional music would now be presented using a chamber-music model, with recitals of traditional music being presented in the wonderful library of Bantry House, one of Ireland's most beautiful stately homes. This was an opportunity to treat the music with the respect I'd always felt it deserved. We also put on concerts in St Brendan's church in Bantry Square and in the local Maritime Hotel.

I have been curating the Masters of Tradition Festival since its beginning in 2002, and it is one of my favourite events of the year. It has been a great opportunity for me to get to know other musicians better and very often to collaborate with them during some of the performances. Over the years we've invited the very best traditional musicians to perform and there have been some really incredible evenings of music. Bantry House and Bantry town itself have proved to be a wonderful home for this music, and West Cork Music and its team of volunteers run this festival very smoothly and professionally.

In early 2002, Dennis and I had a heavy workload. By May, we were ready to embark on a number of Scandinavian gigs. I decided to travel ahead of Dennis as I had a complicated flight itinerary, travelling from Seattle. As I was switching planes in Minneapolis–St Paul, however, I received the distressing news that Gwen, Dennis's wife, had been in a traffic accident near their home in Chicago. Despite the best efforts of the paramedics, Gwen passed away. I was in complete shock. I tried to get a flight to Chicago straight away so I could be with Dennis, but my efforts were in vain. I had no choice but to stay in Minneapolis with my friends Mark and Mary Ann Stillman and fly out the next morning instead. When I got there, everyone was in disbelief about what had happened. Dennis was devastated. The days that followed were spent trying to come to terms with the news.

It was decided that Gwen would be cremated, her ashes scattered on a hillside near where she had grown up in her beloved Scotland. Myself and musician Jimmy Keane travelled with Dennis. For the entirety of the journey, he held Gwen's urn tightly in his arms. My mother travelled from Ireland, as did Matt Purcell and Gary Pepper, from Pepper's Pub in Feakle, where we had been playing for years. We all wanted to be there for Dennis and Gwen's family when they spread her ashes.

I told Dennis to take as much time as he needed; he could come back to doing gigs whenever it suited him. This was something Dennis had already given some thought to. He had already decided he wanted to come back sooner rather than later as playing music would be much more helpful to him than sitting at home in silence. I understood that completely. It was how I had felt after my father's death exactly a year and two days earlier. Music, for Dennis, was his therapy. Playing music provides a healing that not everyone can understand, but for those who do, there's no denying its restorative power. Many years later Dennis would remarry. He met a lovely woman named Mary, who is from New York and, like Dennis, grew up with Irish parents within an Irish immigrant community. They live in Chicago.

Over the next few years, the demand for gigs continued to increase, and in 2008 Dennis and I returned to Australia for another tour. As an indication of how hectic and international things were getting, I booked an around-the-world plane ticket on this occasion, going west from Connecticut towards Australia. We ended up playing a lot of festivals on that trip, including Womad, where Dennis and I performed on a stage under the cover of an enormous tree. The music and sound felt magical in the twilight and quiet of the location. We also played the recital hall of the Sydney Opera House on that tour. In the audience that night was Fergus Linehan, the director of the Sydney Festival and the man who had booked us for it the previous year. After the gig, our agent, Seamus Finneran, was chatting with Fergus and mentioned in conversation the Masters of Tradition festival that I had been curating in Bantry. Fergus was interested in maybe bringing some smaller version of that festival to Sydney. I'd never really considered the idea of taking the festival on the road and wasn't sure I knew how to do that, so I parked it for mulling over on my next flight.

My trip continued to Ireland, to accept the Gradam Ceoil Award in Killarney, a prestigious accolade which I was very honoured to receive. While there, I met a number of colleagues backstage, including singer Iarla Ó Lionáird. I asked Iarla if he'd be up for going to the Sydney Festival the following year. He said yes. I then put the same question to the great piper Liam O'Flynn, who also agreed. When I met accordion-player Máirtín O'Connor and asked him also, he too said yes, and that he'd perform with his bandmembers Cathal Hayden, on fiddle, and Seamie O'Dowd, on guitar. All of these musicians had been at the festival in Bantry and could therefore legitimately represent it in Sydney. And there was no way I was going to Australia without bringing with us our Australian-native son, Steve Cooney. (Steve now performs every year as part of the festival in Bantry, as the roaming house guitarist.) I'd very casually assembled the team just by running into them on my way home from Australia.

I didn't think any more about it for the next few months. Back in Connecticut, I was obsessed with the primary campaign that was taking place between Barack Obama and Hillary Clinton for the Democratic nomination. I wasn't against Hillary and believe she had the capacity to be a very good president, but had been very disappointed in her vote to go to war with Iraq. I was completely convinced that Barack Obama should be the next president. I hadn't been active politically since my teenage years, but Barack Obama was speaking a language that resonated with me. I volunteered for his campaign and went knocking door to door.

Touring was as hectic as ever, taking us to Japan, California, Switzerland, Holland, Italy, and several times to Ireland. Fergus

Linehan, meanwhile, had come back with some proposals for Masters of Tradition at the Sydney Festival. We were to do two nights in a row on the main stage of the Sydney Opera House. I thought he was completely mad, but it was his call. I spent a lot of time mapping out the musical contours of the show and decided I wouldn't just shape up an entertaining package; I wanted to take that audience into the heart of the music, and I wanted to reach out to them with the purest, deepest and most uncompromising version of this music. I also spent a lot of time thinking through the logistics of stage positions, lighting and sound. I had basically become the producer of the show, though not by choice. I simply hadn't thought about this side of things; I hadn't considered the complex logistical challenges of mounting a large show. There was only one hiccup in the process: Liam O'Flynn had to bow out. He was unable to make the tour, which meant I had to find another piper. I asked David Power, who is a truly amazing musician, and in the end he proved to be the perfect choice.

Ruud Kuper from West Cork Music was helping at the Irish end while Seamus Finneran was taking care of things Down Under, so the burden of assembling the show, both musically and technically, was fully in my hands, and I had just two days to pull this whole thing together and make it work. Much to my surprise, both nights at the Opera House were sold out in advance. So, no pressure . . . During the rehearsal, I was simultaneously picking pieces of music, deciding their durations, offering instructions on which microphones needed to be moved and when, where the light needed to be focused during each piece, when people would come on and off the stage, from which side they would enter, along with the task of organizing the section of the show where we'd all play together. I swore I would never again take on so much work. I also vowed that, from then on, I'd always have my trusted sound engineer Matt Purcell by my side. I had mistakenly thought it wouldn't be worthwhile dragging him to the other side of the world just for two gigs, and it was a decision I kicked myself for having made.

I walked on to the stage of this magnificent venue alone and talked to the audience about this music and its deep meaning for me. I was priming them for the nature of this experience. I wanted them to be swept up in the magic and wonder of the sean nós, the piping and our ancient harp tunes. I described our Masters of Tradition festival in Bantry, in order to put the performance in context for them. Then Iarla opened the evening with a solo unaccompanied sean nós song, 'Eistigh Liomsa Sealad'. Even though he was singing in Irish, there was still a deep, communicable meaning in his singing. He was able to convey a beautiful sense of invocation, a signal that this evening was going to be a journey into the heart. Iarla had plenty of experience singing in large spaces and knew instinctively how to work that wonderful hall. David Power was next, playing on his low-pitch set of pipes using the chanter from Willie Clancy's set. They were beautifully in tune and the sound of his pipes was amplified perfectly – his pipes sounded as big and powerful as a church organ. The audience just loved it. The worlds of the old sean nós singers and the great pipers of our past were brought to life on this magnificent stage. Between David's playing and Iarla's singing we had established a very solid grounding for Steve Cooney to build upon with his interpretations of our ancient harp music on guitar. Steve was returning to Australia as a master of a music form in which he had immersed himself after leaving the country. He was now sharing what he had found in the other hemisphere with his fellow countrymen, on the stage of the Sydney Opera House. Dennis and I then played, and we just loved the feeling of that space and loved playing with it. We could play as quietly or as loudly as we wished. This was followed by rousing, high-energy performances by the trio of accordion-player Máirtín O'Connor, fiddler Cathal Hayden and Seamie O'Dowd on guitar. They set the place on fire. We all eventually played together in a large semicircle, slowly working our way towards a musical crescendo at the end of the show.

I felt we'd managed to deliver a very true, uncompromised version of this music. The real thing doesn't have to be watered down, it just has to be presented carefully and with an element of thought that gives the audience a way in. The absolute worst thing one can do is underestimate the intelligence of the audience. Among the old players, there was a sense that audiences were mostly ignorant and wouldn't ever really understand this music, or ever understand who they were. I am convinced that audiences are fully capable of connecting with this music in a very real way; it just needs to be framed and presented with a bit of care and thought. In Sydney, thousands of people were transported by the subtle soulful beauty of Iarla's solo sean nós singing, David Powers' emotionally charged uilleann piping and Steve Cooney's ancient harp melodies on guitar.

I thought to myself that those two nights might also have

worked just as well if Willie Clancy, Darach Ó Catháin and Tommy Potts, from another time, had been onstage instead. Irish music doesn't ever need to be compromised to take the stage. In my world, growing up, any attempt at stage-craft or even any willing embrace of the stage was suspect, but I now knew that by subtly framing and curating the music, it can be given the space it needs without corrupting it; that even the most elemental and raw distillation of this music can become a transcendent experience if the audience is guided toward the true value of the experience. There is a video of the famous violinist Joshua Bell performing in a subway station with people mostly walking by, ignoring him. Many think that this tells us people don't really know the difference between a concert performer and a street musician. Instead, what I believe we are seeing is what happens when something is poorly framed and presented, so in a subway station, which could just as easily be the corner of a noisy bar, even discerning listeners may make a value judgement that stops them from listening with the attention required to hear what is right in front of them. The classical composer Gavin Bryars takes another approach in his most famous piece of music, 'Jesus' Blood Never Failed Me Yet', featuring a looped recording of the faltering voice of an anonymous homeless man singing a line from an old hymn. This framing of a homeless man's frail voice with a subtle orchestral arrangement becomes a deeply moving and powerful piece of music. These two stories tell us how easy it is to overlook the beauty and soulful humanity that is often right in front of us. Those two nights at the Sydney Opera House gave voice to some very subtle, detailed and emotionally powerful music, and for me it validated my sense that this old sean nós music can in fact sit comfortably on the concert stages of the world.

Eugene Downes, who had created the government-funded organization Culture Ireland, had travelled over to Sydney for the festival. Culture Ireland supports touring Irish arts all over the world and had financially supported this Masters of Tradition visit to Sydney. Eugene was very enthusiastic about the two performances and felt I should take it on the road, particularly to the US. So, we ended up doing a few US tours, and this time I remembered to bring my trusted sound engineer Matt Purcell with me. Those Masters of Tradition tours in the States were a big operation logistically, but were tremendous fun.

In 2008, the composer and musician Peadar Ó Riada suggested that we make a record together. Peadar is a powerful composer of tunes; his compositions sound as though they are hundreds of years old already, yet they all have a unique flavour that seems to convey the feeling of the enchanted landscape around his native Cúil Aodha in West Cork. Peadar is also a multi-instrumentalist, playing the concertina, accordion and harpsichord. For the proposed recording, he wanted to also include fiddler Caoimhín Ó Raghallaigh, whose playing I already knew and liked a lot. I had first met Caoimhín when he was a teenager many years earlier, when I was teaching a week of classes at the Fleadh Cheoil in Clonmel. I had also invited him more recently to Bantry as part of a duet with the very fine piper Mick O Brien. We all met in April 2009 at Peadar's home in West Cork, convening in the room known as

Seán's Library, where his famous father Seán Ó Riada had worked on his music. This historic room was still filled with his books, manuscripts and artefacts. For a few days we did nothing except talk and theorize about music. We didn't really know what shape this record might take, and when we came together to record the tracks that December, we still weren't clear. This is basically how the group Triur ('Three') was casually formed.

Peadar had sent ahead some tunes he'd composed, which I had learned. The recording session was very casual; Peadar had set up a minimal recording outfit. We brought our own microphones and just sat down and played some of the tunes that Peadar had written. We didn't listen back to very much of it, and so I assumed we were actually just sketching things out for a more serious recording effort down the road. Peadar kept producing tunes that we'd try to learn on the spot and then record. Caoimhín is really fast at learning tunes; I, meanwhile, was the last one over the hump every time. After a few days, just as we were scheduled to depart, Peadar said to me he thought we had an album there. I was stunned. I couldn't imagine that I'd recorded a whole album of music that I barely knew. I hadn't even so much as checked my microphone position for recording; it just felt like a preliminary exercise. I left it all in the hands of Peadar, thinking that when he listened back he wouldn't be long changing his mind and realize that the recording wasn't up to the mark.

As it turns out, the recording, *Triúr sa Draighean*, sounded really good. It's a recording I'm really proud of. There was something natural, unforced and elemental about it, as if we'd really captured the spirit of this music without overtly trying to do so. It was music that was both new and old at once. The recording came together out of a very relaxed process that was driven by simply letting happen what wanted to happen; there were no grandiose plans or aspirations, I didn't even think we were making a recording. We were just playing music in the moment and enjoying it, without feeling any pressure to produce any particular outcome. The attitude and level of trust we bring to the creative process is hugely important and really does impact the outcome, and sometimes, attempting to control the outcome gets in the way of letting the better music just happen. For me to make good music, the singular most important thing I try to achieve is to become fully present and mindful in the act itself, fearlessly letting go and trusting the outcome. Trying to let go is a bit of a paradoxical instruction, a kind of trying not to try. Freedom in the moment requires just being in the moment. Tibetan Buddhist monks often build mandalas of great beauty, using tiny grains of coloured sand to make sacred images. This is a painstaking exercise where the quality of the process is paramount. These mandalas symbolize the impermanence of life – as soon they are complete they are then ritually destroyed. I like it as a metaphor for the creative process; it's a lesson in loosening our attachment to the outcome and putting our trust in the process itself, as if the outcome was in some way incidental and not the most important part.

Between 2009 and 2010 I started laying the groundwork for a whole series of projects that would be developed over the following years. Dennis and I had finished recording our album *Welcome*

Here Again in 2008. We'd been touring as a duet all over the world and in some ways maybe we'd come to the end of something at an artistic level. We were still putting on good gigs, we were enjoying playing, but there was also the feeling that what we were doing had reached a certain plateau. I was living in Connecticut in a suburban environment and was feeling a bit cut off from the world of music and art that was happening in the big cities, particularly in New York. It felt almost as if those worlds were passing me by.

One day I was looking out across the backyard to the other nice houses of our neighbourhood from the upstairs window, where I had a comfortable office space and a studio. I was beginning to feel trapped and disconnected, and unable to move forward. I was having no new ideas but I had an itch to do something else; I needed to shake things up. Maybe I should go to New York, meet a few people, just see what I might discover? I needed to get connected to something – anything. I phoned Thomas Bartlett, now an adult, having once booked me for a gig when he was just thirteen. We met in New York for a coffee and chatted about what had been going on in our lives and what we were up to musically. Thomas suggested that we jam and maybe even record with a group of his regular go-to collaborating musicians. We set a date in January, just after the Association of Performing Arts Professionals conference, or APAP.

The APAP takes place every year in New York and is where managers, agents, and the people who book festivals and arts venues all over America, all convene. It's a big networking event and artists take part in showcases in the hopes of getting bookings, but it can also be a rather soul-destroying experience. The event is set up just like any trade show selling any commodity. Floors of the Hilton hotel are filled with trade booths and displays from the various agents and management companies. Every minute you're there, you feel like a commodity yourself, with either greater or lesser commercial value. The fact is, no matter how committed to the arts anybody is – and almost everyone there was deeply committed – in the end, whether they like it or not, everyone there is either buying or selling. Tommy Potts once famously said to someone who had embraced a professional career as a musician, 'You've now gone from artist to art dealer!' Whenever I did showcases at APAP, I always tried to keep my blinkers on, to avoid being psychologically sucked into the commodity-trading nature of the event.

As the conference was coming to an end, I met up with Iarla Ó Lionáird and his manager, Gary Sheehan, who were in New York for the APAP gathering. We got together at a diner just a few blocks away from the hotel, during which time Gary and Iarla pitched me on the idea of Iarla coming on the road with Dennis and myself to do some US dates. They knew they were pushing an open door with me, as I'd always been a huge fan of Iarla's singing. I told them that I was planning to get the Masters of Tradition, as a touring entity, off the ground, and naturally Iarla was going to be part of that, but as a separate venture from Dennis and me – I wasn't sure that Dennis and I alone could create a suitable soundscape for Iarla's singing in a trio situation. With the Masters of Tradition touring idea I was developing, however, Iarla could do his solo unaccompanied singing and it would be perfect. I still took on board the suggestion from Iarla and Gary about the trio idea, and I promised to give it some thought and see what I might come up with.

A few days later, in January 2010, I got together with Thomas for a recording session. We had agreed in advance that we'd split the cost of the day's studio time between us. Thomas thought we might come up with an album in a day. This ambition wasn't coming from a place of youthful naivety, just that Thomas is by nature a very confident and fast-moving musician and producer. From his perspective, recording an album in a day was entirely possible. I was more inclined to regard my studio fee as an investment in exploring possibilities. I arrived at the studio and went into an isolated sound booth separate from the other musicians, and there I started to play some tunes, just whatever came into my head, with everyone else doing their thing on bass, drums, guitar, banjo, bass clarinet and piano – the musicians were Sam Amidon, Doug Browne, Shahzad Ismaily and Peter Ecklund. Other than Sam and Thomas, the musicians didn't know the music I was playing, but they were very instinctive players who seemed open to any musical possibility.

From that day emerged some really beautiful moments and lots of interesting ideas, but not enough to make a recording. At the end of the session, I was standing with my fiddle in hand while Thomas was noodling something on the piano. I just started to play some tune that was in the same key, and that rhythmically fitted with the riff he was playing. It sounded very interesting, and from there I could sense a real musical possibility.

I left the studio that day with a sense that Thomas was someone who could do something interesting with traditional music. He still had that instinctive and intuitive feel for it that he'd had when I first met him as a young boy. Over the days that followed, I was still thinking about the conversation I'd had with Iarla and Gary. I began to imagine that Thomas, Dennis and I could really do something interesting with Iarla. Some months later, I learned Iarla was in New York, so I seized the opportunity and arranged for Iarla to meet with both myself and Thomas at the Irish Arts Center. Iarla was cautious and wanted to be sure that Thomas would be a good fit for him. Thomas and I jammed a little bit so that Iarla could listen and get a sense of Thomas. I think it was then that Iarla could see some real possibility.

The main hurdle I needed to overcome was in establishing a clear identity for this new project. Iarla and I had already done the Masters of Tradition touring show at Sydney Opera House. The whole premise of that event was its curated format, where different performers came on the stage to do their thing. If I was going to develop another project, it needed to be different in structure and organization. It simply needed to be a band with its own sound.

I'd spent a good bit of time thinking through how this four-piece band might function, trying to imagine what it might sound like. I felt like I needed another melody instrument, some-one to meet me in the playing of the tunes. I was already working with Caoimhín in the group Triúr and had found his playing very interesting. Caoimhín is a very creative musician and is also someone with a deep love for the old ways of playing, so there was certainly a great deal of compatibility all around.

As if I didn't have enough going on at that time, I had also agreed with composer Dave Flynn to play a fiddle concerto entitled *Aontacht* ('Unity') that he had written for me. This was to be performed in late 2010 at the National Concert Hall in Dublin, with David Brophy conducting the RTÉ Concert Orchestra. Dave Flynn had also made an orchestral arrangement of *Music for the Departed*, which was originally a commissioned work for a trio of guitar, fiddle and classical violin, which I'd only played twice before. This new, orchestrated version was to be performed on the same night, in addition to the fiddle concerto. The concert wasn't until the end of November, but I started working on the concerto that spring. It was thirty minutes of music and *Music for the Departed* was about twenty-two minutes. I had lots of music to memorize.

My plate was full, but the touring schedule continued as normal for Dennis and myself. That included coming back every year, without fail, to play the festival in my local village of Feakle. It wasn't so much an annual booking as a pilgrimage. In 2010 we did our usual Friday-night concert in the local church. A woman who for many years I'd only known by sight came up to me after the concert, while I was putting my fiddle back in its case. She timidly asked me if I knew who she was. I spontaneously answered, 'I always know who you are.' She was a familiar face at my concerts in Clare and there was some essential quality of inner beauty that I'd always been able to see in her. Sometimes we see a person and we just somehow know 'who they are'. In fact, I had first noticed her back in 1998 at a gig in Pepper's Bar in Feakle, when my mother pointed out that the people in the front row that night were all from Spain.

Now, she told me her name was Lina and said something about a children's centre and a new building she was opening. I didn't fully grasp what she was saying because right after a concert my mind tends to be a bit scattered. On the Sunday night of the festival, I joined the Tulla Céilí Band and I spotted her again. She was set-dancing and well able to do it. At the end of the dance, she once again spoke to me about her children's project and whether I might attend the official opening. They hadn't fixed a date for it yet but she said I could come by anytime to see the building. I gave her my business email address and asked her to send me more information – I'd take a look at my schedule and see if it'd be possible to visit.

After the Feakle Festival, I continued with my summer schedule, which took me to concerts in beautiful churches, castle courtyards and plazas around northern Italy, where Dennis and I often perform. While there, I responded to Lina's email: I was coming back to Ireland to do a few more gigs before I headed back to the States and there would be a day when I was going to be driving close by the newly built children's centre. I texted her that day to see if the place would be open, she said it was a good time and that she'd love to show me the building.

Driving down a narrow avenue, I finally reached the gate and saw the most beautiful building. It had thatch on one end, bright white walls, and red windows and doors just like the old, thatched cottages I'd seen growing up. It had a beautiful traditional farmhouse shape but, as Lina explained later, it was also a sustainable building, a stunning blend of new and old that honoured the indigenous farmhouse architecture of rural

Ireland. It was in some ways an architectural model of what I do musically.

As I was getting out of my car, Lina appeared at the red double-door entrance to the inner courtyard. She had made a winding stone path for the children leading to the doors, so I followed the contours of the path and wound my way towards the doorway where she was standing. We chatted as she showed me around, talking about music, education, Ireland, Spain, and before either of us knew it we were very quickly talking about more spiritual and philosophical matters. Our conversation had an ease and comfort to it, as if we'd known each other all our lives. We seemed to see the world in very similar ways.

We wandered around the building and stopped to chat in different parts of it. We ended up sitting beside the sandpit play area outside. I was wearing a pair of new Italian boots that I'd just bought but Lina was sinking her bare feet into the sand while we talked, as if earthing herself, connecting to the natural world. We each talked about our lives. I told her I was in a relationship and she told me about her three sons. Neither of us had ever been married.

We then took a walk down the wooded road, where she pointed to and told me about the thousand-year-old 'Brian Boru' oak tree that was growing close by. We also met her youngest son, Ivan, who was out on his bicycle. Lina had a vitality to her, an almost ageless beauty. As I was looking at her, all of a sudden a thought I'd never had before crossed my mind: 'I could marry this woman!' Now that I'd admitted it to myself, I felt sure of it. Driving away from there, I knew that something both irreversible and transformative had happened to me. We stayed in contact by phone over the next few days while I was doing some gigs before I returned to the States.

I couldn't stop thinking about Lina – there was no going back. I'd spent my life avoiding the deeper commitment of marriage but there was no way I could change direction now. I felt as though I would die if I didn't follow my heart. This was the first time something had become more important in my life than music. My relationship with Liz ended but our friendship continued. She and I still work together and are good friends to this day. She's a wonderful woman, and I'm grateful for the years we spent together.

The touring continued despite all the changes that were taking place in my private life. Nobody knew anything about what was going on, but a number of people said to me that I seemed much happier than normal. I knew why but I didn't say anything. I had my regular gigs to do, and soon it would be time to head for California. Dennis and I had been playing at the Sebastopol Celtic World Music Festival near San Francisco every year since the event had begun, fifteen years earlier. In addition to Dennis and me doing our annual performance, Cloud Moss, the director of the Sebastopol festival, had paired me up with different musicians over the years, and on this occasion Cloud came up with the idea of putting me with the guitarist John Doyle and flute-player Kevin Crawford. He knew that we'd all drunk heavily in earlier years but now were all teetotallers, so we were billed as The Teetotallers. We hit it off immediately, and playing with John and Kevin was a total pleasure – they are both truly powerful and creative musicians. We committed to take things further, to tour and do gigs, which we eventually did, though we have yet to make a recording. Every year the festival would wrap up at Cloud's home with his lovely wife Lori. Performers from the festival would be on the deck, in the kitchen, the living room, the backyard, the trampoline and the hot tub. Those were just absolutely wonderful, music-filled parties with great conversations and great food. We didn't know it at the time, but the Sebastopol farewell party after my partnership with John and Kevin would be our last, as sadly the festival funding fell through the following year.

Around this time, film-maker Art Ó Bríain was making a documentary about me and my relationship with music. This had been prompted by a suggestion from my friend Shane Kenny, who'd been coming to the Bantry festival as an audience member since the year it started. Shane was a prominent national political journalist, who had spent a term as Press Secretary in the 'Rainbow government' of John Bruton. When I got to know him, he had his own private media business. We'd spend long hours talking about politics and music, and still do to this day. He suggested that a film should be made to highlight my thoughts on music, so he approached Art and radio broadcaster Ellen Cranitch, who together managed to get the funding in place to do this.

Art accompanied Dennis and myself on our Japan tour and was also going to capture some of my collaboration with the RTÉ Concert Orchestra in Dublin. We became close friends during this process. We loved hanging out together. He had an infectious enthusiasm for discovering new insights into music, life or creativity. In Art, I found a mentor and confidant. He knew all about my situation with Lina. His advice on the matter was simple. He encouraged me to follow my heart in what I was doing and to fully commit to Lina at this point. He was like an older brother to me during this time of enormous change in my life, and his reassurance proved invaluable.

I had never done anything with an orchestra before and got a churning in my stomach every time I thought about performing the concerto in the National Concert Hall. This concerto was a tricky piece of music that demanded a lot of my attention and was proving to be a real challenge for me. It takes me a long time to absorb music, and this was an extraordinarily lengthy work, which meant a lot of memorization for me. The event was getting closer and closer, yet I felt nowhere near the end of having successfully memorized the piece. This might have been the only occasion where I'd have been relieved to know the hall was going to be half empty.

My part was intended to be performed without a score. The composer, Dave Flynn, wanted me to play this in a traditional music style where I could bend and shape the part around my playing style as I saw fit. The reality was that there was so much detail to be internalized that reaching that place of musical freedom seemed very far off. My whole family, as well as Lina, were going to be there, Art Ó Bríain would be documenting it, and here I was still unsure if I could even play it or not. I practised incessantly, also working on the piece while spending time in Lina's home, in the village of Tuamgraney. This music became the backdrop to the times I spent first getting to know her.

On top of doing the concerto, I also had to remember Dave's piece *Music for the Departed*, which I'd only done twice before. Dave had orchestrated a selection of traditional tunes from Dennis's and my repertoire for the evening also. This was all turning into a heavy lift – almost a full hour of detailed original material to learn by heart. For the first rehearsal, I got together with the orchestra in the same old RTÉ studio where I'd first recorded as a teenager. David Brophy was the conductor, while Dave Flynn was there to oversee this premiere of his work. They both knew how much information I was attempting to hold in my head while simultaneously trying to navigate this environment of unfamiliar cues. I was also trying to get comfortable with the very new experience of having seventy musicians playing alongside me.

In my normal performances I have a very free way of creating variations on tunes – I take tunes in different directions right in the moment of the performance. I play with a lot of abandon and I've normally got everything set up so that with the nod of my head I can alert other musicians to the musical transitions when the feeling is right for me, but I wasn't going to be able to do that on this occasion. We first rehearsed all the pieces in segments, and for the most part I got through with just a few stops here and there, where I'd lost my way. I felt terribly embarrassed in front of all these musicians when I got confused. For much of my time during the rehearsals I actually felt like the least capable musician in the room. It wasn't entirely obvious to everyone there that I was no longer functioning in the zone of my natural competence. Even though the parts written for me resembled how I usually played, it somehow didn't feel natural or instinctive to me to come at it this way. My variations are spontaneously created as I perform, but now the variations were already written for me. My best music emerges from a deep familiarity with traditional tunes, where I play from a place of complete freedom and instinct. This experience was completely at odds with that. Of course, this was just about me trying to adjust to making music in a different way; Dave Flynn had done a great job with the pieces he'd written for me.

The next rehearsal was at the National Concert Hall the day before the concert, where we again went through the pieces section by section. David Brophy is a very bright man and also understands the intuitive world that traditional musicians inhabit, so he was very good at signalling me in a way I could comprehend. I was amazed by his musical ear; he could hear the smallest of details anywhere in the orchestra. He had to manage the rehearsal time very carefully, prioritize what details to concentrate on, and do all this while managing a full orchestra of people. I was in awe of his remarkable skill and focus. Nonetheless, I didn't manage to get through the concerto without stopping up this time either. There was one more rehearsal ahead, on the afternoon of the premiere, so I would need to at least get it right that time. Shockingly, even in that last rehearsal I once again got lost somewhere in the middle of the concerto and we had to stop the orchestra and go back a few bars to pick it up again. I was genuinely beginning to panic. The concert hall was fully sold out.

There were four pieces to be performed in the concert. I had very kindly been invited to choose the first piece of the evening's programme. The orchestra would play this one alone, so I chose *Cantus in memory of Benjamin Britten* by Arvo Pärt. Next, there would be a medley of tunes that Dennis and I would play, with orchestral accompaniment arranged by Dave. Dennis and I would then play *Music for the Departed* with the orchestra. The last thing on the programme for the evening was the concerto. There was no guitar to keep me company on this one.

Backstage after the rehearsal, I was shocked and concerned that I had not yet played the piece correctly without stopping up. *If I get through the concerto without stopping up, it'll be the first time . . . If I can't get through it tonight, I will be humiliated beyond measure.* My first concert performance in Feakle, the night Joe Cooley played, was nothing compared to this. Maybe I was just an untrained fiddler from the mountain who had finally reached too far. I felt like a prisoner awaiting execution. The one bright spot was when Lina came backstage to give me a hug and wish me well. I prayed, I meditated and I surrendered to whatever was about to happen.

The orchestra played Arvo Pärt's *Cantus in memory of Benjamin Britten*, which appropriately starts with a tolling bell. I had a bit of a sickness in my stomach as Dennis and I went onstage to play. We began with our medley of tunes that Dave had arranged for orchestra, which ended with a very driving version of 'Tom Doherty's Reel', seventy musicians playing the chordal ideas that Dennis had originally crafted on his guitar for this tune. The audience absolutely exploded with the loudest, most enthusiastic audience response I have ever experienced. The warmth and welcome of the audience, and knowing that Lina was there, was a really big help going into the next piece, which was Dave's beautiful *Music for the Departed*. Dennis and I managed to get through that one and the audience once again loved it. Next up was the unclimbed mountain, the concerto *Aontacht*.

I took my seat close to David Brophy's conducting stand and the orchestra began their introduction. There is a slightly ominous quality to the orchestral harmonies that open the piece, the orchestra slowly building to a gloriously triumphant and grand crescendo. This was a slow build towards terror for me – my guts were in a knot. The music then resolves to a quiet drone and the fiddle begins along with a harp. I was on my way. Though it wasn't an absolutely perfect execution of the piece, I was none the less holding it together. After navigating the first few challenging sections, we finally made it to a calmer and simpler place in the music, where I finally could relax for just a few minutes.

Then, in the middle of a very simple phrase that needed to be repeated, I couldn't remember whether I'd played it once or twice already. It needed to be played twice and I was unsure. I looked at David Brophy, shifted down dynamically to draw attention, then repeated the phrase – for the third time! The good news was that the orchestra were just holding a drone at that point, so David was able to give them the signal to extend their note just a little longer. The concerto concludes with a demanding seven-part reel that I found to be both challenging and exciting. At the very end it seems as if every instrument is playing at its loudest in a kind of explosive rhythmic frenzy, and as we finished the audience erupted again into a frenzy of their own.

23

In January 2011, Dennis, Iarla and I made our way to New York for the APAP conference. The Masters of Tradition touring project was being showcased there and we were hopeful it would bring in some bookings. Not long after I arrived, I learned that fiddler Caoimhín Ó Raghallaigh was in town also, and I knew Thomas Bartlett was living in New York. I then realized that this was my first opportunity to bring everyone together and make the necessary introductions, with fingers crossed that everyone would just click.

We all met at the Cosmic Diner for a mid-morning breakfast. The name, I felt, was a good omen. It reminded me of that serendipitous book I had bought years earlier, *The Crack in the Cosmic Egg*. Everyone seemed to get along really well; there seemed to be good chemistry. For the first time in my life, I had intentionally assembled a band comprising musicians I'd handpicked myself. There wasn't one person at that table who wasn't capable of carrying a whole concert on their own – each musician was, in his own way, musically unique – yet we all had musical sensibilities and aesthetic preferences that we shared. I had played with each musician at the table already and had a sense of multiple cross-compatibilities that were likely to exist in the band. Caoimhín and I played together in *Triúr*, and I knew that Thomas was a big fan of Dennis's chording ideas. I also felt that Thomas and Caoimhín, when combined, would form a perfect soundscape for Iarla to sing over. I left the diner that day with my spirits high, feeling that we were on to something good. When it eventually came to choosing a name for our band, that honour would go to Caoimhín, who came up with 'The Gloaming'.

At this stage, I was still going back and forth between America and Ireland. Lina was in Ireland but most of the projects and tours that had already been planned were happening on the other side of the Atlantic. Meanwhile, in early March of 2011, Dennis and I received an invitation from the office of John Boehner, the then US Speaker of the House, to perform at the annual St Patrick's Day luncheon on Capitol Hill. The luncheon is a tradition started by Ronald Reagan and the then Speaker of the House Tip O'Neill to acknowledge their Irish heritage and to help Ireland, especially the situation in Northern Ireland. On this occasion, President Obama and Vice President Biden would be there, as would the then Irish taoiseach, Enda Kenny, the Northern Ireland leadership and all of the top leadership figures from the US Senate and House of Representatives, including Nancy Pelosi and Chuck Schumer. This was the ultimate confluence of my music and political interests.

I had seen videos of past musicians at this event, and I was aware how easy it would be for our performance to turn into some sort of background music. To guard against that, I first requested the organizers install a raised platform in the corner where we'd play. I wanted also to be sure that we'd begin the performance after everyone had finished eating. Performing over the chatter of the most powerful politicians in the world isn't any different from playing over anybody else's chatter. I didn't want just the honour of being there; it wouldn't mean that much to me if I couldn't also make some real music. I knew this wasn't a musical occasion – it wasn't even about the music – but I nonetheless intended to turn our segment into a real musical experience.

When we arrived in DC for the event, Dennis and I were met at the airport by one of those big, black, ultra-shiny SUVs, the kind that comes with a sharply suited driver wearing an earpiece. We were first brought to the Speaker's Office, then the House Committee on Ways and Means conference room, before eventually being escorted to the Rayburn Reception Room, where we were to perform.

When we arrived at our stage and took our seats, I was no more than twenty feet away from President Obama. I centred myself before sinking into the haunting air of 'Port Na bPúcaí'. I wanted to give it my all. I knew President Obama had an open musical mind and could potentially understand the music we wanted to express. Dennis and I wove our way through an extended medley of tunes that included the 'Obama Reel', composed by Peadar Ó Riada, ending with a driving version of the 'New Custom House' reel.

As soon as we had finished playing the last note, President Obama stood up from his seat and walked straight over to us: 'That was outstanding,' he remarked as he shook our hands and thanked us for our performance. Rather than bolt back to his seat, he continued to chat with us for a bit, mainly about Chicago. I even got to tell him how I had volunteered on his campaign. I experienced him as being a very warm and fully present human being, chatting to myself and Dennis as though we were the only two people in the room and as though he had all the time in the world to spend with us.

Nancy Pelosi and Chuck Schumer also made their way over to thank us, as did Gerry Adams and Martin McGuinness. It felt like a real gig, where we'd connected with everyone in that room in the way we'd do on any good night. I was thrilled to have met and connected with President Obama and all of these politicians that I'd been following from afar for so many years.

Our day at the White House hadn't quite drawn to a close, as we still had one more performance to go. A few weeks before, we had also received an invitation from the White House social secretary for Dennis and me to play their White House St Patrick's night party. After we had eventually gone through the extensive security check late that evening, we made our way into a room that was packed with senators, congress representatives and governors. We were all mingling when the instruction was issued that we were to form a receiving line, as President Obama and his wife, Michelle, would be arriving soon.

Both President Obama and the First Lady cut quite a dash as they walked through the room, Michelle equally as charismatic as her husband. Both were very warm and approachable, not to mention extremely good-looking. When President Obama reached Dennis and me in the line-up, he introduced us to Michelle and began telling her how much he'd enjoyed the performance earlier in the day and how she needed to hear us herself.

This was a much larger event than the luncheon. The National Chamber Choir of Ireland were performing there, as was singer Glen Hansard. There was a large crowd of people freely moving around the White House, which meant it wasn't as easy for Dennis and me to deliver the musical performance we'd have liked, but we did our bit, still on a high after feeling we'd made a very real musical connection with the president himself earlier that day. We spent the evening rubbing shoulders with senators and governors, including members of the Kennedy dynasty. I also had the pleasure of meeting Senator George Mitchell, an opportunity I took to thank him for his work in Northern Ireland. It's funny how my life of music has occasionally intersected with the world of politics, as if to remind me of the road not taken. But my happiness is in the making of music, and I know that the joy I get from that is one politics could probably never give me.

As much as I cherished our visit to the White House and Capitol Hill, I was even more excited about returning to Ireland to see Lina. Lina and I were madly in love at this stage and were all but counting down the hours until we could be in each other's company again. A few days later, I was on a flight back to Ireland, and after delivering a presentation on the music of Tommy Potts in my role as artist-in-residence at the University of Limerick, I headed straight for Cork, where I got to spend a few days with Lina in Ballymaloe House hotel, home to one of the county's finest restaurants and perhaps the most important culinary centre in the country.

During that time, Lina took me to Glenstal Abbey, a community of Benedictine monks, where her youngest son, Ivan, was boarding at the attached secondary school. The Abbey's Sunday Mass is a particularly beautiful experience, with lots of incense and plainchant sung by the monks along with one woman, Nóirín Ní Riain. I had backed away from the Catholic Church many years earlier, the repressive, controlling Catholicism of my youth made me feel as though I needed to liberate myself from it in some way. The reactionary Christian politics of America had also rubbed me up the wrong way; there was a point where I didn't even want to hear the word 'Christian'. I felt that I could be interested in any spiritual path other than Christianity, with the exception of the mystic Christian saints from earlier times. I also always liked the views of the poet-philosopher John O'Donohue on earlier Irish Christianity and his sense of connection to nature – that, I could relate to and appreciate. It didn't seem as though there was a Christianity of my time that I could connect to in the same way. As a result of this disconnect from the church, it was many years since I had attended a Catholic Mass, outside of the obligatory funeral or wedding services, of course. The Mass at Glenstal Abbey, however, was a beautiful, ritualistic experience amplified by plainchant and incense that seemed to echo the sentiments of a deeper, older and more independent Irish Christianity. At the end of Mass, a church organist played some very edgy modern musical compositions that were completely startling, especially after having just listened to the plainchant. That musical juxtaposition was just a hint of the broader and more expansive thinking that was part of this monastic community. Lina and I went to Glenstal repeatedly for this Sunday Mass, the main purpose being to see Ivan. After Mass, the monks provide tea and scones. In the course of the Sunday conversations that took place around those cups of tea, I ended up getting to know many of the monks, including Abbot Mark Patrick Hederman. I discovered that these monks were freethinking men of faith. This was a different, bolder and more questioning Catholicism than I ever realized existed. The experience of Glenstal was a kind of welcoming-back to a more open and thoughtful Catholicism.

While at Glenstal, Lina bought me a book by Abbot Hederman called *Manikon Eros. Mad Crazy Love* was the subtitle, and a fitting description of how Lina and I were both feeling at that time. Lina was bringing me back to a new Ireland, a new experience of Christianity, and a more complete connection to my own heart. I was deeply in love with her. I wanted for nothing, I hardly even needed food, to be honest. I felt completely alive and satisfied, without that nagging need for something else. We don't stay in that phase for ever, but we do learn what our relationship can give us – we now know its true potential.

On 29 March 2011 I was getting ready to go and do a few European dates before heading over to the States for a few days, then on to Japan for some gigs there. That day, I asked Lina to accompany me on a walk to the 'Brian Boru' oak tree that she had pointed out to me that first day we met. I couldn't think of a more fitting location for me to get down on bended knee and propose.

24

To my delight, it was a yes from Lina. The excitement meant it wasn't long before wedding plans were actively underway. I also had a lot of projects on the go and a number of agents had booked gigs for me to do. I was stretched trying to give attention to all these spinning plates, so I asked Gary Sheehan, Iarla's manager, and Foye Johnson, Thomas Bartlett's manager, if they could handle the logistics of booking rehearsal time and putting together an Irish tour for The Gloaming. We decided on Grouse Lodge Studios in County Westmeath as the place where we'd first get together to work on our music. Here, we'd have both accommodation and a recording space in which to document what would come out of the rehearsals.

Everyone arrived with some material in mind. The first tune I threw into the mix was 'Dick Cosgrove's Reel', a favourite of my father's. It was a tune that Thomas and I had already explored in our recording session in New York. We all started to play with considerable freedom, just letting the ideas emerge, allowing ourselves to be prompted by what the others were doing. Not all ideas survived, but a sound gradually began to develop – a moody, atmospheric sound that was simultaneously old and new. We also split into groups at times just to shape out some rudimentary ideas. This band was going to sound different; it was emerging from places other than the more common strains or styles of traditional music.

Caoimhín was a player whose musical inclinations were more towards the raw, elemental style of Sliabh Luachra fiddle-playing and simultaneously towards the improvised exploration of tone and texture. Iarla, meanwhile, was a genuinely unique sean nós singer, grounded in the rich Cúil Aodha singing tradition, who'd also been working at the margins, with contemporary classical composers, while singing with the band Afro-Celt Sound System. Thomas, while familiar with traditional music since childhood, was able to bring his own colour to the music as a result of his diverse musical experience as a record producer and having worked with the likes of Norah Jones, The National and David Byrne. Dennis and I had already shaped our own interpretation of traditional music, which we brought to the table. The ingredients that made up this band were considerably different from other traditional bands', both in terms of the musical styles and the instrumentation – we had two fiddles, a piano, a guitar and vocals. This wasn't a very typical set-up.

All of us were very sensitive players for whom mood and feeling were paramount. We shared a reverence for the music of people like Tony McMahon, Padraig O'Keeffe, Tommy Potts and Darach Ó Catháin, while at the same time there was also an openness towards bands like The National, Sigur Rós and Radiohead. Thomas and I were both fans of the American jazz pianist Keith Jarrett, Dennis loved the music of Bill Evans, and we all loved the guitarist and composer Bill Frisell. We didn't have a plan to force any particular outcome; our feeling was that it would work best if everything emerged in the most organic way possible, just following our intuition, not trying to make a fusion but also not blocking any influence that might naturally work its way in as we chased the feeling of each piece of music.

A small Irish tour was booked for the end of August that year. The National Concert Hall was our first date and it was already sold out by the time we got together at Grouse Lodge. My only concern was that the band might not have the groove and drive that I felt we'd need to make the concert a complete success. Moody introspection immediately seemed easy to the band, as did ambient soundscapes and minimalism. Iarla brought a selection of his favourite sean nós songs to the table, as well as some Irish-language poems both modern and ancient, which offered an opportunity to create more contemporary-sounding melodies and arrangements around these texts. This is where the band's more modern sound began to emerge. Thomas and Iarla worked closely together to develop these songs.

While we were experimenting at Grouse Lodge, I was keeping track of the various pieces of music that were emerging and was simultaneously constructing a set list for our first performance, both in my mind and on paper. We decided the best way to speed up the operation was to bring in some of the pieces that Dennis and I had been working on and just build out from there, basically expanding on what we'd already been doing. For example, Dennis and I had been in the habit for many years of playing extended medleys of tunes that might sometimes start with a slow air, go from there into some gentle tunes, then maybe into an improvised section, followed by some driving rhythmic reels at the end. We could immediately substitute a sean nós song from Iarla in place of the slow air I'd often play, Thomas could now improvise on sections where Dennis and I might ourselves previously have improvised while he also extended Dennis's chording, and Caoimhín and I could swap back and forth, alternating between being the lead melody and playing a supporting role. Connecting the tunes together eventually became a creative opportunity where we'd make loose arrangements that allowed us to sometimes collectively improvise our way to the next tune.

The set list we were preparing for this debut concert was gradually taking shape and the selections from my and Dennis's duo repertoire were providing the drive and power we needed. The first item was a medley of different tunes that for the moment we just called 'The Opening Set'. They say first impressions are important and I wanted the band to make an impression right from the start. 'The Opening Set' starts with Thomas on piano just hinting ambiguously at the melody of 'Cois an Ghaorthaidh', at which point Iarla then begins singing. This leads nicely into Caoimhín playing a stunning and beautifully textured version of that melody, after which the three of them continue with the song together. I come in at the last bar of the song and start improvising my way from there to the next tune, and so begins a selection of tunes mainly from my and Dennis's repertoire. Some of these melodies were from the record of my father and Paddy Canny, some I'd learned directly from my father in the kitchen as a child. The medley ends with 'Tom Doherty's Reel', which

Dennis and I had performed the previous year with the RTÉ Concert Orchestra.

On 20 August we were met with a full house as we walked on to the stage of the National Concert Hall and went straight into 'The Opening Set'. Having the first gig be a sell-out in a beautiful concert hall is a strong start for any band, but on top of that our opening piece was received with wild applause from the audience, the response every bit as enthusiastic as it had been when I'd performed with the RTÉ orchestra back in November. That first moment of the band onstage was recorded and about a year later we ended up releasing 'The Opening Set' from our first performance as a digital download through the *New Yorker* magazine website.

Less than a month later would come the biggest event of my life. Lina and I got married on 2 September, a year and a day after we sat talking that auspicious afternoon at Brigit's Hearth Early Years Centre. Our wedding day was intimate and beautiful, exactly how we wanted it. People often say they're nervous about getting married and sometimes have doubts, but I can honestly say I had none, which is probably a surprise considering I spent most of my life unable to even envision myself wanting to get married, such was my phobia of commitment. Meeting Lina changed all that in a millisecond. She and I broadly share the same philosophical, spiritual view of life, and she has lived her life with a similar kind of faith and trust as I have. Lina encourages me every day to realize my potential, to become who I really am and to own my own life. Lina and I face the same challenges that all couples do. We can drive each other crazy sometimes, but we always remember the deep, beautiful experience of love that

336

brought us together and continues to sustain us. Our marriage is our commitment to loving and supporting each other as we seek to evolve and grow.

After twenty-six years of living in the States, I had moved back to Ireland. In truth, I'd never lost contact with the country, and even though I had been very happy in Chicago, Seattle and Connecticut, I suppose I always harboured the same quiet wish that most emigrants have, which is to return home. Professionally and personally, 2011 was a very generous year to me.

For a touring musician, the luxury of having time to 'settle into married life' isn't always a feasible one. Some of the bookings I had to do were scheduled before I'd even met Lina. Thankfully, Lina is a very understanding person and she knew the nature of my professional life. After a short honeymoon in Glendalough, County Wicklow, Lina and I found ourselves travelling around Ireland with the Irish Chamber Orchestra – Dennis and I were touring Dave Flynn's arrangement for us of his composition *Music for the Departed*.

About a month later, I was back in New York, this time to the venue La Poisson Rouge to perform for a recording of Philip King's *Other Voices* TV programme. Thomas Bartlett was the house band director for those two nights, while the recording itself included all kinds of famous artists such as Laurie Anderson, Bryce Dessner, Martha Wainwright, Paul Muldoon, Glen Hansard, Roddy Doyle, Damien Rice and Gabriel Byrne. As I walked on to the stage to do my bit with the band, I gradually detected a low-end driving pulse propelling the music forward. I was at the front of the stage so I couldn't see who was actually behind me, much less recognize what instrument was making the pulse. It transpired the sound was emanating from a bass clarinet and the man behind it was Doug Wieselman, whom I'd somehow walked past without spotting. He was completely locked into the groove, his rhythm lifting me off the stage. Remarkably, we'd never played together until that moment, but I knew right there and then that I wanted to play with him again.

Fortunately, it wasn't long before the opportunity to do so arose. When myself and Aidan Connolly, of New York's Irish Arts Center, started brainstorming a series of collaboration ideas that I'd perform there during a two-week residency, Doug was top of my list. He was all up for it, and together with Dennis and Thomas we did an evening at the Center that was just an incredible musical experience. Doug worked particularly well with Dennis, both harmonically and rhythmically. Lina also loved the performance, and felt that I should definitely work more with Doug, suggesting that I create an ensemble where I could work with him on a regular basis. I'd kept this idea of playing with Doug in the back of my mind, but felt that if I were to include Thomas and Dennis, I'd essentially be creating a different version of The Gloaming. The idea of a quartet, however, continued to simmer away in the back of my mind.

When you play with different numbers of musicians in a group, each configuration brings a different dynamic. I had played in duets, trios and quintets, so I was intrigued to discover what the dynamics of a quartet might produce. I didn't have my fourth member yet, so this was still a bit of a puzzle. Luckily, it was a puzzle that didn't take long to complete.

For several years, I'd been teaching at the Celtic Week of the Swannanoa Gathering at Warren Wilson College in North Carolina. It was one of the music camps that I enjoyed most, and where a lot of lifelong musical friendships were formed. One of the regular teachers there was a gifted fiddle-player from Kentucky called Liz Knowles. I'd first met Liz some years previously at a teaching event in Nova Scotia. She was originally a classical violinist but took up Irish music while studying music at Stony Brook University in New York, after hearing New York-based Irish-American fiddler Eileen Ivers perform. Liz and her husband, the piper Kieran O'Hare, along with my own former bandmate the singer-guitarist Pat Broaders, went on to form a lovely traditional music trio called Open the Door for Three. Even though she was a strong traditional player, moving into another genre is always tricky and it seemed as if Liz felt like an outsider to this music. Nonethless, whether Liz fully realized it or not, she had in my opinion worked her way right up to the top tier of traditional fiddle-playing.

I was aware that Liz had previously played in a group called Ensemble Galilei that centred around Baroque, Renaissance and Celtic music. The combination of that background with her solid traditional Irish fiddling made Liz seem a good choice as the fourth member of the quartet. I told Liz I imagined the quartet could offer her an opportunity to pull together all the different aspects of her playing, which has proved to be the case.

As I was now also fulfilling a new position, Irish World Academy Artist, at the University of Limerick, the university board had agreed to fund some of my artistic endeavours. The 'Martin

Hayes Quartet' seemed like the perfect project for this. We decided to rehearse at the university for a few days.

I had already sent Dennis, Doug and Liz the material I wanted to work on, along with Dennis's chording. This gave us a good starting point. The quartet started out as an expansion on what Dennis and I had already been performing. Liz turned up with some beautiful arrangements already in place, while Doug turned up ready to improvise. In a matter of hours, the fundamental sound and character of the quartet had emerged. We gave a small sample performance at Limerick University's Irish World Academy of Music and Dance and went from there to our first official gig, in St Patrick's Cathedral at the Dublin TradFest festival, which seemed to go over really well. We now existed as an actual musical entity.

In 2012, Art Ó Bríain's documentary on my music, *Natural Grace*, was premiered as part of the Galway Film Fleadh. The documentary was launched by my friend Billy Loughnane, son of the fiddler and politician Dr Bill Loughnane, who been such a support to me in my earlier life. It was a special afternoon, made all the more memorable when I received an unusual phone call. As I stood in the lobby of the Town Hall Theatre, an American number appeared on my screen. The caller introduced himself as Paul Simon. I heard the name, but it still took a second for the proverbial penny to drop. For so many years, I had listened to Paul Simon's music, and now here was the man himself on the other end of the line inviting me to play with him at his concert in Dublin that July. He said he'd send me a song from his most recent album that he'd like me to perform with him in his upcoming Dublin concert. As he was talking, I was trying to piece together how I came to be on his radar. I later found out from Iarla that Paul Simon had gone for dinner with his friend, the poet Paul Muldoon, who had brought Iarla along with him. Paul and Iarla brought up my name in the course of the conversation, telling Paul Simon about my music and what I was doing. I can only assume that Paul must have then looked up my music for himself and decided that he'd like to have me involved in his gig.

It was only few days later, after I arrived at Dublin's O$_2$ Arena for the rehearsal, that I met Paul Simon for the first time. He was very friendly and welcoming, and introduced me to the members of his band. We went through the song he'd sent me, then we picked a jig on which he could do some guitar accompaniment. I thought I was done and dusted, ready for the gig, when Paul asked if I'd like to play on his famous song 'The Boxer'. Naturally, this wasn't an offer I was going to turn down. Paul told me I could take the solo section. I didn't actually know this section – I only had a vague sense of it – so I downloaded it to my phone afterwards and found a quiet spot in the catering area backstage where I could quickly learn it.

The concert itself was unforgettable. It was a real privilege to be onstage with Paul and a thrill to be cheered on by the audience when I got to play the solo section of 'The Boxer'. After that gig, whenever Paul knew Ireland was on his schedule, he'd call me up and invite me to join him. On one occasion, I had the honour of joining him on his double-bill show with Sting. Paul and I also flew over from the States to play at the memorial concert to the poet Seamus Heaney at the National Concert Hall. Paul Muldoon was with us at the time, and during the plane journey he helped Paul Simon work on a special song for the event that would merge lines from a number of Seamus Heaney's poems. I spent much of the journey trying to keep up with the constantly-changing melody of the song as it evolved. The event at the National Concert Hall turned out to be a most beautiful tribute to a poetic great whose work I myself had grown up reading.

I was beginning to become very familiar with the NCH as a performance space. My friend Gary Sheehan, who'd previously organized a collaboration and tour for Dennis and me with the great American jazz guitarist Bill Frisell, was now the head of programming at the venue. Gary invited me to curate two concerts for the summer of 2013. Gary loves to brainstorm. He and I would sometimes just sit around chatting and dreaming up project ideas. I regard those conversations and encounters as also being part of the creative process – I try to respond and listen as if already in a creative act. The decisions and choices made in those moments significantly impact how things go.

For the first concert, I would present the touring version of the Masters of Tradition, and for the second we came up with the idea of a collaboration with the great musical master Jordi Savall, whose music I had fallen in love with many years earlier, when living in Chicago. I first heard his playing on the soundtrack of the beautiful movie *Tous les Matins du Monde*. The story of the movie, which is based on the music and life of the seventeenth-century French composer Marin Marais, seemed to echo for me the musical devotion of Tommy Potts. Jordi is one of the most celebrated and renowned figures in the world of early Western music and has recorded and brought to life an incredible amount of music from the medieval, Renaissance and Baroque periods. You can hear the silence around his music, the last subtle granular sound from his bow-stroke on the viol da gamba still retaining his full presence. He had also just started to include some Irish music in his repertoire, having recorded a whole album of Irish and Scottish music that included a tune I love to play, 'The Humours of Scariff', so for me this almost felt like an invitation to reach out. Once again, Gary made it possible for me to collaborate with another of my musical heroes.

I was hoping that I could get Jordi to play some of his solo Marin Marais and Sainte-Colombe pieces from the film, but he seemed very intent on staying within the realm of Celtic music. He wanted to bring harpist Andrew Lawrence-King from Guernsey and Scottish bodhrán-player Frank McGuire, both musicians on Jordi's *Celtic Viol* album. I thought it would be a nice symmetry to this gathering if I included Triúr, my trio with Peadar Ó Riada and Caoimhín Ó Raghallaigh. We were already very familiar with the pieces that Jordi wished to play and we had also shared lots of Peadar's music with him, so we had plenty of material we could work with. The two trios each provided very different takes on this music. Jordi was looking at this music as another ancient European music form that he'd go about interpreting the way he might do with Renaissance or Baroque music. Meanwhile, Triúr had all the sounds of an old Irish music-style that you might have expected to hear sixty or seventy years ago.

To open the concert, I went onstage to introduce Jordi and to play a tune on my own. Since Jordi wasn't going to play any of the early French music I'd hoped he would, I followed a suggestion from Lina and surprised him by playing the first tune on the soundtrack album *Tous les Matins du Monde*, a march by the seventeenth-century composer Lully. The trios did their individual slots and came together at the end as one large ensemble, where the barriers between the musical styles of early Baroque music and traditional Irish music disappeared and the melody just blended into one unified expression.

When I listen to Jordi play that old heavenly music of Marin Marais and Sainte-Colombe, the idea that civilization is advancing becomes questionable. My Italian friend Fabio, who plays the uilleann pipes and with whom I play in Italy most summers, has an apartment in Savona that doesn't have any modern art or furniture. Everything within its walls is hundreds of years old. Even the music he plays and listens to is from a different age. He has no interest in the modernity of the present, he wants nothing more than to nourish his soul with the subtle refinements of bygone times, and he has been a huge fan of Jordi for years. I remember being in the front seat of his car as we drove along the winding motorways of northern Italy, through tunnels and sharp bends, listening at loud volume to the slow-moving, refined subtleties of the music of Sainte-Colombe as played by Jordi Savall. In his playing, each note is savoured, almost as if there won't be another to follow. Fabio, typically Italian and driving at high speed, would hold out both hands, palms up, and exclaim, 'The atmosphere!' I love the music too, even if the trauma of every car accident I'd ever had would run through me at that very instant. Fabio flew in for that NCH gig, and when we reached the hotel after the concert, I had him play a slow air on the pipes for Jordi.

In the early days of The Gloaming, I had a small book in my possession called *Wabi-Sabi: For Artists, Designers, Poets and Philosophers*, which I shared with the band. Wabi-Sabi is a Japanese philosophy of aesthetics that values the natural over the synthetic, the worn over the new, the imperfect over the perfect. It honours earthiness and suggests that beauty can be teased out of the raw and elemental. There was something in these contrasts that I thought could help define a musical and philosophical framework for the band. The language of aesthetics contained within this book was perfect for describing the elemental sources of our music.

Most people tend to like jeans that have a worn feel, clothes with a vintage look or a piece of antique furniture that shows the marks of time. This area of aesthetic appreciation, which is rarely applied to music, provides a language and structure that allows us to artistically describe the raw and elemental parts of the music I grew up with. Traditional music in the hands of the old masters who had influenced Iarla, Caoimhín and me had an earthiness that has often been misunderstood. Caoimhín specializes in exploring this beauty, drawing lots of inspiration from the uniquely textured sounds of the music played by old fiddlers such as Dennis Murphy, Julia Clifford and Padraig O'Keeffe. Iarla and I also draw upon these kinds of older sources. There is a way of actively listening with an open mind to the music of these older players and singers where we can gradually discern their musical intention and join them in their imaginative journey, delving into a place of deeper musical meaning. The Gloaming, while it may have a modern take on Irish music, can also be seen as a homage to the older and more rustic strains of the music. I remember being asked in an interview if I was concerned what the purists might think of what we were doing. I remember I replied: 'We *are* the purists.' Iarla, Caoimhín and myself were three musicians whose whole musical grounding was the distillation of the oldest and most elemental strains of the music. Irish music has repeatedly shaped itself to meet the new day and The Gloaming was simply one more instance of that.

For the next few years, The Gloaming basically travelled the circuit that Dennis and I had been doing, mostly surviving on the fan base that Dennis and I had built up over the years as a duet. It wasn't until 2015 that the band started to generate its own following in a really significant way. The interest in The Gloaming during those early years was wonderful but the band was actually cutting into my income. The most lucrative gigs that just Dennis and I would normally do, in Ireland and the US, were now being done by a five-piece band with a manager. The Gloaming was more or less receiving the same fee as a full band as Dennis and I received as a duet. I didn't mind the loss of income, though. I was enjoying the music we were making, and sometimes you have to take a risk and just accept the loss in order to make things happen.

A significant breakout moment for the band came when we were invited to play the Royal Albert Hall in London in April 2014, in a concert put on as part of President Higgins' state visit to the UK. The broadcast would be viewed by millions. Most importantly, however, we wanted to make President Higgins proud. He had been regularly coming to see the band and we were always honoured that he'd take the time out of his busy schedule to see us perform. The first night he showed up, we were playing Dublin's Vicar Street venue. He came in ahead of the gig in a very low-profile way and made his way to the green room, where he took a seat. We all knew him, except for Thomas and his buddy, singer Sam Amidon, who was joining us onstage that night. After a half-hour of chatting with Thomas and Sam, President Higgins got up to leave and bade goodbye to the two lads. It was only afterwards that they were made aware they'd just been shooting the breeze with the president of the country.

For the gig at the Royal Albert Hall in London, President Higgins requested we perform 'The Opening Set'. He wanted it to be the penultimate piece of the evening, just before all the artists would come back to the stage for the finale. It was an exhilarating experience for us, and the night itself was one for the history books. We were honoured to have played our part.

The producer of that live broadcast, for BBC and RTÉ, was Philip King, whom we knew well. Philip had already made a documentary about The Gloaming called *Moment to Moment*, which was released in 2014 and centred around how we first came together. We had also appeared on Philip's TV programme *Other Voices* that same year. Philip's work in filming the band and championing our work contributed significantly to the growing popularity of our music. You could make the most beautiful music in the world, but the music won't find its listeners without the help of people like Philip who can provide the platform to bring it to the masses. These are the people who bring the magic to life on a stage far bigger than any venue. Philip's work played a very big part in the overall success of The Gloaming.

25

T HE SOUNDS OF India have remained with me since the mornings in Chicago when I would listen repeatedly to my first CD featuring the Indian violinist L. Shankar. That was just my introduction – I went on from there to listen to lots of Indian music. India's music, much like Ireland's, has so much history behind it. The *ragas* that form the basis of the music can be traced back at least a couple of thousand years, to the sacred Vedic chants of the Hindu temples. For any musician with an interest in tradition, India holds a very captivating energy.

Fortunately, I was able to explore this for myself in December 2014, after Cork-born business consultant Áine Edwards, who was living in Chennai, proposed that Dennis, myself, and the Ireland-based Australian-Indian sarod-player Matthew Noon, travel to India for a music tour. I didn't have to be asked twice – neither did Lina, Dennis or Matthew! India appealed not only to my musical side but also to my spiritual side, its mysticism having always attracted me.

With the Christmas lights of Dublin Airport glittering behind us, we headed for India, excited for the trip ahead. Filming the whole tour was my friend and Dublin-based music film-maker

Myles O'Reilly, who was there with his lovely wife, Aideen. The documentary he made of the tour is called *The Sound of a Country*. On the first evening, as we were driving along a highway in Delhi, we saw an elephant casually walking along one of the many lanes. You wouldn't see that in Chicago! I nudged Dennis and said, 'Remember the "Psychic Elephant" you used to wake up hearing on the stereo when we lived on St Louis Ave?'

We met so many interesting people in India, including a young pianist by the name of Utsav Lal, who had been invited to do a musical collaboration with us. I was just going along in good faith; I didn't know anyone in India or have any idea who I was going to be collaborating with beyond Dennis and Matthew. One evening we visited the home of Utsav's parents to rehearse for a gig that would be taking place a few days later in Delhi. At one point during the rehearsal, Utsav turned to me and asked if I knew some particular piece. Despite repeated attempts, I just couldn't make out the name of the tune he was asking for. Eventually, I realized he was asking me if I'd play 'N'Fheadar', a tune of Peadar Ó Riada's that we'd recorded with Triúr. Both Utsav's enunciation and pronunciation of 'N'Fheadar' were perfectly clear; it was just that I wasn't expecting to hear any request like that in Delhi! Utsav is a truly amazing pianist. During our visit, I found out that he had spent a great deal of time in Dublin in his youth and that in addition to playing Indian classical music, he also knew how to play traditional Irish music quite well. Since our trip, I've been fortunate enough to collaborate with him on a number of other occasions.

We all had a wonderful time in India. We absolutely loved the people we met there and the music we got to hear. We met the most extraordinary Indian musicians there, such as tabla-percussionist virtuoso Zakir Hussain and the great Indian violinist L. Subramaniam. We also spent time in Chennai at the Brhaddhvani music centre with the great vina-player Professor Karaikudi S. Subramanian, with whom we also did a concert.

One of the highlights of the trip was being able to see the master-musician himself, my old mentor, Tony McMahon. Tony was now spending part of his year in India, and Áine Edwards, who made the trip possible, knew Tony very well and had arranged for us to meet up. It was incredible to see Tony again and to have such a beautiful place to provide the backdrop to our memories. We caught up on everything, from life at home to life on the road. It was just one of the many special moments I experienced during such a beautiful, soulful trip.

We had a wonderful time everywhere we went, making connections and friendships with lots of people. We found the people of India to be very open and friendly, and full of warmth. We were struck by the bright, vibrant colours everywhere. On a free day during the tour, Lina and I sneaked off to the spice market in the centre of Old Delhi. It was like a glimpse of life from another time, a place that looked as though nothing had changed in a thousand years. The sounds, smells and feeling of India are something we will never forget.

Back in Ireland, success for The Gloaming was on the up. As a result of our increasing popularity, we won Album of the Year in the 2015 Meteor Choice Music Prize, fending off some serious competition from the likes of Hozier, U2 and Sinéad O'Connor.

We were the first traditional music band ever to win this award. It was a moment when the division between mainstream culture and traditional music no longer seemed to exist. The Gloaming was just music.

That same year, we sold out three nights in a row at the National Concert Hall. Ticket sales gradually grew in the years following, to the point where our dates would be extended to seven consecutive nights, with some of the first concerts selling out in under fifteen minutes. I had never imagined that our music would be this appealing or popular. We then toured all over the US, Europe, Australia and even Mexico. My father would have liked to know that we finally made it to Carnegie Hall. My mother was there this time, to celebrate her eighty-fifth birthday, having been at the Royal Albert Hall performance for her eightieth.

Whether it is Carnegie Hall, the Sydney Opera House, the Kennedy Center in Washington DC or the National Concert Hall in Dublin, walking on to a stage with this band is always a joy. There is a comforting feeling of safety and confidence, as if nothing can really go wrong. I'm filled with anticipation for the night's unknown musical twists and turns that have yet to emerge. The band has a capacity for improvising that allows anyone to feel free to toss in some musical idea in the knowledge that the other musicians will collectively respond and embrace whatever was offered. The music is flexible and different every night, the energy changing from one performance to the next, and we relish the moments of uncertainty when we're all engaged in a collective improvisation, not knowing how or when it will end. We love that we don't know.

All of the musicians in the band like to live on that knife-edge of instantaneous response. One of my things, going onstage, is that I never want to establish in advance a fixed number of repetitions for any melody. I prefer to sense where the music's going and see how far the band might want to develop the tune on any given night. I prefer to give the nod across the stage that I am going to switch to the next melody. We'll often keep pushing and repeating the melody until we break through into some new territory, but sometimes I'll go one round too many where nothing new emerges or no deeper feeling is achieved, and Thomas will smile at me, always knowing when I've overshot it. There was one occasion when I gave the nod for a change of tune but felt that the transition was a little bit sloppy, so I broached the matter gently before we went onstage the following night. The lads looked at one another as if to exchange words unspoken yet understood. It was at this moment that Thomas pointed out to me that it was I who had mistakenly skipped over an entire tune in the medley. What sounded like a slightly sloppy transition to me was in fact the whole band adapting at almost lightning speed to an enormous and unanticipated change that I had initiated myself. That just showed me how intense the listening on the stage with this band really is.

For the Martin Hayes Quartet, it was time to make a recording. I knew that I'd like to have this new album project filmed, so together with Lina we set about figuring out the best way to make that happen. The first person who came to mind was Myles O'Reilly, who had done a beautiful job filming the tour in India.

We now needed a suitable location for the recording, one that would work in terms of sound-space and accommodation, and also look beautiful on film. Lina suggested Bantry House. From my years playing there as part of the Masters of Tradition festival, I was already very familiar with the place, and in particular the atmosphere and acoustics of its magnificent library room. I knew it would be a very inspiring space. The plan was to spend a week there; however, no sooner had we arrived at the house than we realized we had overlooked an important detail. We were in the depths of December, and as the house closes up for the winter, the library, where we were going to record, was very cold. We had to light and maintain two roasting fires in the room for two days straight before we got the place to a comfortable temperature, but in the end the beauty and atmosphere of the space made it all worthwhile.

Matt Purcell set up the recording equipment and did the mike placement to get the best sound, while Martin Torpey did the rough tracking of the recording, saving and documenting all the different takes. Myles is a very tall guy yet he somehow managed to make himself invisible and film the whole thing without us barely being aware of his presence in the room. For the recording, we sat in a circle and followed the loose plans we'd come up with for the pieces we wanted to perform, while still leaving plenty of room for new ideas as we went along. Playing the fiddle across from Liz is invigorating. She can meet me solidly in the playing of the tunes, yet also create counterpoint and contrast on the fly. Doug, meanwhile, is a rhythmic powerhouse who is constantly alternating between shadowing the melody I play, extending Dennis's chords and weaving himself into the parts that Liz had created. One of the most beautiful rooms in Bantry House is called the 'Blue Room' – the colour of its walls is very striking. Lina, who helped produce this recording, also named the CD *The Blue Room*.

In The Gloaming we tend to take turns being the lead voice, with the rest of the band often playing support. I think that is a dynamic that emerges when five people are working together. The quartet, however, has a different dynamic. Here, all four voices are simultaneously weaving their musical lines together. It's like an intricate machine of interlocking parts; we all have to be fully engaged with one another or it won't work. The quartet has become a great source of musical joy for me.

During my years of presenting collaborations at the Kilkenny Arts Festival as part of the 'Marble City Sessions', and also in my collaborative residencies at the Irish Arts Center in New York, I'd often find myself creating impromptu house bands with whoever was available at that moment. From these experiences, I started dreaming up my ideal house band, one that could work with me in exploring and presenting traditional music and that could also help me reach out to make further collaborations with musicians from diverse backgrounds all over the world.

Gary Sheehan once again asked me to do a couple of nights at the National Concert Hall and suggested I build and direct a band purely around my own musical vision. Lina was also pushing me to try that idea. This seemed to fit in with my 'ideal house band' that I'd been thinking about. I'm not a music arranger or composer in any formal sense but I do have very definite ideas about how I like things to sound. I started playing around with different instrumentation in my mind and scrolling through my experiences with different musicians until I finally settled on the people I wanted to invite. I then began to sketch out a general direction for each piece of music I'd like to play, with some basic cues for all the instruments in terms of the chording and rhythmic feel I wanted to pursue. My experience with Dennis, where we'd sift through lots of chordal possibilities, just searching for something that felt good, made me confident that I could at least chart out some basic harmonic ideas for a new band, make broad arrangements and sketch parts for the different instruments. My efforts are about charting a direction and creating a space of common ground within traditional music where musicians can freely create and be themselves. The best music happens when each musician has the freedom to be the maximum of who they are.

The band is called the Common Ground Ensemble. Cormac McCarthy is a very accomplished jazz pianist who grew up inside the world of traditional music. His father is an accomplished and well-known fiddler and flute-player, and Cormac himself has played Irish music. Kyle Sanna is a New York guitarist and composer who moves between worlds of modern composition, free jazz and traditional music. Kate Ellis is a very accomplished and versatile cellist who is artistic director of the contemporary music group Crash Ensemble, and she and I have had the opportunity to collaborate on a good number of previous occasions. Brian Donnellan is the grandson of fiddler Francie Donnellan, who was in the Tulla Ceílí Band with my father when it was formed in 1946. Brian plays bouzouki, harmonium and concertina in the band. He has the rhythm of the dancers in his music and the full repertoire of the music of East Clare at his fingertips. We were two days away from our first live performance when it was cancelled due to the pandemic. We immediately switched gears and used that time to instead make a recording at Grouse Lodge Studios in County Westmeath. In those confusing days at the beginning of lockdown, we were inside a joyful little bubble of musical discovery and exploration. We now have a recording of the music that we were going to perform and therefore have a starting point for when we resume performance in the post-pandemic world.

For years, I had a little chip on my shoulder about never having finished college. Becoming one of the University of Limerick's artists-in-residence and sitting on its governing body were certainly big steps towards healing this wound, but I think I finally put the issue to bed for good when, in November 2018, I was conferred with an honorary doctorate of music by the National University of Ireland, Galway. This doctorate came as a complete surprise to me. What made it particularly special was that my mother, Peggy, who had done so much to support me in those days when I was going through my college experience, was there to see it happen.

Less than a year later, my mother, who had been unwell for just a couple of weeks, was told she had terminal cancer. Even for this robust-minded woman, who had already overcome many health battles, the news was a blow. But after her diagnosis, she never once showed even so much as a hint of self-pity or fear. A lot of people in those situations invest their energy in fighting the inevitable, but my mother took the opposite approach. Drawing on the same courage with which she had lived her life, she accepted that it was her time to go. In the following days she started making her own funeral arrangements. She chose the clothes she wanted to be wearing when laid out, the music she wanted in the church for her Mass – she even put in place the arrangements for her own cremation. She then gathered her energy and spoke to each member of the family individually so we could all have an opportunity to say goodbye. It was quite a display of character.

My mother remained her determined self right through to the end. Her doctor's prognosis was that she might be with us for many weeks, maybe even a couple of months. My mother, however, had other plans. Her exact words to us were, 'I'm ready to go now.' She was diagnosed on the Thursday and left us the following Monday. She left on her own terms. I always thought it was funny how my parents both left this world in a manner that was perfectly in keeping with their characters. My father, in his final days, faded gently like a slow, shimmering light, whereas my mother left in a flash.

The death of our loved ones can be a rattling experience. Our faith can be shaken but it can also be a moment where we begin to think about the meaning of our own lives. Living with the awareness of our own mortality helps us to focus on what is most essential in our lives. Love, forgiveness, kindness and generosity seem to me to be essential things worth focusing on. I certainly don't have answers to life's bigger questions, but I can't help thinking that it's the questions themselves that we most need. For me, just pondering on the big questions of our existence is a way of gaining perspective, of becoming inspired, of staying connected with my own sense of wonder and curiosity.

Since those years of discovery in Chicago, I have tried to live my life as an act of faith – a belief that, if I'm on the correct path, I can face all uncertainty without much worry or fear. I do not walk this path consistently; I wander off it repeatedly – every day, in fact. I can get hooked on materialism, selfishness or moral judgement of some sort, I'm continuously falling and failing, but I relentlessly correct my way as I go.

In my musical life, I have placed my faith in the intangibles, giving them first priority. Music is so much more than scales, notes and sound-vibrations. Technical skill can impress and produce moments of real excitement, but the truly soulful and transformative expression of music is of a different nature – it comes in a moment of surrender.

Back in my Chicago days, I had no idea where my little metaphoric monk's sailboat would take me. Certainly, I would not have been capable of scripting a more fulfilling life than the one I have discovered along this mysterious path. I have found love and meaning, made wonderful friends along the way, and have been fed and sheltered all of my life. The precarious, uncertain path of music has ended up blessing me with the confidence to embrace the unknown. Not knowing what comes next is the only certainty. This book, like my music, is all I can say for now. So there you are!

ACKNOWLEDGEMENTS

I WOULD LIKE to thank all the people who have supported me in writing this book.

My editor Fiona Murphy, who helped me believe I could do this and who, along with Tara King, helped give shape to the book. They were kind, patient and open-minded.

My managers Ken Allen and Michael Roe, who, along with Jackie Joseph, shepherded this project.

Patrick O'Donoghue, who was the first person who tried to get me to write a book and who therefore led me to first contemplate this idea.

My good friends and wonderful photographers Christy McNamara and Nutan, Mick O'Connor, who helped source photos, and the Traditional Music Archive in Dublin for their contribution.

Marco K. von Knobloch, who, with his refined aesthetic sense and graphic skills, did a wonderful job in designing the book cover.

Behind the scenes of my music career there are many people who have supported, encouraged, managed, booked, promoted and recorded my music: Helen Bommarito, Elizabeth Roth, Amy

Garvey, Ellen Byrne, Seamus Finneran, Yoko Nozaki, Judith Joiner, Foye Johnson, Wim and Ria Wigt, Ruud Kuper, Fabio Rinaudo, Music Works International, Green Linnet Records, Real World Records, Compass Records, Brassland Records, Faction Records, 251 Records, Adastra Music Agency, Kilkenny Arts Festival, Irish Arts Center NY, West Cork Music, Culture Ireland, and also Gary Sheehan and the National Concert Hall in Dublin.

My music engineer and faithful friend Matt Purcell, who has been beside me all over the world, always making sure the sound is the best it can be.

My lifelong friend and musical partner Dennis Cahill, with whom I have circled the world a few times.

I also have to thank my family and friends, and my audiences: you were all in my thoughts on this writing journey.

And finally, I want to thank my wife Lina, who pushed me to sit and write this book, kept fresh water on my desk, cooked meals and kept our home going while I locked myself away for days and months to write. She read my initial draft and with her own writing intuition offered me many valuable suggestions.

PHOTO CREDITS

INDEX

Abbey Pub, Chicago, music sessions
    182–3, 186, 189–207, 254
Adams, Gerry 328
Adams, Rob, art gallery 240–1
Adare 94
African–American community, art
    gallery 240–1
Afro-Celt Sound System 333
agriculture, modernization 64–5
All-Ireland Fleadh Cheoil 78, 79–83
American Irish music, early
    recordings 42–4
Amidon, Sam 280–1, 313, 347
An Fhidil Scraith record 89
Anderson, Laurie 281, 337
Anger, Darol 224, 246
Art Institute of Chicago 223
Association of Performing Arts
    Professionals (APAP) conferences
    311–12, 325
Athlone bar gig 260–1
Augenblick bar 212–14, 220
Australia
    First (Aboriginal) People,
        Dreamtime 264
    Sydney Masters of Tradition
        Festival 302–8
    tours 263–7, 302

Baal Tinne (band) 196, 206
Baile na nGall (Ballydavid) 204
Ballinakill, Galway 63
Ballymaloe House 329
Bane, Joe 104, 105–6, 108,
    238, 247
banshees 31
Bantry festival 319
Bantry House 300, 353–4
Bantry, Masters of Tradition Festival
    299–301, 302
bar owner's advice 137–8
Barnett, Armin 20
Barry, Christy 202
Barry, Gerald 125
Bartlett family 280–1
Bartlett, Thomas 275, 280–1, 347
    and The Gloaming project 325–6,
        332–6
    house band director 337
    Irish Arts Center gig 338

MH recording session with
  311, 313–14
Bays, Randal, MH musical
  partner 255–8, 263, 267–8,
  275–7, 281
Begley, Séamus 272, 275, 282
Béla Fleck and The Flecktones 284
Bell, Joshua 307
Benedectine community, Glenstal
  Abbey 330–1
Benn, George 155–62
Biden, Joe 326
Big Tom and The Mainliners 95
Bill Malley 104
Black, Mary 100
Blaney, Neil 127
Blasket Islands 203
bodhrán players 197, 213, 214–5,
  263, 265, 286, 343
Boehner, John 326
Bohan, Fr Harry 142–3
Boland, Kevin 127
Bolands' Cross 49
Bommarito, Helen 244, 245–7,
  253–4, 255, 269, 280–1
  and MH's recording studio
    290
  relationship ended 297
Bono 279
Boston College fiddle recording
  247, 251
Bothy Band 72, 101, 105
Brady, Paul 100
Brhaddhvani music centre 350
'Brian Boru' oak tree 317, 331

Brigit's Hearth Early Years Centre
  315–17
Bring Down the Lamp (TV) 102
British Overseas Airways
  Corporation 12
Broaders, Pat 242, 243, 253, 258, 339
Brody, Ita 21
Brody, Jimmy 21, 22, 104
Brogan, Sonny 243
Brooklyn Rider quartet, The
  Butterfly 237
Brophy, David 315, 321–4
Brown, Peter 88
Browne, Doug 313
Bruton, John, 'Rainbow
  government' 319
Bryars, Gavin, 'Jesus' Blood Never
  Failed Me Yet' 307
Buddhist texts 226, 227–8
Buncrana fleadh cheoils 78–83,
  117–18
Burke, Fr 111
Burke, Kevin 246
Butlers of Bunnahow 23
Byrne, David 281, 333
Byrne, Gabriel 337
Byrne, Gay 279
  radio show 276–8
  The Late Late Show 278

Cahill, Dennis 131, 165–6, 194–5,
  197–202, 204–5, 208–9, 212, 215,
  216, 224, 226, 246, 250, 254, 312
  and death of Gwen 301–2
  and Martin Hayes

working up musical
partnership 282–7
on the road 287–8, 293–5,
301–3, 315–19, 346
Feakle Festival 287
setting up recording studio
289–90
'Lament for Limerick' 291
'Poll Ha'penny Selection' 291
The Lonesome Touch, recording
290–3
exploring standard
interpretations 291–3
Australia tour 2008 302
Masters of Tradition 306
Welcome Here Again album 310–11
Gloaming project *see*
Gloaming, The
Flynn concert 323–4
at White House 326–9
touring Flynn's *Music for the
Departed* 337
Irish Arts Center gig 338
Martin Hayes Quartet 340,
353–4
India tour 348–50
Cahill, Gwen, death and funeral 301
Cahill, Mary 302
Cahills (Killanena) 50
Callaghan, Dave ('The Rave') 197
Campbell, Francie 193
Canny, John Joe 48
Canny, Paddy (PJ's musical partner)
14–16, 43, 72, 76, 77, 82, 94, 104,
105, 257, 335

marries Philomena 14
Dublin Records LP 39–41
Canny, Paddy 'The Volunteer'
(neighbour) 49, 114, 116, 123–4
Canny, Pat 14
Canny, Philomena 14
Canny family (neighbours) 48,
52, 62
Carey, Christy 155–62
Carey, Gerry
and Maggie 155–64
Irish Village regular gig 168–9
Carnegie Hall 15, 351
Carney, Fr 111
Carroll, Liz 190
Carthy, Martin 265
Casey, Bobby 41, 252
Casey, George 164–6
Cassidy, Pat 159
Cavanmen association 159
CD and 'Tom Doherty's Reel' 323
céilí bands
heyday 96–7
in decline 95–6, 99–100
comeback 101
Celtic Music and Arts Festival 1993
262–3
Celtic World Music Festival,
Sebastopol 318
Ceoltóirí Chualann 84, 100
Ceoltóirí Laighean 100
Chennai 350
Chicago, St Patrick's Day 180–3
Chicago futures market 175–8
FBI sting 176

Chicago Irish Musicians
 Association 158
Chicago Ridge 186–7
Chieftains, The 74, 84, 100, 101
Clancy, Willie 96, 305, 307
 The Minstrel from Clare 109
Clancy's Pub, Chicago 181, 182,
 234–5
Clannad band 83
Cleland, Seán 190, 196–7, 206,
 213, 223
Clifford, Julia 345
Clinton, Hillary 303
Clonmel fleadh cheoil 308
Cloonagrow 48
Cloonan, Pat 189
'Cois an Ghaorthaidh' 335
Coleman, Michael 43, 81, 292
Collins, Jimmy 89
 and Eileen's house 50, 55
Collins, Kathleen 41
Collins, Neiley 213
Common Ground Ensemble 355–6
Connecticut 298
Conneely, John (teacher) 85–6
Conneely, Pauline 202
Connolly, Aidan 338
Connolly, Séamus 80, 82, 247
Connors, Danny 117
Conroy, Julia 21
Conroy, Willie 21
Conway, Kieran 194
Conway, Mrs (teacher) 66
Cooley, Joe 70–4, 96, 103, 126,
 244–5, 323

homecoming concert 72–4
funeral 74
Cooney, Steve 272–5, 282, 303, 305–6
 Ceol Ársa Cláirsí 275
Corn Uí Ríada Oireachtas 235
Corry, Dennis 84
Corry, Mary 84
Cosmic Diner 325
countercultural folk revival 100
Cox, Pat, and Fianna Fáil 128–9
Coyle, Jimmy 189
Cranitch, Ellen 319
Crash Ensemble 355
Crawford, Gaynor 265
Crawford, Kevin 272, 318–19
Crehan, Junior 75, 82, 108,
 252, 257
Croom Orthopaedic Hospital 152
Crusheen 12, 34, 36, 60–1
Cuffe, Tony 268
Cúil Aodha singing tradition 308, 333
Cullinan, James 67, 78
Culloo, Joan 84
Culture Ireland, and Masters of
 Tradition 308
Curtis, PJ 91

Dale Haze and The Champions 95
dance 'feis' 62–3
Daniel O'Connell Hotel,
 Melbourne 265
Darlin' Girl from Clare festival 3
Davis, Miles 224
De Dannan 101, 102, 105
De Valera, Éamon 122–3

'Dear Irish Boy, The' 90
Dearborn 157
Delhi 349, 350
Derry Bogside gig 274–5
Dessner, Bryce 337
Detroit Gaelic League 157
'Dick Cosgrove's Reel' 332–3
Dillon, Bob (Irish-American) 213
Dillons 50
Dixie Dregs (band) 209
Doherty, John 43
Donnellan, Brian 355–6
Donnellan, Francie 94, 116, 250, 355
Doorus 50
Douglawn National School 50–4,
   62, 63–4
   closed 66
   walking home in darkness 86–7
Downes, Eugene 308
Doyle, John 318–19
Doyle, Roddy 337
Drovers, The (band) 196–7, 213
Dublin
   National Concert Hall 315,
      320–4, 334, 336, 341–4, 351, 354
   O2 Arena 341
   St Patrick's Cathedral 340
Dublin Records LP 39–41
Dublin TradFest 340
Dungarvan 79
Dyer, Wayne 137

Early, Biddy 32–3
East Clare
   Fianna Fáil branch 129–31

modernizations 64–5
newcomers 113–16
see also specific places
East Clare music x–xi, 44
see also specific music/
   musicians
East Galway melodies 132
Ecklund, Peter 313
ECM catalogue 225
Edwards, Áine 348, 350
'Eistigh Liomsa Sealad' 305
Ellis, Kate 355–6
Emily (child student) 238–9
England, Tulla Céilí Band playing
   in 100
Ennis 24, 272–4, 275
Ennis, Seamus 44, 102
Ensemble Galilei 339
European Economic
   Community 65
Evans, Bill 333

Fabio (uilleann piper) 344
faeries 30–3, 34–5
Fahey, Marty 182–3, 206
Fahey, Paddy 132, 291
Fahy, Bridie 63
Fahy, Máirín 62–3
Fahy, Marty 190
Fairport Convention 201
Feakle 31, 33, 72, 233
   Joe Cooley concert 323
   phoning home to 161
   'Start Your Own Business' course
      140–2

Feakle Festival 274, 287, 315–16
Feakle Mass 123
　drive to 58–9
Fennessy, Éamonn 151
'Fermoy Lasses, The' 78
Fianna Fáil 122–31, 138–9
Field, Gerry, mends PJ's broken
　fiddle 185–6
Finneran, Seamus 263–7, 302, 304
Fionn mac Cumhail 261
Flagmount 24
Flagmount School 66
Flahertys 50
Flatley, Michael 190
fleadh cheoils 66–7, 78–80, 83–4,
　117, 132, 196, 308, 340
Flippen, Ryman 174
Flower, Robin, *The Islander*
　translation 203
Flynn, Dave
　Aontacht ('Unity') concerto 315,
　　320–4
　Music for the Departed
　　arrangement 315, 323, 337
Fox, Tom 164–6
Fox's Pub 164–6
Friday, Gavin 279
Frisell, Bill 195, 334, 342

Gael Linn 83, 87
Gaelic Park club 159
Gallagher, Rory, Park West gig
　231–2
Galligan, Joe 61, 102
Galligan's pub (Highway Inn) 61, 102

Galtymore ballroom, Cricklewood
　13, 100
Galway Film Fleadh 340
Galway International Arts Festival
　259–60
Garbarek, Jan 195, 224
Garvey, Amy 258, 276, 278–9
gender stereotyping 125
Gerry and Stefan (of Melbourne)
　264, 267
Gibbons, Tom 186
gigs, organizing equipment for 208–9
Gina (band) 95
Glackin, Paddy 87, 251
Glackin, Séamus 87
Glendalough 337
Glendora House Ballroom 157,
　158, 196
Glenstal Abbey mass 330–1
Gloaming, The 89, 101, 275, 345–6,
　350–2, 354
　as project 325–6, 332–6
　at Carnegie Hall 351
　debut concert planning 333–6
　Irish tour 332–6
　Meteor Album of the Year 2015
　　350–1
　Moment to Moment documentary
　　347
　Royal Albert Hall concert 346–7
　'The Opening Set' 335–6, 347
'Golden Castle' 82
Gort, Classic Ballroom 95–6
Gradam Ceoil Award 303
'Graf Spee, The' 82

Graham, Bill 258, 278–9

Green Linnet Records 265, 289, 290
   Martin Hayes album 255–61

Greengrove lounge bar gig 273–4

Greg, Gloria 245

Gregory, Mark 250

Gresham Ballroom 100

Griffin, Vincent 104

Grouse Lodge Studios 332–4, 356

Half Time Rec, St Paul 214–17
   friends from 238–9

Halloran, Francie 156

Hammond, John 265

Hannon, Aidan 184

Hansard, Glen 329, 337

Harrah, Randy 199–202, 214, 216,
   223, 226

Haughey, Charles 127–8, 138

Hayden, Cathal 303, 306

Hayes, Anna Marie (MH's sister)
   6–7, 60, 113, 249

Hayes, Helen (MH's sister) 7, 60,
   175, 249
   and music 113

Hayes, Liam (MH's uncle) 5–7
   farm work 26
   moves to Killanena farm 56–8
   'pioneer' (non-drinker) 133

Hayes, Lina (MH's wife) ix, x, 212,
   315–18, 320–4, 326, 329–31, 332,
   344, 348–50, 352–3
   wedding 336–7
   Brigit's Hearth Early Years Centre
   315–17

Hayes, Maggie (MH's grandmother) 5

Hayes, Martin
  family
    see Hayes family and specific
     family members
  early life
    childhood 3–22
    early escapology/ independence
     46–7, 51–2, 56
    first school 47, 50–4, 56, 62,
     63–4
    journey 47–50, 54–6
    Flagmount School 66, 68–9
    secondary school 69–70, 75,
     84–7, 111
    and English literature
     85–6
    leaves without plan
     119–23
  and farm work 27–30
  first bicycle 115–16
  and music
    alienation feelings fuel
     69–70, 75–7
    first fiddle 37–44, 62–9
    developing technique and
     style 67–8
    early competitions 62–3,
     66–7, 78, 110
    first concert 72–4
    first recordings 87–9
    joins Tulla Céilí Band
     69–74, 88–91
    wins Munster Fleadh
     Cheoil 78

wins All-Ireland Fleadh
Cheoil 78, 79–83
East Clare playing style
104–5
as young adult
Business Studies at Limerick
NIHE 120–3, 128–32, 134–5,
136, 139–40, 148–9
on Students' Union
Executive 131, 134–5
at Lorient Music Festival
132–4
and politics 122–32, 135,
138–9
Fianna Fáil 129–30,
138–9
joins 'Start Your Own Business'
course 140–2
and frozen food business
142–7, 148
in debt for van 143, 153,
156, 162
makes final debt repayment
250–1
and Irish expat video business
147–8, 154, 159
and Tulla Céilí Band USA 1984
tour 148, 153–4
hay tower accident 150–1
leg seriously damaged
150–2, 153
Chicago 'visit' 1985 with Careys
155–60
construction labouring 160–8
tries music teaching 164

gigs with Paul, wrong music
168–85
Kitty O'Shea's bar gigs 174, 178
Houston, Kenneally's Irish Pub
gigs 177–8
futures market runner 175–8
enjoying diversity 178–9
breaks PJ's fiddle over Paul
180–6
at Abbey Pub 189–206, 214
Midnight Court (band) see
Midnight Court
at Half Time Rec, St Paul
214–17
teaching Irish traditional music
238–41
homesickness/ identity crisis
166–8, 170–4, 179–87
depression/ loses heart 136–40
drinking & partying 132–4,
134–5, 136–8, 170–2, 178–9,
216, 217–20
quits drinking 220, 221–2
quits smoking 219–20
rebuilding life at Abbey Pub
202–7
begins resolution 218–22,
226–32
as secular humanist 230
and relationships 298
and Catholicism 330
meditation 227–30
vegetarianism 227
immigration status illegal
172–3, 176, 184

robbed by fake lawyers
172–3
legalized 251
life as act of faith 358
Ireland
returns home 248–53
RTÉ TV programme 1992 251
teaches at Willie Clancy
Summer School 251–3
leaves for Seattle 253–5
Australia tours 263–7, 302
organizes Sydney Masters of
Tradition Festival 302–8
Ireland tour 267–8
gigs with Steve Cooney 272–5
Under the Moon album 275–9,
282
recording with Willie Keane
set-dancing 286–7
San Francisco 244–5
Seattle
with Liz Roth *see* Roth, Liz
Murphy's Pub, Seattle 245–6
and Green Linnet Records
255–8
West Coast gigs 262
seeks new musical partner 281–3
Ballard apartment 297
Martin Hayes album 255–61
Ireland promotion tour 258–61
Galway gig 259–60
Sligo gig 258–9
Athlone bar gig 260–1
Connecticut, summers in
Ireland 298

Ireland and USA, projects and
awards
Gradam Ceoil Award 303
with Ó Lionáird and Bartlett
311, 313–14
Triur 314, 343–4
Triúr sa Draighean 308–10
Flynn's *Aontacht* concerto 315,
320–4, 337
Art Ó Bríain *Natural Grace*
documentary 319–20, 340
Gloaming project *see*
Gloaming, The
Limerick University artist-in-
residence 329
NY Irish Arts Center
residency 338
Irish World Academy Artist
339–40
Martin Hayes Quartet 340,
352–4
Paul Simon Dublin concert
340–1
two trios NCH concert 342–4
India tour 348–50
Common Ground Ensemble
355–6
honorary doctorate
of music 356
on music/ musicianship
aesthetic appreciation 344–5
audience guiding 306–8
curating musician recitals 300–1
group configuration dynamics
338

ideal collaborations 354–5
musical discovery/
    experimentation 201–7,
    210–18, 223–6
musical freedom, first
    experience 44–5
playing in large spaces 265–7,
    268–9
playing only as entertainment
    233–4
returning to roots 247, 249,
    251–3, 255–61, 279
seeking authentic musical
    vehicle 188–9, 202–7,
    233–7
structuring own concerts
    299–300
The Gloaming musicianship
    351–2
work with Dennis Cahill
working up musical
    partnership 282–7
on the road 287–8, 293–5,
    301–3, 315–19, 346
Feakle Festival 287
setting up recording studio
    289–90
'Lament for Limerick' 291
'Poll Ha'penny Selection' 291
The Lonesome Touch, recording
    290–3
exploring standards
    interpretations 291–3
Australia tour 2008 302
Masters of Tradition 306

Welcome Here Again album
    310–11
Gloaming project see
    Gloaming, The
Flynn concert 323–4
at White House 326–9
touring Flynn's Music for the
    Departed 337
Irish Arts Center gig 338
India tour 348–50
Hayes, Pat (MH's brother) 5–7, 59,
    60, 62, 175, 249
and family farm 27–30, 112–13
and Fianna Fáil 123
Hayes, Peggy (MH's mother) 5,
    6–10, 17–21, 62, 63, 64, 249
early life 10–14
farm work 26
and school 53–4
on MH's own style 67
at All-Ireland Fleadh Cheoil
    79–83
on college 120
and Sunday lunch 125–6
and 'Start Your Own Business'
    course 141
and frozen food business 148
at Gwen's scattering 301
85th birthday 351
death and own preparations 356–7
Hayes, PJ (MH's father) 1, 3, 5–12,
    18–22, 104, 247
early life 13–17, 24
and farm work 24–30
and Fianna Fáil 122–8

and Maghera mountain 24–5
and MH
   and MH's first fiddle 37–42
   as teacher 238
   make recordings together
     249–50
   misses All-Ireland Fleadh
     Cheoil 79
   on classical music career 119
   track in *Under the Moon* album
     275
and the Sampsons 113–16
as musician
   and Paddy Canny, recordings
     291, 335
   and Tommy Potts 78
   band *see* Tulla Ceílí Band 295
   fiddle music development 67
   early recordings 42–3
   Dublin Records LP 39–41
   on tradition in music, PJ on
     15–16
   playing 116, 256, 257
   and céilí bookings 92–4
drives a car 58–60, 289
ill-health and death
   Addison's disease 248–9, 295
   Parkinson's disease 295
   final days 356
   MH at bedside 295–7
Hayes, Quillan (Martin) (MH's
   grandfather), 47, 184
and farming 5, 23–5, 32
Hayes family farm, change and
   technology 29–30

cattle farming life 23–30
herdsmen ancestors 23–4
MH rejects succession to 112–13
Pat and 27–30, 112–13
PJ and 24–30
Quillan and 5, 23–5, 32
working 23–30
Hayes family home 5–10, 236, 286
and music 38–9
visitors 17, 18–22
MH returns to 248–53
Heaney, Seamus 247
memorial concert 341–2
Hederman, Abbot Mark Patrick,
   Manikon Eros 331
Hedges, Michael 224
Henry, Kevin 189
Herbert, Michael 138
Higgins, President Michael
   346–7
Highway Inn, Crusheen 61, 102
Hill, Noel 99, 102
Hogan, Hannie, cottage 57–8
Houlihan, Mary 48
Houlihan's Cross 49
Houlihan's house 48, 55–6
Hozier 350
Hughes, Maureen 259
'Humours of Scariff, The' 343
Humphrys, Francis 299
Hussain, Zakir 350

Inchicronan lake 36
India tour 348–50, 352
Indian music 224, 348–50

Indian philosophy
  Upanishads 226
  meditation 228
Indians, The (group) 95
Irish American Heritage Center
  Chicago 164
Irish Arts Center, NY 314, 338, 354
Irish Arts Office, San Francisco 269
Irish cabaret clubs, Chicago 165
Irish Chamber Orchestra 337
Irish expat video business, MH and
  147–8, 154, 159
Irish independence, and land
  redistribution 23–4
Irish language, old words and
  farming 27–9
Irish traditional music (in general)
  x–xi
  bodhrán players 197, 213, 214–5,
    263, 265, 286, 343
  céilí bands (in general) 95–7,
    99–100, 101
  early recordings 39–44
  East Clare ethos x-xi
  new performance model 100–1
  no career path to 119–22
  popularity increases 299
  PJ on 15–16
  sean nós singing 43, 234–5, 275,
    305, 333, 334
  set-dancers/ dancing 21, 97–9,
    101, 117, 272, 286–7, 316
  sessions, traditional *vs.* modern
    pub 190–4
  traditional players 102–9

uilleann-pipers 43, 189, 262, 289,
  306, 344
  see also Tulla Ceílí Band; specific
    performers
Irish Musicians Association
  (Chicago) 189–95, 206
Irish Press 74
Irish rebel songs 168
Irish step-dance lessons 62
Irish War of Independence 123
Irish Village, Chicago 165, 168–77
Irish World Academy 122
Irish-American songs 168
Irvine, Andy 100, 102
Ismaily, Shahzad 313
Ivan (Lina's son) 317, 330
Ivers, Eileen 339

Jacobsen, Colin 237
Janet from Kilkenny 215
Jarrett, Keith 333
jazz–rock fusion music 197, 200,
  201, 223–5
John and Seamus (uncle James's
  sons), at All-Ireland Fleadh
  Cheoil 79–80
Johnson, Charlie 216–17
Johnson, Foye 332
'Jolly Frog, The' 21
Jones, Norah 333
Jones, Tom and Mary
  (neighbours) 116

Kathleen (Emily's mother) 238–9
Keane, Jimmy 190, 206, 301

Keane, Kathleen 197
Keane, Mike 157, 158
Keane, Willie 98, 286
Keegan, Kevin 245
Kelly, James 243
Kelly, John 43, 252
Kelly's Post Office 64
Kenneally's Irish Pub, Houston 177–8
Kennedy dynasty 329
Kennelly, Patricia 245
Kenny, Enda 326
Kenny, Shane 319
Kerrymen Association 158–9
Kilclaran Mass 114–15
Kilfenora céilí band 41
Kilkenny Arts Festival, 'Marble City
    Sessions' 354
Killanena 4, 31, 50, 57–8
Killarney, Gradam Ceoil Award 303
King, Paddy 21
King, Philip
    Moment to Moment
        documentary 347
    Other Voices TV 337–8, 347
King, PJ 272
King, Rita 21
Kirkpatrick, Mike 196–7, 213
Kitty O'Shea's bar, Chicago
    Hilton 174
Knocknageeha (Cnoc na Gaoithe) 50
Knocknagree 99
Knowles, Liz 339
    and Martin Hayes Quartet 340,
        353–4
Koning, Jos 20

Krauss, Colby, Midnight Court
    manager 208
Kuper, Ruud 299, 304

La Poisson Rouge, New York 337–8
Ladig, Sherry and Don 216
Lafferty, Bridie, Dublin Records LP
    39–41
Lal, Utsav 349
Lally, Mick 212
'Lament for Limerick, The' 291
landscape, family names 48–50
Latimer, Jim 216
    The Irish Piper 254
Lawrence-King, Andrew 343
Leaghort 30
Lenehan, Francie 258
Lennon, Maurice 87
Letterkenny Folk Festival 79–80
Levy, Howard 284
Lewis family 132
Liffey Banks 90, 109, 236–7
Limerick, University of 329,
    339–40, 356
    MH appointed to board 149–50
Lind-Waldock futures brokerage
    174–8
lineage tracing 35–6
Linehan, Fergus 303–4
Lingenfield, Lord 23
listeners and music 116–18
Looney, Tom and Breege 183,
    189–94, 198–9, 254
'Lord Gordon's Reel' 81
Lorient Music Festival 132–4

Lough Graney 24, 49, 54

Loughnane, Billy 340

Loughnane, Dr Bill 13, 72–4, 340
and Tulla Céilí Band 126–7
dies 138
Fianna Fáil TD 126–8, 130

Loughrea 79
dance feis 62–3

Lully, Jean-Baptiste 344

Lúnasa 101

Lunny, Dónal 100

Lydon House TV dinners, MH and 146–7

Lyons, John 61

Lyons, Tim 61

Mac Gabhann, Antóin 20

Mac Gabhann, Bernie 20

Mac Mathúna, Ciarán 18, 44

MacNamara, Andrew 98, 156, 231

MacNamara, Ita, MH and 103

MacNamara, Mary 83–4, 87, 89, 117–18, 256

Macra na Feirme 150

Maghera mountain 4, 23–5, 49

'Maghera Mountain, The' 25

Maghera telecommunications mast 25

Maharishi Mahesh Yogi 228

Malley, Bill 104, 105

Malley's Stream 49, 55

Malone, Éamon 160

Marais, Marin 342, 343, 344

Maritime Hotel, Bantry 300

Marsh, Pat 259–60, 268

Martha (MH's girlfriend) 218, 222

Martin Hayes Quartet 339–40
recording *The Blue Room* 352–4
St Patrick's Cathedral gig 340

'Mason's Apron, The' 174

Masters of Tradition festivals 302, 342, 343, 353
Sydney 302–8
project showcased at APAP 325
USA tours 308, 312

Masterson, Tom 189

McCarthy, Cormac 355–6

McCullough, Larry 20

McDonald, Jack 92–4

McGann, John 268

McGlinchey, Brendan 67

McGreevy, Johnny 189

McGuinness, Con 142, 156

McGuinness, Martin 328

McGuire, Frank 343

McGuire, Seán 74

McGurk, John D., St Louis pub 242–4, 253, 258

McHugh, Jamie 265

McHugh, Paul 214
MH gigs with 168–85
MH breaks fiddle over 180–6

McKee, Gerry 235–6

McKee, Jocelyn 236

McLaughlin, John 195

McLaughlin, Martin 162

McMahon, Brendan 21, 75, 243

McMahon, Christy (MH's uncle) 58, 61, 102

McMahon family 49

McMahon, James (MH's uncle)
79–80
McMahon, John 21
McMahon, John Joe 48
McMahon, Margaret (teacher)
50–4
McMahon, Mary and Kate (MH's
aunts) 12
McMahon, Molly and John
(MH's maternal grandparents)
34–6, 60–1
McMahon, Paddy and Nora 121
McMahon, Seamus 21
McMahon, Tony 41, 72, 74, 75, 96,
99, 102–4, 243, 251, 333, 350
McMahon's house 48–9
McMillan, Shona 246
McNamara, Biddy (MH's aunt)
13, 21
McNamara, Christy 21, 60
McNamara family 60, 84
McNamara, James 60
McNamara, Joe 13, 21, 60
McNamara, Mary 60
McNamara, Michael 149
Meehan, Mrs (teacher) 68–9
Meenaghan, Ann (Aine Ní
Dhonncha) 182, 234–5
Meenaghan, Seán 235
Melbourne 264–7
memoir writing ix-x
Mensa club 214, 215
Merriman, Brian 50
Merriman Tavern, Scariff 102
Meteor Choice Music Prize 2015 350

Metheny, Pat, and Charlie Haden,
Beyond the Missouri Sky 290–1
Midnight Court 199–207,
208–17, 234
at Half Time Rec, St Paul 214–17
at McGurk's pub 242–4
confuses audience 199–202
not progressing 241–2
Mikkelborg, Palle 224
Miltown Malbay 3–4, 98
Minogue, Susan 142
Mitchell, Senator George 329
Molloy, Matt 72, 73
Moloney family 50, 98–9
Moloney, Fr TJ 157–8, 164–5
Moloney, Geraldine 117
Moloney, Johnny 160
Moloney, Kathleen 117
Moloney, Mick 100
Moloney, Seán 132
Moloney, Tim 84
Moment to Moment documentary 347
Montgomery, Seán 87
Montreux (band) 246
Moore, Cathy, batiks 83
Moore, Christy 100
Moore, Jimmy 194
Moore, Liam 196
Moore, Mike 184
Moran, Jackie 197
'Morning Dew, The' 291
Moroney, John 'The Geg' house 49
Moroney's Flat 49, 55
Morrison, James 43
Moss, Cloud 318–19

Moss, Lori 319
Moynihan, Johnny 100
Muldoon, Paul 212, 337, 341–2
Mulkere, Dessie 72
Munster Fleadh Cheoil 78, 80
Murphy, Dennis 345
Murphy's Pub, Seattle 245–6
Murray, Chris 157

'N'Fheadar' 349
National Ballroom, Kilburn 100
National Chamber Choir of
    Ireland 329
National Concert Hall, Dublin 315,
    320–4, 334, 336, 341–4, 351, 354
National, The 333
National University of Ireland 356
Natural Grace documentary 340
Naughton, John 104
Naughton, Rosaleen 21
Naughton, Young John 21, 22
New Age music 224–5
'New Custom House, The' reel 327
Ní Dhonncha, Áine (as Ann
    Meenaghan) 234–5
Ní Riain, Nóirín 330
Nolan, Sean 129
Noon, Matthew, India tour
    348–50
Norman (Timmy's mentor)
    234, 252
Norway, Førde Traditional and
    World Music Festival 283, 287
Nugent, George 182–4
Nugent, Jim 141

O'Beirne, Gerry 268
Ó Bríain, Art, MH documentary
    Natural Grace 319–20, 340
Ó Brien, Mick 308
O'Brien, Paddy 94, 96, 242, 243–4,
    253, 258
O'Brien, Pat 194
O'Briens 50
Ó Catháin, Darach 235, 307, 333
    The Star Above the Garter 109
O'Connor, Máirtín 212, 303, 306
O'Connor, Sinéad 212, 279, 350
'O'Connor Dunn's reel' 252
O'Crohan, Tomás, *The Islander* 203
O'Dea, Mick 212
O'Dea, Willie 129
Ó Domhnaill, Mícháel 246, 255
O'Donnell, Sheila 212
Ó Donohue, John, 'A Morning
    Offering' vii
O'Donohue, John 330
O'Dowd, Seamie 303, 306
O'Driscoll, Mary 244
O'Driscoll, Seán 244–6
Ó Dwyer, Jim 129
O'Flynn, Liam 303, 304
O'Grady, Tim, and authenticity
    210–12
    I Could Read the Sky
    154–5, 212
Ó Halloran, Francie 143
O'Halloran, Tom 158
O'Hare, Kieran 339
Ó Kanre Seamus 194
O'Keeffe, Padraig 43, 333, 345

O'Leary, Helen 212

Ó Lionáird, Iarla 89, 212, 303, 304, 312–13, 314, 341, 345

O'Loghlin, Éamonn 157

O'Loughlin, Miss 62

O'Loughlin, Peadar 18, 72, 74, 77, 94

Dublin Records LP 39–41

O'Malley, Brian 206

gives MH electric violin 201

Ó Móráin, Micheál 129

O'Neill, Francis 189

O'Neill, James 40

O'Neill, Tip 326

Ó Raghallaigh, Caoimhín 308–10, 314, 343, 345

and The Gloaming project 325–6, 332–6

O'Reilly, Aideen, and India tour 348–50

O'Reilly, Myles 352–4

films India tour 348–50

Ó Ríada, Peadar 308–10, 343

'N'Fheadar' 349

'Obama Reel' 327

Ó Riada, Seán 44, 74, 84, 97, 100, 308–9

O'Rourke, Tony 264–7

O'Shea, Brendan 196

Ó Súilleabháin, Mícheál 247

O'Sullivan, Timmy 'The Bard' 202, 203–6, 213, 220, 234, 254

O'Toole, Helen 212, 241

Obama, Barack 303, 326–9

Obama, Michelle 328

Ogonnelloe church 130

Ono Lennon, Yoko 281

Open the Door for Three (trio) 339

'Opening Set, The' 335–6, 347

'Orange Blossom Special' 173–4

Oskay, Billy 255, 256–8

Our Lady's College, Gort (secondary school) 69–70

pagan community, at Half Time Rec 215

Páirc na Tarabh 60

Palace, The 242–3

Palais des Congrès, Lorient 133

Pärt, Arvo 225–6

Cantus in memory of Benjamin Britten 323

Tabula Rasa 225

Pearce, J. C., The Crack in the Cosmic Egg 218–20, 222, 325

Pelosi, Nancy 326, 328

Peoples, Tommy 72, 73, 252

Pepper, Gary 301

Pepper's Bar, Feakle 116, 295, 315

Planxty 101, 105

Plough and the Stars Pub, San Francisco 244–5, 261, 263

'Pol Ha'penny' 291, 293

politics 122–31, 138

polyrhythm 200

Ponty, Jean-Luc 201

Port Fairy Folk Festival 265

'Port Na bPúcaí' 327

Portland, Oregon 246

Potts, Tommy 18, 43, 76–8, 90, 94, 243, 292, 307, 329, 333, 342
  'The Butterfly' 237
  The Liffey Banks 90, 109, 236–7
Power, David 304, 305, 306
Public Dance Halls Act 96
púca 31–2
Puff, Teresa 216
Purcell, Matt 249–50, 301, 272, 275–7, 305, 308, 353
  and hay tower accident 150–1
  video business 147–8, 159

Quality Kitchens, MH and 142–6
Queens Hotel, Ennis 12
Quinn, Fr 80–1
Quinn, Mick 274
Quinn, Ruairí 149

Radiohead 333
ragas, and Vedic chants 348
Rayburn Reception Room 327
Rea, Stephen 212
Reavey, Ed, 'The Whistler from Rosslea' 252
Regan, Ronald 326
Reid, Seán 77
Rice, Damien 337
Rice, Noel 196, 206–7
Rochford, Martin 72, 75, 104, 106, 108, 238, 257
Rodger's Well 49
Rodgers, Joe 56
Rogers, Michael 55
'Rolling in the Barrel' 291

Roth, Danielle (Liz's daughter) 298
Roth, Liz 297–8, 318
Royal Albert Hall concert 346–7
RTÉ Concert Orchestra 315, 319, 320–4, 336
RTÉ Radio studios 88–9
Russell, Micho 104, 105
  Ireland's Whistling Ambassador 109
Ryan, Joe 252
Ryan, Mattie 92–4

Sainte-Colombe, Jean de 343, 344
Sampson, Bill and Anne, buy derelict house 113–16
San Francisco 244–5
  Celtic festival 268–9
  unknown mentor 269–71
Sanna, Kyle 355–6
Savall, Jordi
  and two trios NCH concert 342–4
  Celtic Viol album 343
Scariff 50, 56
  sports day 1984 150–1
Schumer, Chuck 326, 328
Scotland, Gwen's ashes scattered 301
sean nós singing 43, 234–5, 275, 305, 333, 334
Seattle 20
  Lake Union bike trail 297–8
  train to 254–5
Seiler, Madeleine 258
set-dancers 21, 117, 286–7, 316
  rhythm 272, 286–7
set-dancing 97–9, 101
Shakti with John McLaughlin 223–4

Shankar, L. 348
  'Psychic Elephant' 225, 349
  Vision 224–5
Shaskeen Céilí Band 95
Shaughnessy's Garage 58
Sheedy family 33–4
  house, Leaghort 30, 33–4
Sheedy, Paddy 33, 34
Sheehan, Gary 312–13, 314, 332,
  342, 354
'Ships in Full Sail, The' 22
Sigur Rós 333
Simmone, Dave 217
Simon, Paul 341–2
  'The Boxer' 341
  Dublin concert 340–1
Slattery, Mahon 141–2, 147, 150, 159
Slattery's Pub, Bodyke 147
Sliabh Luachra playing 43
Sligo fiddle-players 42–4
Slógadh competitions 83, 87
Slógadh Náisiúnta record 89
Spancilhill Inn 98
Spanish Point, County Clare 83
Spillane, Davy 262–3, 289
St Brendan's church, Bantry 300
St Patrick's Cathedral gig 340
St Patrick's Day, White House
  luncheon 326–9
  party 328–9
Stack, Eddie 262
'Start Your Own Business' course
  140–2
Stillman, Mark 215–16, 301
Stillman, Mary Ann 215, 301

Sting 341
Stockton's Wing 272
storytelling 35–6
Stray Leaf Folk Club 274
Studio Eyewear, frozen food disaster
  144–5
Subramaniam, L. 350
Subramanian, Professor
  Karaikudi S. 350
Surette, David 268
Swannanoa Gathering, Warren
  Wilson College 339
Sydney Masters of Tradition Festival
  302–8
Sydney Opera House 302, 304–8

Taibhdhearc Theatre, Galway 259–60
Talty, Pat 249
Taoism: 'The Way' experience 229–30
Taylor, Barry 20
Taylor, Jacqueline 20
Teehan, Terence 'Cuz' 189
Teetotallers, The 318–19
telephone comes to East Clare 64
Thompson, Séamus 87
Thornton, Jim 189
Tipperary Pub, Warrendale 158
'Tom Doherty's Reel' 335–6
Tommy Gun's bar, Chicago 181–3
Toonagh fleadh cheoil 66–7, 78
Torpey, Martin 353
'Toss the Feathers' 291
Touhey, Patsy 43
Tous les Matins du Monde 342, 344
tracing (storytelling) 35–6

traditional music *see* Irish traditional
   music
Transcendental Meditation 228
Triur 314, 343–4
   Triúr sa Draighean 308–10
Tuamgraney 321
Tuath Éachta Cooperative 141–2
Tulla 31
Tulla Céilí Band 3, 13–22, 39, 41,
   60, 81, 148, 151, 189, 208, 233, 278,
   295, 316, 355
   céilí bookings 92–4
   history 94–102
   MH and 69–74, 135
   musicians, morally upstanding 94
   rosary on journeys home 93–4
   UK tour 111
   USA 1984 tour 148, 153–4
Tulla Junior Band 84
Tuomey, John 212
turf cutting 28–30
Tyrrell, Seán 262–3

U2 350
uilleann-pipers 43, 189, 262, 289,
   306, 344
Upanishads 226
US Christian politics, reactionary 330

Vaughan's pub gigs 208–12
Vermont booking 280–1
Vicar Street, Dublin 347

Wabi-Sabi: For Artists . . . 345
Wainwright, Martha 281, 337

Walsh, Louis (Half Time Rec) 214
Waterboys, *Fisherman's Blues* 196
Weather Report (band) 209
West Cork
   Chamber Music Festival 299
   Masters of Tradition Festival
     299–301
   Music 299–301, 304
Whelan, Brid (teacher) 50–4
Whelan, Mike 216
'Whiskey in the Jar' 169, 201
White House, St Patrick's Day
   326–9
Whyte, Aggie 63, 72
Whyte, Bridie 72
Wieselman, Doug 338
   and Martin Hayes Quartet
     340, 353–4
   Irish Arts Center gig 338
Williams, John 190, 213
Williams, Tony
   'Some Hip Drum Shit' 223
   Ultimate Tony Williams 223
Willie Clancy Summer School,
   Miltown Malbay 251–3, 258, 268
wise woman 32–3
Womad festival 302
Wood, Martin 104
Woods, Tommy 48
Wrigleyville 223

Yasukawa, Erwin 196, 197–202,
   209, 216

Zeta electric violin 201